THE *PARMENIDES* AND PLATO'S
LATE PHILOSOPHY

ROBERT G. TURNBULL

The *Parmenides* and Plato's Late Philosophy

Translation of and Commentary on
the *Parmenides* with Interpretative Chapters on
the *Timaeus*, the *Theaetetus*, the *Sophist*,
and the *Philebus*

UNIVERSITY OF TORONTO PRESS
Toronto Buffalo London

© University of Toronto Press Incorporated 1998
Toronto Buffalo London
Printed in Canada

ISBN 0-8020-4236-8

Printed on acid-free paper

Toronto Studies in Philosophy
Editors: James R. Brown and Calvin Normore

Canadian Cataloguing in Publication Data

Turnbull, Robert G.
  The Parmenides and Plato's late philosophy : translation of
and commentary on the Parmenides with interpretative
chapters on the Timaeus, the Theaetetus, the Sophist, and
the Philebus

(Toronto studies in philosophy)
Includes bibliographical references.
ISBN 0-8020-4236-8

1. Plato, Parmenides.   2. Plato.   Dialogues.   I. Title.
II. Series.

B378.T87 1998   184   C97-931703-7

University of Toronto Press acknowledges the financial assistance to its publishing program of the Canada Council for the Arts and the Ontario Arts Council.

This book has been published with the help of a grant from The Ohio State University.

To the memory of
Wilfrid Stalker Sellars
Master Teacher, Philosopher's Philosopher, Friend

Contents

PREFACE ix

1 Introduction 3
2 Zeno's Stricture, Predication, and 'Having Shares' (126A–35C) 9
3 The Needed Exercise and Supposition One (135C–42A) 37
4 Supposition Two as the Clue to the *Parmenides* 60
5 Supposition Two, Part One (142B–48D) 71
6 Supposition Two, Part Two (148D–55E) 93
7 The 'Coda' and the Remaining Affirmative Suppositions (155E–60B) 111
8 The 'One' and the 'Others' on Both Versions of *If One Is Not* (160B–66C) 124
9 The *Timaeus* 142
10 The *Theaetetus* and the *Sophist* 156
11 The *Philebus* 169
Afterword 185

APPENDIX: OTHER APPROACHES TO THE *PARMENIDES* 189
NOTES 201
BIBLIOGRAPHY 205

Preface

This book has been many years in the making. The project was conceived in the middle 1960s. What gave impetus to it was manifold. First, I could not help believing that the *Parmenides'* account of the numbers was seriously intended and connected with Plato's ancient reputation as a mathematical philosopher with close ties to the Pythagoreans. Second, I was sure that the *Sophist* account of false belief or 'not being' was related to various of the suppositions or hypotheses of the *Parmenides*. Third, Plato's representations of Parmenides in the *Theaetetus* and the *Sophist* promised to have some sort of justification in the *Parmenides*. Fourth, I simply could not bring myself to believe that Plotinus had got the late Plato right, despite the profundity and influence of Plotinus' work. Fifth, though I could not in the 1960s articulate my problems with the tendency to treat Plato's forms as 'universals,' whether Aristotelian or Russellian, I could not reconcile the tendency with Plato's texts. Sixth and finally, as one greatly influenced by Wilfrid Sellars, I could not credit the late Plato with an 'acquaintance' account of our awareness of either sensibles or forms.

Much has happened in the intervening years both to hinder work on the project and to provide means of sophisticating and justifying the several convictions just listed. Not the least of those happenings has been the production by several scholars of books on the *Parmenides*, all of them helpful but none of them totally convincing. Even so, I must note here that, despite serious disagreements with his book, I have learned from and have been provoked to much thought and reconsideration by Kenneth Sayre's scholarly and imaginative work, *Plato's Late Ontology: A Riddle Resolved*.[1] The present book provides a total explanation of the text of the *Parmenides* and uses that explanation in accounting for the first philosophy of other late dialogues. To undertake careful and appropriate critique of other purported explanations of the text would require greatly complicating an already complicated account and at least doubling the size of the book. I try to take note of other accounts of the text of the *Parmenides* at various points, undertaking only a relatively brief critique of their lines of interpretation and explanation in an appendix.[2] I proceed here to other relevant happenings in those intervening years.

Directing the 1970 Summer Institute in Greek Philosophy and Science in Colorado Springs brought many relevant discussions with several distinguished scholars (notably, G.E.L. Owen) and the beginning of long association with younger scholars, many of whom are by now well-known. Working with Peter Machamer at Ohio State University in the mid-1970s on a two-year grant from the National Endowment for the Humanities greatly improved my understanding of the history of science and Plato's place in that history. A research semester at the University of Pittsburgh in 1980 resulted in the first draft of my translation of the *Parmenides* and began a valuable intellectual relationship with Alexander Nehamas. Hindrances came in the form of serious administrative burdens both at Ohio State University and with the American Philosophical Association – to say nothing of the task of editing a journal for six years.

Only in the past four years have I been able to give myself over to completing the present work. The first full draft of the manuscript included Greek text in addition to translation of and commentary on the *Parmenides*. It did not include chapters on other late dialogues. And it failed to incorporate many insights that are in the present volume. A serious reading of that manuscript draft was done by my former student, Dirk Baltzly, while he was working with the Aristotle Commentary translation project at King's College, London. Another was done by James Bogen and Charles Young of the Claremont Graduate School. In the light of their critical comments I have changed many things. Indeed, their comments and my own critical reading of the manuscript led to a complete recast and rewrite. Most of the rewriting has been in the interest of clarity and, where possible, simplification. Though the interpretation of the *Parmenides* remains intact, many changes (and cross references) have resulted from the task of writing the chapters on other late dialogues. I have benefited as well from critical comments made on papers that express major features of the present interpretation of the *Parmenides*, most recently from the comments of Patricia Curd and Steven Strange at a conference held in Vanderbilt in May 1994. I must as well acknowledge the useful critical comments of readers for the University of Toronto Press. They have led to several clarifications in the text, increased reference to alternative interpretations, and some expansion and development of the last chapters.

Even if I were able to list the external influences that have helped bring the articulations of the sixties to fruition in the present book, they would only partially explain the occasional insights growing out of more or less constant preoccupation with the workings of Plato's mind. The history of philosophy, fortunately, is still in large part *philosophy* and requires the assumption that great figures made serious efforts to explain themselves and to work out solutions to problems. Let me suggest several relevant examples.

First example. Given that Socrates in the *Parmenides*, confronted with the Zenonian claim that predication leads to contradiction, responds with the doctrine of forms and having shares, it is very likely that the Plato of the *Phaedo* was similarly responding to the Parmenidean/Zenonian attack on predication. Since having a share is not *being* something different, the problem of Helen's *being* beautiful is obviated. It is not the case that she *is* the same as beautiful; rather she *has* a share of the Beautiful. The *Parmenides* appears to include an attempt to state objections to the forms/shares account of the *Phaedo* in the first part and to provide a defensible account of predication in the second part.

Second example. How is change possible? If it occurs in a given stretch of time, then one must say that the changing thing both is and is not F for any given value of F. But how can it occur otherwise? One seems to need to deny that anything can change without remaining the same in some respect and to affirm that the change occurs in a non-time. To allow for 'smooth' change one seems to need the possibility of an actual infinite. Plato seems to require the first in the *Theaetetus*[3] and to accept the second in the third supposition of the *Parmenides* (the one I call the 'Coda'). Given the infinity of the numbers of the second supposition, this appears to be a genuine possibility.

Third example. Even though one may find that something, A, may *be F* for various values of F, how is one to think of B in connection with A? A can hardly *be B* without ceasing to be itself. B could, however, be *non-A*, provided that expression is non-vacuous. But non-A (other than A, different from A), need not be nothing, though it lacks specificity. And Plato, in the *Parmenides*, devotes a great deal of attention to the *others* (that is, things gotten at by non-X expressions) in the several suppositions of the second part of the dialogue. Indeed, explorations of the 'consequences' for the 'others,' whether as such or relative to whatever is supposed, are required by *Parmenides*' 'laborious game.'

Fourth example. Zeno in his treatise finds the 'consequences' of the supposition that many are to be contradictory, thus requiring by *modus tollens* that the supposition of the 'many' be rejected. Plato, turning the tables on Zeno, finds that, unless the supposition that *one is* requires the duality of *one* and *being*, the claim that *one is* is self-destructive. Given that duality, the supposition of the many (in a somewhat different form) is reinstated.

But enough. My point has been to show that a great deal of the effort to explain the *Parmenides* (and the other late dialogues) requires the attempt to understand the sorts of philosophical problems Plato was looking at and the language in whose terms he stated them. Even though in the end the explanations must conform to the text as we have it (unless there is good reason to believe it corrupt), coming up with adequate explanations is at least as much a philosophical task as it is a philological one.

And, in the end, of course, objectivity in the history of philosophy is lost if texts are either patronized or ignored. So let us proceed to the real task of explaining the *Parmenides* and its connections with several of Plato's late dialogues.

THE *PARMENIDES* AND PLATO'S LATE PHILOSOPHY

1

Introduction

Plato's long and astonishing career produced not only a large and arguably the most influential output of intellectual writing in Western, if not human, history but also the establishment of a research and educational institution that maintained its identity for more than nine hundred years. But the general features of these events have been written about and celebrated through many centuries of adulation, polemic, and relatively neutral scholarship. It is not the intent of this book, however, to comment on or celebrate these general features but rather to concentrate on the interrelations of some of Plato's later writings and to provide the detail necessary for explanation of the interrelations. To begin with reference to Plato's remarkable career and influence does, nevertheless, suggest the need for appropriate humility in approaching the actual task of this book. Indeed, it is intended to function rather as a substitution for Plato's common invocation of the gods when undertaking an intellectual task.

The centrepiece and, shifting the metaphor, the focal point of this book is Plato's *Parmenides*, a dialogue that from antiquity has been taken to be an enigma (though, among others, the most prominent of the Neoplatonists, Plotinus, relied upon it heavily). The first and larger part of the book offers a translation of and detailed commentary on that dialogue. The second part undertakes an interpretation of relevant portions of four other dialogues in the light of the commentary on the *Parmenides*. The other dialogues are the *Timaeus*, the *Theaetetus*, the *Sophist*, and the *Philebus* – all generally conceded to be late works of Plato. The translation of the *Parmenides* omits, where possible, non-significant comment of interlocutors, and is primarily to provide quick reference for readers in working through the detail of the dialogue. Though the translation is deliberately literal (in the interest of preserving the sense and flavour of both problems and presumed solutions), it embodies no effort to improve upon or correct the Burnet text.[1]

I join in the standard scholarly assumption that there was never any such conversation between Socrates and Parmenides as that detailed by Plato. This obligates an interpreter of the *Parmenides* to attend carefully to Plato's intentions throughout, for it is unlikely that he would include characters, events, and patterns of argument and exposition without set purpose. As I try to show, there is a genuine rationale for all of the following: the introductory meeting of visitors from Clazomenae with the chief interlocutors of the *Republic* (Plato's brothers, Glaucon and Adeimantus); the choice of Plato's half-brother, Antiphon, as narrator; the initial exchange of Socrates with Zeno; the critical questioning of Socrates by *Parmenides*; Parmenides' claim that Socrates needs 'exercise' of the sort exhibited in Zeno's treatise; and *Parmenides'* exhibition of the 'exercise' using 'his own' supposition, viz., *If one is*.

I think that the critical questioning of Socrates after his response to Zeno is seriously intended and invites emendation of the rationale and doctrine stated in Socrates' response, roughly, those of the *Phaedo*. Major questions in the critique are those concerning the 'separation' of the forms and the doctrine of 'participation' or 'having shares.' Socrates is told that somehow the forms are needed, but that he has tried to define various forms before he has been properly 'exercised.' (As we shall see in the text commentary, this passage does not require that, after 'exercise,' definition be the same activity that is displayed in the earlier dialogues.)

The 'exercise' procedure, which I call the Method of Suppositions, is the vehicle for the most telling insights of the *Parmenides*. It first appears in the dialogue as Zeno's procedure for showing that contradictions follow from the supposition that *many are*. Zeno's express purpose is to show, against those who ridiculed Parmenides' thesis of the One, that there is greater absurdity in the thesis of the Many. In the first part of the dialogue, Plato concedes the damaging character of Parmenides' critique of Socrates' reply to Zeno. But in the second part, making use of the very procedure of Zeno, that is, the Method of Suppositions, he puts in the mouth of Parmenides himself the utter barrenness of the doctrine of the One as Parmenides understands it. And, using the same procedure, Parmenides serves Plato's purposes by exhibiting what I shall call the 'logical structure' of the world.

The procedure requires taking a 'supposition' of the form 'If X is,' and proceeding to explore a patterned set of its 'logical' compatibilities or 'consequences.' Proposed values for X include *Many* (Zeno's supposition) and *One* (*Parmenides*' supposition), *Likeness* and *Unlikeness*, *Motion* and *Rest*,

Coming to Be and *Perishing*, and *Being* and *Not Being*. Exploration is to include compatibilities for whatever is supposed and also those for the 'others.' Finally the procedure is to involve compatibilities or 'consequences' both for the supposition that whatever is supposed is but also those for the supposition that whatever is supposed *is not*.

In Parmenides' example, using the supposition of the One, there are actually eight explorations of compatibilities or 'consequences.' Four are obvious: 1) the consequences for the One, if One is; 2) the consequences for the Others, if One is; 3) the consequences for the One, if One is not; and 4) the consequences for the Others, if One is not. This number is to be doubled, for there are two quite different readings or versions of the One Supposition. The first, which I call the Parmenidean Version, requires that there be no predication at all. The second, the Platonic Version, allows for predication, indeed, introduces duality (of *One* and *Being*) throughout everything.

No special significance is to be attached to the *One* of *Parmenides*' supposition other than its contrast with the *Many* of Zeno's supposition. I shall therefore cease the capitalization of 'One' and 'Many' – unless the context requires capitals. What the eight explorations come to (following the order of Plato's presentation) could be put as follows, using F and G as terms: 1) F is G, but really simply F (Parmenidean); 2) F is G (Platonic); 3) *Not-F* is G (Platonic); 4) *Not-F* is G, but really simply *Not-F* that is not (Parmenidean); 5) F is *Not-G* (Platonic); 6) F is *Not-G*, but really simply F with the additional liability of its being considered not to be anything (Parmenidean); 7) *Not-F* is *Not-G*, the appearance of predication (Platonic); 8) *Not-F* is *Not-G*, total non-being (Parmenidean). Generally, the Parmenidean versions produce 'neither/nor' consequences, and the Platonic versions produce 'both/and' consequences (with an effort to show how both might be allowed).

The first Platonic Version, supposition two, commences with the recognition of the duality required by understanding 'if one is' as involving *both one* and *is*. It proceeds to use this duality for generating all of arithmetic (and, *pari passu*, geometry) before proceeding to 'both/and' consequences. The generation of 'both/and' consequences is a function of the Platonic versions' allowing *predication*. The several expressions above that use 'Not' followed by a hyphen are to be understood in the light of the account of not-being in the *Sophist*, thus as indicating *different from X*, whatever term replaces X, that is, as indicating what in the *Sophist* are called the 'parts of Different' (257C–D). And it is worth noting that both Plato and Aristotle think of negation rather as negation of terms than as a sentential connective.

Plato's use of the Method of Suppositions shows respect for the procedure and thus indebtedness to Parmenides, but it is used for the purpose of exhibiting the foundations of arithmetic and for exhibiting the grounds of the intelligibility of whatever can be commonsensically said. Using the term broadly, Plato uses the Method of Suppositions as a means of exhibiting the *logical* foundations of the world. Its use in undermining Eleaticism is of a piece with the insistence in the *Sophist* (244D) that Parmenides' claim that *one is* is self-destructive in requiring more than one.

Chapters 2 through 8 go through the *Parmenides* in appropriate detail. Chapters 9 through 11 are designed to show, respectively, interrelations between the *Parmenides* and the *Timaeus* (chapter 9), the *Theaetetus* and the *Sophist* (chapter 10), and the *Philebus* (chapter 11).

The generation of the numbers in the second supposition of the *Parmenides* is completely dependent on the forms Being, Same, and Different, forms that may be taken as making up the foundation of intelligibility. The *Timaeus* takes those same forms to be the 'ingredients' of the soul of the World Animal, thus ensuring intelligibility and rationality for the movements of the heavens. In the 'second start' (47E ff.) of the *Timaeus*, the Receiver (*hypodoche*) is informed by the intelligible numbers and shapes (presumably as derived from the foundational forms), thus bringing about space and the physical world as Plato conceives it. The whole universe, though 'limited' spatially and temporally repetitive, is conceived to be a living animal, its soul supplying intelligibility to a physical world that is derived from the eternal intelligible and mathematical order and the Receiver. Human beings, with souls and bodies akin to the World Animal, are subject to perception and sensibles by the need for sustenance and rectilinear motion. Though there is mathematical and physical explanation of sensibles, the sensibles, playing as such no role in the intelligible causal order, are both a hindrance and a precondition for human understanding of the great order of things.

The *Theaetetus*, in denying that it is the eyes that see, the ears that hear, etc., asserts that it is the soul that perceives, using the various sense organs as *tools* (organa). Socrates gets *Theaetetus* to agree (185C–E) that the soul also has *tools* of its own that are essential to perception. These are Being, Same, Different, and Number. They enable the soul to take things as being such and such; as being the same as themselves and, in respects, other things; as being different from various things; and as being two, three, or some other number. Once again we have the foundational forms, this time in the guise of innate abilities of human souls. The argument proceeds by taking true belief as a definition of knowledge, but it founders for lack of an explanation of how false belief is possible. The problem of false belief carries over into the *Sophist*, notably in the guise of Parmenides' insistence on the unintelligibility of not-being. After insisting against the 'friends of the forms' that there is life and mind in the *all* (the World Animal again!) and not simply in the static forms of intelligibility, the Eleatic Stranger proceeds to discuss the interrelationships of the 'greatest forms,' viz. Being, Same, Different, Motion, and Rest, and to exhibit the pattern of their intermingling. *Different* and its 'parts,' for example, Different from F, Different from G, etc., carry the burden of the being of not-being. Thus, for example, '*Theaetetus* flies' is false, the truth of the matter being not the non-being of anything, but rather *Theaetetus*' having a share of the Different-from-Flying.

The *Sophist* begins with a rather elaborate set of definitions of the Sophist, all arrived at by the procedure of Collection and Division. The *Statesman*, an obvious sequel to the *Sophist*, with the Eleatic Stranger continuing as protagonist, consists entirely of the use of the procedure of Collection and Division. The *Philebus*, despite its return to Socrates as protagonist, treats Collection and Division as a remarkable procedure that has saved Socrates from the despair of failing to arrive at satisfactory definitions (very likely a reference to the *Parmenides* Socrates who has tried 'too soon' to attempt definitions). The idea is to find or select a 'one' under which or included in which what a person is seeking to define falls, then to divide on down, making sure to omit no steps. If the procedure has been done properly, what one has is a genera/species tree by means of which s/he can say exactly 'how many' what is to be defined is and by means of which a useful definition can be formulated.

In all of the examples given in the three dialogues there is no clear statement that the procedure leads to definition of eternal forms or even that it makes reference to forms as described in earlier dialogues. A major contention of the present book is that Collection and Division makes use of linguistic/conceptual abilities of persons using tried and tested languages. It must be pointed out that, in the procedure, the languages are *used*, not mentioned, and that their semantic targets are genuine features of the world – the physical world being the mathematized Receiver of the *Timaeus* (or, as we shall see much later, the *mixture* of the *Philebus* – the form of which is given by the intelligible numbers and the basic forms that generate them). One may therefore use Collection and Division without necessarily being familiar with Plato's fundamental ontology, though the intelligible numbers and the basic forms are needed to make the procedure possess such authenticity as it has.

8 The *Parmenides* and Plato's Late Philosophy

In the *Philebus*, as part of the effort to determine the relative places of pleasure and mind in the good life for a human being, Socrates speaks of four factors in the universe: *Unlimited, Limit*, the *Mixture of Unlimited and Limit*, and the *Cause of the Mixture*. Pleasure and the other sensibles as such are invariably 'more or less' and containing no metric. *Limit* seems to be whatever in itself contains number, ratio, or proportion. *Mixture*, in human beings, seems to consist of ratio or proportion in the body plus whatever sensibles may obtain along with that condition. More generally, it seems to be the mix of proportion or ratio and the lack of either in physical things. As one might expect, Socrates takes the *Cause* to be mind (whether perception, belief, memory, or knowledge), and he thinks of mind generally as introducing or maintaining order and harmony in things.

At one point in the *Philebus*, the image of the World Animal is invoked. Socrates' interlocutor, Protarchus, agrees that earth, air, fire, water, and soul in us are all derivative from the great order of things. And Protarchus readily agrees that the whole order is as good as it can be. The distinction between the practical arithmetic and geometry of the artisan and those of the philosopher is set out in terms redolent of the *Parmenides*' account of the numbers. In the end, the good life for a human being is taken to consist in theoretical and practical competence plus the pleasures that don't interfere with the work of mind, including the pleasures of learning and knowing. And it is obvious that, in the end, the sense of the marvellous intelligibility of the world and one's place in it is taken to be the crowning achievement of the well-lived life.

2

Zeno's Stricture, Predication, and 'Having Shares' (126A–35C)

Introductory Narrative (126A–30A)

Text:

Cephalos After we came to Athens from our home in Clazomenae, we happened upon Adeimantus and Glaucon in the market-place. Seizing my hand, Adeimantus said, 'Welcome, Cephalos, if we can do anything for you while you are here, you have only to say it.'

'How very timely,' said I. 'I am here for just that purpose – to ask a favour of you.'

'Tell us the favour,' he said.

[126B] And I said, 'What was the name of your half-brother on your mother's side? For I don't remember it. He was just a boy when I came here from Clazomenae earlier, and it has been a long time since then. I think that the name of his father was Pyrilampes.'

'It was indeed,' he said.

'And his own name?'

'Antiphon. But what especially are you interested in?'

'These,' I said, 'are fellow-citizens of mine and much taken with philosophy. They have heard that this Antiphon met many times with a certain Pythodorus – Zeno's friend – and that he had heard recounted so often the [126C] conversation which Socrates, Zeno, and Parmenides once had that he can relate it by heart.'

'What you say is true,' he said.

'Then,' said I, 'we wish to hear that conversation.'

'That's not difficult,' he said, 'for as a youth he took great pains with it, though now, like his grandfather who had the same name, he devotes himself to the care of horses. If that's your need, let's go to him. For he has only just now gone home from here, and he lives nearby in Melite.'

[127A] Having said as much, we started walking, and we found Antiphon at home, giving a smith instructions for making some sort of bit. When he was free from him, the brothers told him our purpose in coming. He recognized me from the earlier visit and welcomed me, and we asked him to recount the conversation. At first he hesitated, for he said it was a hard task. Finally, however, he went through it.

That Plato chose to open the dialogue with the arrival in Athens of visitors from Clazomenae suggests, of course, Anaxagoras. There is therefore considerable temptation to find some linkage between the content of the *Parmenides* and the philosophy of Anaxagoras. And there is in fact a little evidence. Anaxagoras Fragment 12, which deals with *mind (nous)*, does invite making the linkage, and a bit of speculation may be justified, especially since nothing in my interpretation of the dialogue depends upon it. The second supposition of the *Parmenides* argues for the indefinite or infinite division of *one* and *being* and the presence of both in absolutely everything. Fragment 12, in keeping with Anaxagoras' claim of the infinite divisibility of everything, equally claims that mind is present and active throughout everything. And the second supposition, linking the divisibility of *one* and *being* with the generation of numbers, equally suggests intelligibility in everything that is. It may be worth remarking as well that Anaxagoras' pluralism is commonly thought to be a response to Parmenides' and Zeno's attack on multiplicity and change, in that Anaxagoras, though keeping a form of pluralism, strongly insists that nothing comes to be from or perishes into nothing. What one has according to Anaxagoras is simply arrangement and rearrangement of things that *are*. Since the *Parmenides* is, as I read it and as we shall see, a pluralistic response to Parmenides and Zeno, it is likely that Plato's introduction of visitors from Clazomenae invites a parallel between Anaxagoras' response and his own. But both of these comments are, of course, a bit speculative, however reasonable the case for them.

I take it as established by others that a conversation between Zeno, Parmenides, and the young Socrates did not actually take place and that the choice of dramatis personae was Plato's. The presence of Plato's older brothers, Glaucon and Adeimantus, in the introduction suggests linkage with the *Republic* – in which they are Socrates' chief interlocutors. I am prepared to claim that the *Republic*'s breathtaking images of the Line and the Cave and their surrounding text, though lacking detail, represent Plato's first attempt at a really comprehensive account of the place of everything (*Republic* 509E–20E). Better, those images invite a comprehensive account of the rationale for determining or making explicit the place of everything. And that account, however promissory, requires thinking of the forms as interconnected and not simply as *beings* in splendid isolation from each other. The *Parmenides* actually does attempt to supply the intellectual framework in terms of which detailed inquiry into everything can go on. Thus the evocation of the *Republic* by the presence of Glaucon and Adeimantus is, I believe, intended by Plato. It is noteworthy that the *Timaeus* is also linked with the *Republic*, as a longish part of a conversation taken as occurring the day after the *Republic* conversation. As we shall see in sequel, the mathematized world of the *Timaeus* (chapter 9 below; also presaged in the *Republic*) is a major part of what I take to be the late philosophy of Plato.

That Antiphon, a younger half-brother of Plato (the son of Perictione's second husband, Pyrilampes), is the narrator of the dialogue has no obvious explanation. But the following suggestions do not seem entirely speculative. Antiphon has given up philosophy for the care of horses, and this removes him from any hint of philosophical advocacy at the time of the Parmenides' composition. That he had been closely associated with Pythodorus obviously suggests youthful fascination with Zeno and probably Parmenides as well. Unless he were to invent a character to serve as narrator, Plato needed someone who could not have been present at any such actual encounter, who was credibly interested in Zeno and Parmenides, and who would not resent being represented as narrator. Indeed, it is likely that Antiphon was pleased by his famous half-brother's choice.

Zeno's Argument (127B–28E)

Text:

[127B] Zeno and Parmenides once came to the Great Panathenaea. Parmenides was already fairly old, grey and of good and noble appearance. He was about sixty-five. Zeno was nearly forty, tall, and elegant looking. And it was rumoured that he was Parmenides' lover. He said that they lodged with [127C] Pythodorus outside the wall in Cerameicus. Thence Socrates came with many others – eager to hear Zeno's writings read, for they had been brought to Athens for the first time by Zeno. Socrates was then quite young. Zeno himself read aloud to them. At the time Parmenides happened to be outside. When only a little remained of the reading of the [127D] arguments, Pythodorus said that he himself, Parmenides, and Aristotle (who became one of the Thirty) came in, so they heard only a little of the writings. Pythodorus had, however, heard the readings from Zeno before.

Socrates heard Zeno out and then entreated him to read the first supposition of the argument again. Zeno read it again.

Socrates [127E] Zeno, how does your argument go? If the beings are many, then they must be likes and unlikes. But this is impossible, for likes cannot be unlikes, and unlikes cannot be likes. Is this not the thrust of your argument?

Zeno It is.

S And so, if it is impossible for unlikes to be likes and for likes to be unlikes, it is also impossible for many to be. For, if many were to be, they would be impossibly characterized. And so is the burden of your arguments nothing other than to contend – against everything commonly said – that many are not? And is it your belief that each of your arguments is a proof of just this, so that you undertake to supply as many proofs as your written arguments – all to the effect that many are [128A] not? Have you written to this purpose, or have I not understood you rightly?

Z No. You have put together very well the import of the entire treatise.

S I have discovered, Parmenides, that Zeno wishes to be quite close to you not only in friendship but also in authorship. For he has written to much the same effect as you have yourself, but, by turning things about, he tries to trick us into thinking that he is saying something different. For you, in your poems, say that the [128B] all is one, and of this you lay out proofs in fine and excellent style. He says, on the other hand, that it is not many, and he also lays out numerous and weighty proofs. That one of you says *one*, the other *no many*, and thus each, while appearing to have no contention in common, says almost the same things appears to be an expressive accomplishment that is quite beyond the rest of us.

Z Yes, Socrates, but you have not fully perceived the real nature of my treatise, though you are keen, [128C] like a Spartan hound, at chasing and running down arguments. But a primary fact has eluded you, namely, that my writing is not so pretentious as to have been produced with the intention you say it has: to deceive men in the guise of some great performance. What you speak of is something incidental; the truth is that these writings are simply support for the argument of Parmenides, coming to his aid [128D] against those who set upon him with caricatures to the effect that, *if one is*, many ludicrous conclusions follow and, as well, conclusions that are contrary to his contention. This treatise of mine argues against those speaking on behalf of the many and returns to them the same and more. For it undertakes to show that *their* supposition, *if many are*, must allow, if one pursues it sufficiently, even more ludicrous conclusions than the supposition, *if one is*. It was from such love of controversy and while yet quite young that I wrote it, and then someone stole the manuscript, so that there was no chance to consider [128E] whether to publish it or not. Not being aware of this, Socrates, you think that it was written, not from youthful love of controversy, but from mature love of honour. Even so, as I said, your representation of it is not bad at all.

Plato would have helped subsequent scholarship a great deal if he had reproduced Zeno's book (whether or not there was but one book) completely or, at any rate, had given us a great deal more of it. We must assume, however, that Socrates produces a reasonably accurate statement either of one of the book's arguments or of the general thrust of all of them. Plato does, however, supply us with quite a bit of additional information when, at the end of the first part of the dialogue, Parmenides describes the sort of 'exercise' that Socrates needs and refers to it as the procedure followed by Zeno. And there is good reason to believe that the procedure followed by Parmenides (in the dialogue) for 'his own' supposition, *If one is*, (notably in determining the 'consequences' for what I have labelled suppositions one and two) is like Zeno's procedure. These, as well as the other suppositions, follow a more or less set pattern in which *part/whole, same/different, like/unlike*, and other pairs of opposites appear. *Like/unlike* is used here.

As Socrates states it, Zeno's supposition is: *If the beings are many* (εἰ πολλά ἐστι τὰ ὄντα). Later (136A) Parmenides refers to Zeno's supposition as *if many are* (ἐι πολλά ἐστι), so I doubt that much, if anything, turns on the precise formulation given it by Socrates in the present section. The Zeno argument, as stated by Socrates, is of the form *modus tollendo tollens*:

If the beings are many, they must be likes and unlikes. But it is impossible for them to be likes and unlikes. Hence, the beings cannot be many.

It is important to insist at the outset that, in considering the argument, it will not do to claim an obvious difference between the *is* of identity and the *is* of predication and then fault Zeno for failure to recognize it. Precisely what is at stake is the intelligibility of the or an 'is' of predication. And Socrates shortly attempts to show how *he* can make predication intelligible for at least some 'beings.'

I think that the simplest way to explain and give relevant point to Zeno's argument is to suppose that there are several 'beings' (and it makes no difference *what* beings, whether horses, trees, reds, larges, or whatever – though it may help to note that adjectives and some other forms of speech are rather easily nominalized in Attic Greek with the use of the definite article or a demonstrative). Let them be A, B, and C. Suppose that A is B. Obviously A is A, for they are the same or, in the vocabulary of the second part of the dialogue, *sames*. But we have supposed that A is B and thus that *they* are *sames*. But we have also supposed them to be different, so they are *differents* as well as *sames*. Since *sames* are *likes*, and *differents* are *unlikes*, A and B must be *likes* and *unlikes*. But if A really is the same as B, it cannot also be the same as itself. Hence it must be different from itself and thus unlike itself. But surely A is A and thus the same as and like itself. If this reasoning is played out for any number of beings, the conclusion must be that they are all *likes* and *unlikes* both of themselves and the others. But this is impossible, so there cannot be many beings.

It may be thought that this dialectic is avoidable. But if beings are many and are *somehow* related, whatever term is used to express their being related will stand to them as B to A in the above paragraph. Even if it is merely said that each of them is, there is a problem. Are A and is two names for the same being or for different beings? If the former, then the supposition is frustrated in the stating of it. If the latter, we are back to the argument of the above paragraph. It is noteworthy that, when Socrates turns to Parmenides at 128A–B, he has Parmenides saying 'One' (*not* 'One is') and Zeno saying 'No many' (*not* 'Many are not' or 'Not-many are').

This sort of reasoning leads to what I have elsewhere[1] called 'Zeno's Stricture': *For any two terms replacing A and B, if A is B, then B cannot be different from A.*

There are a great many allusions by Plato and others to people who took Zeno's Stricture or something akin to it quite seriously, and I think that Plato was motivated by it in adopting his theory of forms and participation. In the *Phaedo* and in the next section of the *Parmenides*, the response to it is to understand predication in sentences about individuals as *having a share* (or *shares*) *of* rather than *being*. Thus 'Helen is beautiful' is parsed as 'Helen has a share of the Beautiful.' Since *having* is not being, this appears to get past Zeno's Stricture. As I have suggested earlier, however, it invites another equally disturbing problem, namely, that of giving an intelligible sense to 'having a share of.' The effort to do so sets the agenda for the remainder of the first part of *Parmenides*. And the failure of that effort sets the agenda for at least part of the complex second part of the dialogue.

Before moving to Socrates' response I might avoid future confusions by saying something about *use* and *mention*. So far as I can tell, Plato throughout his writings is, in using words, inviting us to attend to what words are used to *mention*. He makes it quite clear when he is writing about a particular word or letter or numeral, and normally in so doing he is writing about a geometric shape as *type*, not about a certain individual shape. Except for proper names of individuals he appears to think of words as used to mention features or things that yet other words or phrases can also be used to mention. Most, if not all, of the Socratic *What is X?* questions invite an answer by means of other words or phrases that are appropriately used to mention exactly what *X* is appropriately used to mention. They are not questions about two *different* things' being literally the same. They seem to be questions about the 'unpacking' of *X* and thus seem to assume that *X* is something that is compound or complex.

Socrates' Response (128E–29E)

Text:

Socrates I accept that and believe it is as you say. But tell me this. Don't you acknowledge there to be just by [129A] itself a form of Likeness and yet another, opposite, which is Unlike? And you and I and others that we call *many* come to have shares of these two beings? Those coming to have shares of Likeness come to be *likes*, in the same way, those coming to have shares of unlikeness, come to be *unlikes*, and those coming to have shares of both come to be both? And even if everything should come to have shares of both opposite beings and, as having shares of both, are *likes* and *unlikes* [129B] of themselves, what is there to be surprised at? If, however, one could exhibit likes themselves coming to be unlikes or unlikes themselves coming to be likes, that would, I think, be a wonder. But, if one merely exhibits those having shares of both as admitting both, it seems to me, Zeno, that there is nothing strange about that – not even if he shows everything to be *one* by having shares of the One and the same things to be *many* by having shares of Multitude. But, if he showed what *is* One as itself *Many* and what *is* Many as itself [129C] *One*, I would then really be amazed.

And the same holds for all of the rest. If one could exhibit the kinds and forms themselves in themselves as themselves admitting [undergoing?] opposites, there would be just cause for amazement. But if someone shows me to be one and many, what is there to be amazed at? He may say, if he wishes to exhibit me as many, that my right, my left, my front, my back, my upper, and my lower are all differents. And, indeed, I think I do have a share of Multitude. If he wishes to exhibit me as one, he may say that, while we are [129D] seven, I am one man and have a share of One. And so he shows me to be both. If, therefore, anyone undertakes to exhibit that the same things are one and many – such things as stones or sticks – he will show that the same things are many or one, but he will not show that One is Many or that Multitude is One. Nor will he say anything amazing but simply what we all should agree to. If, however, as I said just now, one should first separate out the forms just by themselves, for example, Likeness and Unlikeness, Multitude [129E] and One, Rest and Motion, and all such, and then show them able to intermingle and separate from one another, I would be astonished and amazed, Zeno. I believe that you have handled these matters boldly. But, as I say, I would be much more impressed by anyone who could produce this same difficulty among those that are grasped by reasoning – that is the [130A] intertwining of every kind – that you detailed in the visibles.

After noting the collusion of Parmenides and Zeno in defending Parmenides' One and hearing confirmation of it from Zeno, Socrates proceeds to state, in effect, the *Phaedo* doctrine. First, distinguish the forms as beings each of which is *just by itself*. Second, grant that the things we call *many*, that is, individuals, may have or come to have shares of the forms, and, in so having, be called by the appropriate names. Thus, those having shares of the Like itself are called *likes* (though, strictly, this is only in virtue of their having shares of the Like itself, not of their *being* likes). Such individuals may, as having shares of both Likeness and Unlikeness, even appropriately be called both *likes* and *unlikes* without any problem. On this ground, Socrates responds to Zeno by denying for the *many* (that is, individuals having shares) the impossibility of being *likes* and *unlikes* (in virtue of their having shares) and thus holding to the antecedent of Zeno's argument, namely, *The beings are many*.

Socrates flatly denies for his forms any sort of *having shares of*. Indeed, they cannot even be thought of as *many*, for Socrates states that things are many only by having shares of the form, Multitude. It is even difficult to suppose that each form is *one*, for Socrates describes himself as one only by having a share of the form, One (or, perhaps, what it is to be One). There can be no 'communion' (Plato's term in the *Sophist* for the linkage of the 'greatest kinds') of such forms; each is, as it were, a splendid solitaire.

It is interesting to note that most of Parmenides' arguments in the first part of the dialogue against Socrates' account have the result that the form cannot be one (an unacceptable conclusion). Even allowing self-predication for the form One, only that form could be one. On the doctrine here stated, no other form could be one. There is some indication in Socrates' response here, however, of worry about *opposites* and thus the suggestion that One could hardly tolerate Multitude but that it might get on with Largeness or Likeness. *How* it might get on is quite unclear, for the doctrine of having shares of is invented for predications made of individuals. And, without significant transformation, it could hardly do the job for, say, Likeness' having a share of One. For the time being, however, and until we get to the second part of the dialogue, I think we shall have to go along with Parmenides and treat accounts of *having a share of* that lead to the form's not being one as unacceptable. Even so, it may be worth noting at this point that, should a form fail to be one, it would either have parts or simply be a non-holistic many. In either event, granting the *difference* among the parts or the many, such a form would be different from itself and, *prima facie* at least, the grounds of univocity would be lost.

Another way of pointing out the difficulty of the form's being many is, of course, to note that, with the form's being many, we are back with Zeno's argument. If a form is many, then its 'parts' (each assumed to be different from every other) must somehow be related. The 'parts' will then play the role of A, B, and C of my original illustration. But, for them, we cannot appeal to the *Phaedo* doctrine of having shares, as Socrates did in showing how there could be many individuals having shares of different forms. If we were to try, we would have to treat the 'parts' of a form as individuals having shares and thus not as forms at all. Treating each 'part' as a separate form, identical with its essence (what it is to be F, for whatever value of F), would not exhibit any relation between 'parts.' With the failure of such efforts we would be back with the Zeno problem – this time for forms.

The forms mentioned in this section are somewhat unfamiliar ones to *Phaedo* readers: Likeness, Unlikeness, Multitude, One, Rest, Motion. All of them (except Multitude) figure in the exercise of the second part of the dialogue, and they are probably among those spoken of by Zeno in his treatise (and alluded to by Parmenides in his first question to Socrates in the next section). It is difficult to come up with an appropriate general name for these forms. Since they figure a great deal in the second part of the dialogue, however, it will be useful to have one. Let me start now referring to them as *framework* forms and justify the use of the term in the arguments to follow.

It may be worth noting that Socrates' response to Zeno requires the recognition that individuals having shares of 'opposite' forms do so only as specified in certain respects. Thus Socrates has a share of the One itself *as being one man among many.* And he has a share of Multitude *as being made up of parts*. With Parmenides' later criticism of the 'pattern/copy' account of having a share, it is noteworthy that individuals may be said to be 'likes' (having shares of the Like itself) in virtue of having shares of one and the same form (other than the Like itself); and 'unlikes' in virtue of having shares of different or opposite forms (other than the Unlike itself). Thus having a share or shares of at least some framework forms seems to presuppose being specifiable in some other respects.

What Things Have Shares of Forms? (130A–E)

Text:

Parmenides   [130B] How admirable you are in your zest for argument, Socrates! Tell me, have you yourself made the division you speak of, separating on the one side some forms themselves and on the other those having shares of them? And do you think that there is Likeness itself quite separated from the likeness we have in us, and also One, Multitude, and all the others of which you have just heard Zeno speak?
Socrates   I do.
P   And also such as these: some form of Justice by itself, of Beautiful, of Good, and of all of the others like them as well?
S   Yes.
P   [130C] And what about a form of Man separate from us and from all such as we are, a form of Man just by itself, or a form of Fire, or a form of Water?
S   I have often been puzzled concerning these, Parmenides, whether one must speak concerning those in this manner or in some other way.
P   And, Socrates, what about some which may even seem ludicrous, such things as hair, mud, dirt, and other unvalued and unworthy things – are you puzzled concerning them whether there is a separated form for each of [130D] them, a form different from what we can hold in our hands?
S   Not at all. What we see of them is just what they are. Since it would be strange to believe that there are forms for them, there is no incentive to do so. Still, it has occasionally disturbed me that the same should not obtain for all cases. But then, when I have taken this stance, I take flight, fearful that I may perish in an abyss of prattling. And so, coming back to those which we just now acknowledged to have forms, I work away at various matters concerning them.
P   [130E] That's because you are still young, Socrates, and philosophy has not yet gripped you as firmly as I think it will later, when you will despise none of these. Now, because of your age, you are still overly attentive to the opinions of men.

Parmenides' first question invites a distinction between *forms, individuals*, and *the shares* that individuals have. Socrates' use of *metechein* (μετέχειν), a verb taking the genitive of share and translated as *have a share of*, invites the question. Plato obviously took a term commonly used to characterize various things (as 'He has a share of the brave' for 'He is brave') and gave it a technical usage. With that technical usage and Socrates' description of its function in the section just presented, Parmenides' asseveration of a *separation* (*chorismos*, χωρισμός) between forms and individuals that have shares appears justified, and Socrates does not object to it. The distinction and the asseveration do, however, invite the arguments of the next section. They justify Parmenides' talk of the *share in us* as contrasted with the form. And Socrates readily accedes to there being *framework* forms (those mentioned by Zeno) on the one side and shares of them *in us* on the other. Thus the worrisome separation is not just between forms and individuals; it is also between forms and shares of forms.

The question about Justice, Beautiful, etc., gives us, of course, Platonic old friends. And Socrates readily grants that, in their case, there are forms, the shares in us, and ourselves. Parmenides might well have included the whole class of forms that, in imitation of Strawson,[2] I shall call *characterizing* forms, that is, forms corresponding to adjectives and adjectival uses. In all these cases, there is at least initial sense to be made of distinguishing the form, the individual, and something the individual *has* – the *share*. There is nothing obviously untoward in talking about the beautiful in Helen, the large in Dumbo, and so on. And, of course, the last argument of the *Phaedo* (103C10–107A1) depends heavily upon our being able to do so.

Parmenides' next question, inquiring about a form for man, raises genuine difficulties. For here we have what, following Strawson again, would be a *sortal* form, that is, a form corresponding to a noun or a nominal use. *Prima facie*, one could distinguish between the form of Man itself and an individual man. But could that individual be said to be a man by virtue of having a share of the Man itself and thus having a man in him? Here, if you please, is a third man we don't need. And Parmenides is careful to say 'separate *from us*,' not 'separate from the man in us.' It is very doubtful that the *Phaedo* account or Socrates' account in the *Parmenides* can accommodate sortal forms without revision, and Socrates does well to answer that he is puzzled about them (and, one adds, the general applicability of his account to sortals).

At this point in the *Parmenides* there is, I believe, at least the making of a Third Man argument, which has some appropriate resemblance to what Aristotle calls 'the third man' and which he describes in some detail in

Sophistical Refutations (178b37–79a11). It is not the largeness argument of *Parmenides* 132, as I hope to show in discussing the latter. Though the topic of the Third Man has achieved great prominence since Gregory Vlastos' 1952 article[3] (and we shall soon be briefly discussing that article), it is not of crucial significance at this point in the *Parmenides*. The issue, however, of how Plato is to handle sortals is significant. I discuss it at some length in commenting on the second part of the dialogue in connection with the Platonic interpretation of the One supposition.

'Fire' and 'water' are not, strictly, sortals. They are what Strawson calls 'bulk' terms, and they invite prefixing by such expressions as 'piece of,' 'expanse of,' and the like. Except for the *Phaedo*'s argument (103C–E) in which the presence of fire necessitates that it or what has it also be or have *a hot* and the account of earth, air, fire, and water in the *Timaeus* (53C4–55C6), Plato has relatively little to say about stuff or materials. In the *Phaedo* I think Plato is careful *not* to commit himself to the pattern of forms, individuals, and shares for fire and snow. Though the question is a bit different when posed for *man* from that to be posed for *water*, one must ask: What is it that has a share of Man or Water (assuming these to be forms)? And no answer fits the pattern readily.

As I read the *Timaeus*, the 'Receptacle' (better, *Receiver*, ὑποδοχή), after the work of the demiurge, is completely formed by a vast number of elementary mathematical solids (tetrahedra, cubes, octahedra, and icosahedra), separately and jointly conforming to an appropriate mathematical pattern. (As we shall see in the *Timaeus* chapter, the Aristotelian issue about the construction of solids from surfaces is *strictly* irrelevant and based on a misunderstanding.) Thus the Receiver, as completely unformed, is the non-characterizable *non-what* (50A–D) that is so informed. My point for the moment and for the present text and context is simply to note that the *Timaeus* doctrine does not easily, if at all, accommodate the form-individual-share pattern here being discussed. In the *Timaeus*, Plato appears to be speaking 'in some other way' concerning water and fire. Indeed, Timaeus explicitly rejects 'standard' accounts of water and fire, in favour of a mathematical account, at least partially on the ground of preference for knowledge over opinion (51D3–52A7). We shall return to this set of issues in discussing the second part of the dialogue (and in the *Timaeus* chapter) where, to anticipate, I shall claim that, for a physical *thing* (as the object of a sortal term) to have a share of a form is to have or embody a certain mathematical configuration or number.[4]

As we shall note at the end of this chapter, Plato in the *Parmenides* is prepared to recognize that there is a general form of Knowledge and also a number of forms for the specific kinds of Knowledge that human beings may have or come to have shares of. And this figures as a consequence of each of the several Platonic interpretations of the *One* supposition in the second part of the dialogue. The *Theaetetus* (184C1–86D5), in a passage that I shall advert to again and at length, insists that it is the *soul* that *sees* various things using the eyes as instruments (*organa*) and, as well, using *itself*. The implication in context is that the soul has a set of aboriginal abilities, abilities suggested by the *Timaeus* account of the soul as 'made of' Being, Same, and Different and thus appropriately akin to the most foundational of the framework forms (34C–35B). Since souls do not come to be or perish and are the principles of any actual motion in the universe, their having in them the fundamental abilities to move bodies, to use bodies' organs for perceiving, talking, building, etc., and knowing are not features that they *come to have* (but, rather, come to *exercise*). Though 'made of' in the *Timaeus* may be a metaphor, Plato offers no means of getting behind it and thus suggests that soul has a place in his fundamental ontology on a par with the forms themselves.

The *Timaeus* suggests, if it does not state, a doctrine of more complex bodies as made from the simpler regular-solid bodies mentioned above. The simpler of *these*, constituting what we should ordinarily call *materials* (wood, stone, etc.) are, like their constituents, structures according with intelligible mathematical formulas. As such, however, they are still 'stuffs' (though mathematically determined and not the stuffs of crude materialism) and not individual things except as pieces, chunks, heaps, etc. More complex but not animated bodies are also structured according to intelligible mathematical formulas. Yet other more complex bodies, however, are *organ*ized (that is, having organs) and thus capable of being ensouled. As ensouled, they cease to be *stuff* and, while ensouled, are individuals – *a man, this horse, that bird*, etc. Though Plato's account certainly suggests that the bottom-level solids can be thought of as individuals, the primary application of individuals-talk is to items in the vast domain of animals (ensouled things – leaving plants, as Plato does, out of account). And Plato certainly suggests that at least some of the differences between individual (kinds of) animals are due to possession of or lack of effective *organs* (that is, bodily tools to be used by the soul). All of this requires, of course, that one must, indeed, speak in a different way (from the form-individual-share manner) concerning genuine individuals.

Manufactured things are individual things and not simply stuffs because of their serviceability for human needs and desires, because of their resemblance to ensouled things, and/or because their organization of stuffs results from human patterns (that is, thought of by human being and, in the interesting cases, form-patterns) that are analogous to or identical with the form-patterns or number-patterns embodied in 'natural' bodies. As in the 'natural' cases one commonly says what a thing *is* (that is, what sort of individual it is) by adversion to what it does or is capable of doing, so, in the manufactured cases, to say what things *are* is to specify their role or use or their resemblance to things so specifiable or their being produced in the manner of things so specifiable. The latter part of the *Timaeus* is filled with anatomical individuation of bodily organs by reference to their role or function (69D ff.). Generally, therefore, Plato's settled account of sortals and their application is teleological in character. *Caveat*: reference to role may *be* reference to form or mathematical configuration embodied (where the form is complex), or (in simpler cases) the sortal's application may *be* the embodiment of a form (with no teleology specified).

Parmenides' final question to Socrates in this section adverts to earlier Platonic accounts of forms as ideals or paradigms that, in the words of the *Phaedo*, things 'strive to attain' (*bouletai einai, βούλεται εἶναι*, 74D) but fall short of. Can there be forms for 'unworthy things'? And what is Socrates talking about in saying that hair, dirt, etc. are 'just what we see them to be'? Holding these two questions in abeyance for a moment, I think that *Parmenides'* comment on Socrates' answer rather more anticipates the second part of the dialogue than predicts Socrates' future philosophical activity (though it may well predict his future activity in the *Philebus* – but of this more in sequel). In effect it invites Socrates not to confuse the intelligibility of everything that is or comes to be (including hair and dirt) with its desirability. Both the *Sophist* and the *Timaeus* urge that the universe is the best it can be and that it is patterned on the forms, but neither urges that every part of the universe considered in isolation, even though intelligible, is as such desirable. When, at the end of the first part of the dialogue, Socrates is told that he has tried 'too soon' to define Beautiful, Justice, etc., part of the point is that he is not in a position to determine desirability before he has a grip on the principles of intelligibility.

In this light Socrates' comment that hair, etc., are 'just what we see them to be' is a symptom of the conflation of intelligibility and desirability. This is the Socrates of the condemnation of Anaxagoras in the *Phaedo* – Anaxagoras who wrote about bone, sinew, etc. and thus, though recognizing *mind* formally, confused the material conditions for action with the cause of such action (97B8–99B6). Socrates surely is prepared to concede that he can hardly walk to Boeotia without legs, but, should he walk, the *cause* of his walking there is not his legs, but rather his thought that going there is somehow good. Here in the *Parmenides* Socrates is prepared to grant the framework forms as needed for intelligibility and the 'value' forms (Good, Beautiful, etc.) as needed for desirability, but he is uncomfortable about 'stuff' or 'thing' forms. And now he denies forms for trivial and in themselves undesirable things. This is the more or less expected response from a Socrates who starts with concerns about the excellences (*aretai, ἀρεταί*) and who models action on the assumption of a universal desire for *good*. The conception of the form-explanation of *everything* comes late and with the recognition that the whole universe is the best it can be, though parts of it in themselves are not.

'What we see of them is just what they are' invites discussion of perception and its objects, and we cannot assume in the young Socrates the accounts of the *Theaetetus* and the *Timaeus*. It is worth noting, however, that the *Timaeus* gives us two 'worlds of becoming': one the deceptive and contradictory sensible world; the other the 'world' of Plato's changing (in place and combination) mathematical solids.[5] The former is, of course, causally derivative from the latter. And only the things in the latter, strictly speaking, have shares of numbers or forms, that is, are literally structured in accordance with form-principles. I shall explain this comment at length later. But the present point is simply that for the Socrates of the *Parmenides*, who has been given roughly the views of the *Phaedo*, there can hardly be the two worlds of becoming of the *Timaeus* or the distinction between the goodness of the world and the goodness of individual things in it. Since he cannot find 'value' in hair, dirt, etc., he has no alternative than to say that 'what we see of them is just what they are.' The comment about Socrates' concern with men's opinions is probably to be related to the comment at the end of the first part of the *Parmenides* concerning exercise that is 'what most people call mere talk.' It is thus not simply the shift from moral concerns that is involved; it is as well Socrates' failure to be preoccupied with ontological or metaphysical issues that have no obvious practical import.

Having the Whole or Part of the Form as a Share (130E-31E)

Text:

Parmenides [130E] But then, tell me this. Does it seem to you, since you say there are some forms, that those coming to have shares of them have their [131A] names, for example, those coming to have shares of Likeness come to be *likes*, those of Largeness, *larges*, those of Beauty and Justice, *justs* and *beautifuls*? And does each which comes to have a share come to have the whole form or part of the form as its

share? Or could there be some other coming to have a share besides these? Then does it seem to you that the whole form, while remaining one, is in each of the many? How is this possible?
Socrates But, Parmenides, what hindrance is there to its being in each of them?
[131B] **P** The fact that, while being one and the same, it would then simultaneously be in many separated things and would thus be separated from itself.
S No it wouldn't, for it may be like a day that, while being one and the same, is in many places simultaneously and remains in no way separated from itself. If this were the case for each of the forms, it would be one and the same in all of those having shares of it.
P How pleasantly, Socrates, you make it one and the same simultaneously in many places! It's as though you were to cover many people with a sail and then say that it is one [131C] whole over many. Isn't this the sort of thing you think it appropriate to say? But then would the *whole* sail be over each, or would a *part* be over one and *another part* be over another?
S A part would be over each.
P Then, Socrates, since the forms themselves are divided into parts, those having shares of them would have shares of parts; only a part and not the whole form would be in each of them. Are you prepared, Socrates, to tell us that one form can really be divided into parts and yet remain one?
S Not at all.
P Then consider this. Doesn't it seem unreasonable that, given the division of [131D] the Large itself into parts, each of the many larges should be *large* by having a share of a smaller part of the Large than the Large itself? And what of this? If something has received some small part of the Equal, will it, by virtue of the less than Equal itself, be equal to something?

And if one of us should have a part of the Small, the Small will be larger than it (since it is a part, the Small itself will be larger). But that to which the part taken away is added will be [131E] smaller, not larger, than it was before.

In what way, then, Socrates, can the others come to have shares of your forms, if they can come to have shares neither of parts nor of wholes?
S Good Lord, I think it's no easy matter to make any sort of determination.

Parmenides starts serious critical discussion by getting Socrates to agree that the form-names transfer to the individuals having shares of them, so that those having shares of the Like itself, for example, are *likes*. In total context, this really seems to require *three* items with the name: the form (the Large itself), the individual having a share of the form (the elephant that has a share of the Large itself), and the share (the large in the elephant). There is, as I see it, no question but that each of the latter is are or can be a many or a multitude. But one might wish to argue (as several have)[6] that the shares are somehow 'universal' characters, so that the large in our exemplary elephant would somehow be distributed through all of the individuals that have shares of the Large itself. If one so argues, s/he has, I believe, compounded a problem, for there will be not only a one/many issue for forms and individuals (or forms and characters in individuals) but yet another one/many issue for universal characters and individuals. And the last argument of the *Phaedo* will be made virtually unintelligible. If the hot in this fire can 'retreat or perish' at the approach of a cold, then the universal characters account would require that the perishing of the hot from this fire would remove hot altogether from the world. It must be conceded, however, that Parmenides' initial question to Socrates and, later, the Slave/Master argument suggest the universal characters interpretation. But we shall be at this issue again in discussing the so-called Third Man argument and the Slave/Master argument.

The next few arguments (with one exception) conclude that a form cannot be one – given that individuals have shares of it. In the first argument Parmenides seems to be taking *have a share of* or *come to have a share of* (*metechein*, μετεχείν or *metalambanein*, μεταλαμβάνειν) quite literally. So understood, several people may all have shares of, say, a cake, each having a piece as his/her share, and in the limiting case a person may have the whole cake as his/her share. So Parmenides asks whether each of a group of individuals (all having shares of a given form) has the whole form as his/her share. If so, the whole form, being 'in' each of the many individuals must be divided from itself and cannot be one. And, of course, the form, as a many, provides all the problems of Zeno's original argument.

If the focus is on the literal sense of 'have a share,' then Socrates' use of the metaphor of the *day* is simply hopeless. And Parmenides calls him back to the literal theme with the comment about the *sail*, a part of which is over each item it covers. Indeed, it is impossible to make sense of Socrates' suggestion *and* Parmenides' comment unless literalness is the issue. Efforts to save Socrates' suggestion have been based on the assumption that the dialogue as a whole is an exercise inviting the detection of *Parmenides'* errors. And, of course, the present volume is an attempt to show that the dialogue is serious.

If the form, like the cake, is divided into parts, then the oneness of the form is given up before one gets started. The same holds, of course, for the sail, a *part* of which is over each item it covers. Parmenides does not note that, assuming a finite number of parts, the form would with many participants be – like the cake – exhausted. The final comments of the section about the paradoxicality of having parts as shares of the Small, the Equal, and the Large are really humorous overkill.

The Largeness Regress (132A–B)

Text:

[132A] **Parmenides** I think it is for some such reason as the following that you believe each form to be one: when many things seem to you to be large, there seems to you as you look at them a single look (*ἰδέα*) that is the same in all of them, and hence you take the Large to be one.

Now what if, in like manner and, as it were, using your soul, you should look at the Large itself and the other *larges*? Would there not appear yet another Large that is one and in virtue of which all of them appear *larges*?

And so yet another form (*εἶδος*) of Large will appear besides the Large itself and those having shares [132B]of it. And then yet another for all of these in virtue of which they all will be larges. And each of your forms will in no way be one but rather an unlimited multitude.

This argument has in relatively recent times come to be called 'the Third Man argument,' though there is no ancient tradition for giving it that name, and I do not believe that it is appropriately so termed. Crucial here are the use of a *characterizing* (*not* a sortal) form, that is, the Large itself, and the vocabulary in which the argument is stated. This argument marks the first appearance of *idea* (*ἰδέα*) in the dialogue. Up to this point only *eidos* (*εἶδος*) has been used, though Plato in other dialogues commonly uses 'idea' and *eidos* more or less interchangeably as terms for *form*. That this is the first appearance of 'idea' is, I believe, intentional, for this argument, like the first one, focuses on the literal meaning of terms.

This time, however, the focus is on one of Plato's two terms for forms (rather than on the term for 'having a share'). Both terms are participial nouns from the verb *eido*, a verb that had in Plato's time no employment in its present tense but whose second aorist means 'see' or 'look at' and whose perfect means 'know' (probably from the notion that to have seen is, in one of its senses, to know). *Eidos* commonly has the meaning of 'form' or 'shape.' *Idea* commonly has the meaning of 'look' or 'appearance.' In the present argument, Parmenides is exploiting the common meaning of '*idea*,' as we shall presently see.

I shall start with the crucial first sentence and then reproduce the Greek text:

I think it is for some such reason as this that you believe each form (*eidos*) to be one: When many things seem to you to be large, there seems to you as you look (*idonti*) at them a single look (*idea*) that is the same in all of them, and hence you take the large to be one.

Οἶμαι σε ἐκ τοῦ τοιοῦδε ἓν ἕκαστον εἶδος οἴεσθαι εἶναι· ὅταν πολλ' ἄττα μεγάλα σοι δόξῃ εἶναι, μία τις ἴσως δοκεῖ ἰδέα ἡ αὐτὴ εἶναι ἐπὶ πάντα ἰδόντι, ὅθεν ἓν τό μέγα ἡγῇ εἶναι.

The previous argument has just concluded that, if *having a share* is understood as *having the whole or part of the form as a share*, then the form cannot be one or single. Here Parmenides is offering a suggestion of how Socrates might have been led to think that the form is one. He starts by using *eidos* but, when he gives the suggestion, he switches to *idea* and deliberately uses a cognate dative participle, *idonti*, in the sentence. The sense is: 'To you as you look at several large things, they will all present one and the same appearance or look; they will all look large.'

Whether using English or Attic Greek, we may indeed say of several things that they all have one and the same look or appearance (identical twins, sunsets, uniformed soldiers, etc.), and we refer to and talk about such looks. We may even look at and invite others to look at looks. 'Look at the look on his face!' 'Come and look at the appearance (or look) of the house in the fading sunset.' Parmenides' juxtaposition of *idea* and *idonti* is a similar invitation. Language allows us to invite someone to see a thing or to see the look or appearance of that thing. In this way one might say that looking at or seeing can generate looks or appearances, for, without looking at or seeing, there could be no looks or appearances. (I am not, of course, recommending any solution to the philosophical problems of looking and appearing. I am merely attempting to get clear about the sense of a text.)

Parmenides immediately exploits this generating of looks by the 'looking at' or 'seeing' features of the language. He also exploits the possibility of looking at or seeing a look. He invites Socrates to make a thought experiment. Granted that you cannot literally see or look at something without using your eyes, consider the generating principle, and with or by means of your soul (*tei psychei* – the dative of agency, not to be translated as *in* your soul or 'mind's eye') and in a metaphorical way allowed by the language 'look at' the look or appearance (the *idea*) *and* the many large things. Does not the generating principle require that there be yet another look or appearance that is in all of these? And, obviously, replications of the thought experiment would produce any number of fresh looks or appearances.

The fact that some things look the same and others don't may as a matter of fact lie behind some linguistic development and language learning. And there is a whole family of problems for philosophers in the subtleties in our complex language of appearing and being. The fact is also that Plato gave a technical significance to two words drawn from the Attic Greek language of appearing. And we should not let our being inured to the technical usage prevent recognition of the peculiarity of the terms and their association with appearance. It is hard not to believe that Plato, in writing the *Parmenides*, with its serious intent of defence and sophistication of the theory of forms, had any number of discussions in and out of the Academy in mind. And his getting around Zeno's Stricture in the *Phaedo* and elsewhere makes use of what speakers of Attic Greek must have regarded as metaphor. (Aristotle, in *Metaphysics* A, 987b10–12, still regarded *having a share* as useless metaphor.) So it does not seem unduly odd for Plato to put the present argument in the mouth of Parmenides if only to show that, if *idea* is taken literally for the theory of forms and having shares, there is trouble in holding to the claim that each form is one.

Gregory Vlastos made this small portion of the *Parmenides* very well-known indeed, and much sophistication has gone into discussion of his famous article. This literature is well-known, and I shall not attempt either to summarize it or even to enter the discussion (though the bibliography of this book lists the article and much of the discussion it generated). It may be worth noting, however, that something akin to Vlastos' *Self-Predication* and *Non-Identity* assumptions enter into the argument as I have attempted to explain it. Parmenides assumes that the first idea is itself a large that can, as it were, be looked at by the soul (thus the analogue of Self-Predication). And he assumes that, if the idea is looked at, there is generated yet another idea (the analogue of Non-Identity). Without these there is no regress.

I should note, finally, that calling this argument a *regress* invites the question: vicious or benign? For the present argument, raising the question would be a category mistake. What is at stake is not whether the regress makes knowing or even being aware of something impossible. And Parmenides draws no such conclusion. What is at stake is simply the failure of the account (unsophisticated as it may be) to explain how the form can be one. The conclusion is simply that there will have to be many different things with the form name, that is, 'the Large itself.' And thus the form will be an indefinite multitude. And we are then back with Zeno's argument.

Forms as Thoughts (132B–C)

Text:

[132B] **Socrates** But, Parmenides, might not each of these forms be a thought and thus fittingly come to be nowhere else but in souls? Then each would be one and unaffected by the argument you made just now.
Parmenides Tell me, must not each of the thoughts be a thought of something that [132C] is? And will it not be a thought of some one thing that, as being of them all, that thought thinks – a certain one look (ἰδέα)? And will not this thought-of that is one and always the same in all be a form?
S That seems necessary.
P Well then, does not the necessity by which the others have shares of the forms seem to you to require that everything is made of thoughts and that everything thinks or that, despite being thoughts, everything is unthought?

Having, through the suggestion of Parmenides, just seen the demise of the form as a *look* (and thus linked with perception), it is not surprising that the next attempt takes the form to be a *thought* (*noema*, νόημα). Even as many things may have one and the same look, one and the same thought may be *of* many things. This argument is unique among those in the context in that it does not conclude that a form cannot be one. It concludes, rather, that absurdities follow from the assumption.

The argument is simple. If forms are thoughts, then whatever items have shares of them must be thoughts. It follows that everything thinks, and that is absurd. Thoughts, as relatives (*pros ti's*), must be *of* something other than themselves. But, of course, the things that the thoughts are *of* need not be thoughts. Having a share *of* a *thought-of* loses the purported advantage of thought, for at least some *thought-ofs* cannot be *of* many. Taking the form as a *thought-of* thus opens the possibility that things may have shares of thoughts (in the thought-of sense) and yet be unthought.

Simple as the argument is, its purport can be missed. It is important, first, to recognize that the *of* in *thought of something* is relational and not necessarily intentional. Plato and Aristotle both think of 'relations' as *pros ti's*, that is, as items that require relata. *Double* is *pros half*, *parent* is *pros child*, *name* is *pros named*, and so on. *Thought, knowledge*, and *perception* are all *pros thought-of, known*, and *perceived*. What Parmenides is appealing to in commenting on Socrates' suggestion is the notion that thought without the thought-of is as incomplete as double without half. And more specific or particular thoughts are incomplete without the specific or particular thought-ofs. Thus, if any thought-term has application, there must be a thought-of term that has application. And Parmenides is appealing to something obvious to Socrates in asking for recognition of a thought-of that is and is 'a certain one *idea*.' (The use of 'idea' is surely deliberate as calling attention to the largeness argument just made.) Such a thought-of need not, of course, be itself a thought – except as being the relatum of a *pros ti*. The ambiguity of 'thought' as thought and thought-of is reflected in Parmenides' conclusion. Either (*qua* having shares of thoughts) everything thinks, or (*qua* having shares of thought-ofs) everything – though a thought – is unthought.

Pattern and Copy (132C–33A)

Text:

Socrates That too makes no sense, but, [132D] Parmenides, what seems to me most promising is this. The forms stand as patterns in nature, and the others resemble them and are likenesses. And for the others to come to have shares of the forms is nothing more than for the others to copy them.
Parmenides So if anything were to copy a form, could that form fail to be like that which copies it and then just so far as the thing has been made like the form? Or is there some means for the like not to be like its like? And is it not quite necessary that the like have a share of [132E] one and the same form as its like? And will not that by having shares of which likes are likes be the form itself?
S By all means.
P Then it is impossible for anything to be like the form or for the form to be like an other. If it were possible, then, in addition to the form, another form would always appear; and, if *that* form were like an other, yet [133A] a different form, and there would be no end to the continuous generation of fresh forms – if the generated form were to be like what has a share of it. And so it is not by likeness that the others have shares of the forms, and we must search for some other means by which they come to have shares.

With Socrates' statement that a form might best be thought of as a *pattern* or *paradigm* (*paradeigma*, παράδειγμα) and that those having shares as *copies* or *likenesses* (*homoiomata*, ὁμοιόματα), we are in what looks to be familiar Platonic territory. Parmenides' treatment of it is simple (and the principle appealed to will play a large role in the second part of the dialogue). The principle is: If something is like another thing, then both are like each other. With this in mind, two things can be like each other only if there is some form of which they both have shares. The pattern and the copy are like each other. So there must be a form that both have shares of. But, by hypothesis, *this* will also be a pattern and thus like its copies., And if these are to be like each other, there must be yet *another* pattern. And so on. As in the case of the largeness regress, the problem is that there will be an indefinite number of things gotten at by the form-name, thus destroying the univocity of the name and, *pari passu*, the singleness or unity of the form.

It may be worth noting that at no point in the Platonic corpus are forms treated as *universals* (*ta katholou*, τὰ καθόλου). Aristotle regularly uses the term, and I think it is his settled opinion that universals are or are rather like *concepts*, linked rather with the order of knowing than with the order of being. There is, as well, nothing in Plato like Russellian universals or propositional functions (though, as we shall see in the second part of the *Parmenides*, there may be part-whole constructions that have *some* structural resemblance to Fregean saturated concepts or functions). Here, Socrates is articulating what most readers take for granted in reading the *Phaedo*. The Beautiful itself is paradigmatic beauty. Helen, as having a share of it, is like the form, though she and any other beauty would lose in a contest with the Beautiful itself. But Helen and the Beautiful itself are presumably like each other. Even so, there is an apparent blur in the thought of the *Phaedo*. If the Beautiful itself is beautiful in the sense of *what it is to be beautiful*, it can hardly be beautiful in the sense of *having a share of the Beautiful itself*. And the beauty in Helen can hardly stand to the Beautiful itself as copy to paradigm or pattern. True enough, what it is to be beautiful would seem to be unchangingly and eternally just that and nothing else, whereas Helen may have a share of the Beautiful itself in young womanhood and later cease to have such a share. But the Beautiful itself, so construed, could not enter a beauty contest at all. Thus the paradigm, so construed, could not stand to a 'copy' (a share or a thing having a share) as like to like. The blur lies between this way of construing the relation of form and share (or thing having a share) and construing the form as 'perfectly' beautiful and the share (or thing having a share) as imperfectly beautiful. What is being developed in the *Parmenides* is, I believe, a move from the second construal to the first. But of this much more in discussing the second part of the dialogue.

Though he was not obviously ruling it out, Plato was not willing to accept a Tractarian view of the world as consisting of *facts* or *states of affairs*. His world is one of individuals (where for the present purposes *forms* are individuals), and the problems of the *Parmenides* are the problems of accounting for diversity and change while construing the principles of intelligibility as somehow individuals. As we shall see, this requires some fairly remarkable applications of the part/whole distinction and, with the present argument in mind, the drawing of respects or distinctions in which things may be like or unlike.

This argument is commonly referred to as 'the second Third Man Argument in the *Parmenides*.' Again, as in the case of the Largeness regress, I do not think it is appropriately so called – if we are using Aristotle's references to and characterization of the Third Man. The upshot of the present argument is the unacceptable conclusion that the form must be many, not the unacceptable presence of some third. Aristotle's testimony and the discussion of the Third Man by Alexander Aphrodisias[7] do seem to require an unacceptable third. The proper paradigm for what I take to be a real Third Man Argument is one that has a first man (the individual) having a share of the second man (the Man itself) and thus coming to have a third man (the copy or share) in it. *This* third is not another form, but rather an unnecessary copy or share.

Relational (*Pros Ti*) Forms (133A–35C)

Text:

[133A] **Parmenides** Do you see, Socrates, how great the difficulty is for anyone who determines that forms are just by themselves. Be assured, however, that as the story unfolds, the real dimensions of the difficulty have not yet been [133B] touched, if, having distinguished it, you always posit each form as one of the beings. There are many other difficulties, but the greatest is this. If anyone should assert that the forms are not appropriate objects of knowledge if they are such as we say they must be, no one would be able to show a person asserting this that he is wrong unless he were uncommonly experienced and skilled in argumentation and quite willing to follow the many details and intricacies of a [133C] laborious demonstration. But if he were unconvinced, he would compel their unknowability. Because, Socrates, I think that you or anyone else who determines that there is just by itself an essence (οὐσία) of each thing will agree right off that none of the essences is in us.
Socrates How could it be in us if it were just by itself?
P Quite right. But consider as well such forms as *are* and have their essence (οὐσία) relative to one another, but not relative to likenesses (whatever they are determined to be) [133D] in us, having shares of which we are named whatever each of them is. And those joined to us that have the same names as the forms *are* relative to themselves and not relative to the forms, being of themselves and not of those

after which they are named. I mean, for example, if one of us is master or slave of someone, he is not a slave of Master itself [133E] (which *is* Master) nor a master of Slave itself (which *is* Slave), but rather, being a man, is master or slave of a man. Mastership itself is *of* Slavehood itself, and Slavehood itself is likewise *of* Mastership itself. But those in us are not relative to *them*, but, [134A] as I say, the forms are of themselves and relative to themselves. And these in us are likewise relative to themselves.

And also Knowledge itself (which *is* Knowledge) is *of* that which *is* Reality (ἀλήθεια), if it is to be Knowledge of That. And each of the Knowledges (which *is* Knowledge) must be of each (which *is*) of the Beings, if it is to be knowledge. Would not the knowledge which is in us be knowledge of reality in us and each of the knowledges [134B] in us be of the beings in us if each is to be knowledge? And you agree that we do not have the forms themselves nor can they be in us. And each of the kinds which *are* is known by a form of Knowledge itself.

Thus none of the forms is known by us, since we do not have a share of Knowledge itself. And so the Beautiful itself, the Good [134C] itself, all of those we take to be forms themselves cannot be known by us.

Now attend to what is even more dire than that. You would say, of course, that, if there is just by itself a kind or form of Knowledge, it is far more precise than the knowledge in us – and so also are Beauty and all of the Others.

And thus, if anything has a share of Knowledge itself, you could say nothing better than that a god has this most precise Knowledge. [134D] Then can a god, having Knowledge itself, know those things which are in us?

S Why not?

P Because we have agreed, Socrates, that those forms have no relation to things in us, nor do things in us have a relation to them, but the forms are relative only to forms, and things in us relative only to things in us. And thus, if the most precise Mastership and the most precise Knowledge are in a god, his Mastership cannot be mastership of our affairs [134E] nor can his Knowledge be knowledge of us or anything in us. And likewise we do not rule them with the authority in us nor know anything of a god with our knowledge. And again, by the same reasoning, they, being gods, exercise no mastery over us nor do they know human affairs.

S But this would be a most astonishing argument if it would deprive a god of knowledge!

P [135A] And yet, Socrates, the forms must carry with them these consequences and a great many others, if there are forms of beings, and one marks off each form by itself. And so one who hears them is puzzled and disputes whether there are any such things and argues that, even if there were, they would of necessity be unknowable by human beings. And saying these things, what he says seems reasonable, and, as we just now said, he is amazingly hard to convince. Only a man who is naturally very gifted will be able to learn that there is some kind or essence just by itself for each thing. [135B] Only an even more amazing man will search these out and be able to teach another all these things sufficiently for analysis and careful arrangement.

On the other hand, Socrates, if anyone, looking steadfastly at all of these and other such objections, will not allow that there are forms of the beings and will not see some form of each one, then he will have nowhere to turn and fix his thought, since he will not allow for each of the beings a [135C] form that is always the same. And in this way he will completely destroy our ability to engage in discourse. But it seems to me that you are quite aware of this.

Immediately after the pattern/copy argument Parmenides says to a somewhat dejected Socrates that there is another set of issues that must be faced by anyone who maintains that there are forms and that many things may have shares of them. In the preceding arguments there has been only a hint (in the 'forms are thoughts' argument) of the problems of making *relational forms* intelligible. Parmenides says that, if one were to claim that the forms cannot even be known, s/he would be very hard to convince and then only after going through 'the many details and intricacies of a laborious demonstration.' The reference is, I believe, to the sort of 'demonstration' that is given in the second part of the dialogue, but what is needed here is a statement of a special problem.

The problem comes in the recognition that, if a form is posited for each of the distinctions made among things, then there will have to be *relational* (*pros ti*) forms, important among which is *Knowledge* and its relatum, *Known* (and, of course, the various kinds of Knowledge and *their* relata). The issue is not the giving of a serious definition or account of knowledge, important as that may be. It is rather that of recognizing that an important set of forms are what they are only relative to (*pros ti*) other forms and then asking how we can have any connection with them. If Knowledge and its relatum are 'just by themselves,' and it is not made intelligible how we can have a share of Knowledge, the denial of our having any knowledge seems obvious enough. And, if each form is just by itself, how can there be forms that are *pros ti*? Thus, how could there be Knowledge at all? There is no attempt to answer this last question in the present section, though there is the presupposition that there are relational forms and that knowledge is possible. Interestingly, in each of the affirmative Platonic versions of the one supposition (in the second part of the dialogue), the claim of knowledge (whether of the *one* or the *others*) appears in the very last section.

I think that this sort of reflection as well as thought about several other texts of Plato leads to the idea that there there are knowledge forms indeed, and that persons who have knowledge have shares of Knowledge itself (or one of its species) and thereby have a purchase on the appropriate form-relatum. Given this, we have to think of a Plato who treats knowledge (in us) not as some sort of Moorean or Russellian diaphanous 'act' of awareness (despite some Platonic metaphors) but rather as an appropriately structured conceptual ability whose exercise is fitted to the appropriate form-relatum. This idea in a slightly different form is used in the final argument of the first part of the *Parmenides*. The god is said to have in him a knowledge form and thus a connection with the relatum. What the god does not have is a connection with *us* or anything in *us*.

Parmenides invites Socrates to consider the *pros ti*'s, Slave itself and Master itself. And he contrasts them with slave and master in us, that is, someone's being a slave and another's being a master. The same remarks apply *mutatis mutandis* for knowledge and its relatum. Parmenides suggest that, given the failure of making a connection between forms and those in us, if a god were a Master or had Knowledge, he would have in him the Mastership or Knowledge that has a *pros form* relatum, and he would not have in him Mastership or Knowledge that is *pros* anything in us. It follows, of course, that the god cannot be our master or know us (or anything in us). These conclusions are obviously both unacceptable and, indeed, horrifying to the young Socrates.

Parmenides speaks of 'the most precise' (*akribestate*, ἀκριβεστάτε) Mastership and Knowledge as being in the god. A curious expression, and it has given aid and comfort to interpreters who speak of degrees of reality or degrees of participation in forms, thinking of the participants as failing to measure up to the exacting standards of forms. Suitably understood, I think this is correct. But it wants explanation. I have suggested earlier and argued at some length elsewhere that forms for the late dialogues of Plato are usefully thought of as *principles of structure* that are not themselves *structured* things.[8] They are not, therefore, perfect embodiments of themselves, and self-predication, so-called, is best taken as Alexander Nehamas has suggested, that is, as being *what it is to be* whatever the form is.[9] Thus the *F* itself is *F*, that is, *what it is to be F*. So understood, the form cannot fail in itself to be precise for reasons analogous to the necessary precision of definitions and theorems in a calculus. They couldn't be what they are and fail in precision. *Our* conceptions, that is, structured shares of knowledge (or name) forms, may be imprecise and messy (cf. Aristotle's distinction between what is evident to us and what is evident in nature, *Physics* I,1). In the *Timaeus* Plato assumes several ways in which structur*ed* things may imperfectly embody principles of structure, if only because what is being described is a copy. If Master (or one of the 'moral' forms) is thought of as a principle of structure, its embodiment would, of course, be an ordered temporal series; and it is easy to see how an embodiment in us may be inexact and messy. But this paragraph is only the first of several comments to be made about the use of *precise* in characterizing Platonic forms. It is a start towards explanation that will be continued in the treatment of the second part of the dialogue.

The text being discussed ends with another claim to the effect that it takes a remarkable person to make out how it can be 'that there is some kind or essence just by itself for each thing' and a more remarkable one to search them out 'and be able to teach another all these things sufficiently for analysis and careful arrangement.' And the last few sentences insist that there must be forms, lest we have nowhere to fix our thoughts and lest we 'completely destroy our ability to engage in discourse.' From both these comments we have every reason to expect a rescue operation in the sequel. The problem has been how to understand the so-called second part of the dialogue, so that it can be seen as a rescue operation for some defensible version of the doctrine of forms and having shares. I think that it is, and in the next few chapters I try to explain how it is done in the *Parmenides*.

3

The Needed Exercise and Supposition One (135C–42A)

Definition and the Need of an Intellectual Frame (135C–37C)

Text:

Parmenides [135C] What then will you do about philosophy? Where will you turn while these things remain unknown?
Socrates At the moment I do not see that at all clearly.
P The reason is that you have, Socrates, undertaken too soon, before being exercised, to define Beautiful, Just, Good, and each one of the forms. I noticed that yesterday when I heard you in conversation with Aristotle here. Believe me, the zeal that you have for arguments is noble, even divine. But you must bring yourself to exercise in what is seemingly unprofitable and what most people call *mere talk* while you are yet young. If not, the truth will elude you. This is the sort you heard from Zeno. I admired your [135D] reply to him, because you would not permit the enquiry to wander in and among the visibles but rather kept it to those that one grasps by argument and takes to be forms.
S It seems to me that in this way it is not difficult to show that the beings can be likes, unlikes, or whatever.
P Good enough. But you must undertake something that goes beyond Zeno's practice. You must attend to the consequences of a given supposition – not only to those of the supposition that what you suppose [136A] *is*, but also to those of the supposition that what you suppose *is not*: both of these if you wish to be well exercised. Take as an example, if you wish, that supposition of Zeno: *If many are*. You must attend to the consequences both for the *many* themselves relative to themselves and relative to the *one*, and the consequences for the *one* relative to itself and relative to the *many*. You must as well take the supposition *If many are not*, and again attend to the consequences for the one and for the others both relative to

themselves and relative [136B] to one another. Once more, if you suppose, *If likeness is* or *If likeness is not*, you must attend for each to the consequences both for what is supposed and for the others both relative to themselves and to one another. And the same procedure is to be used concerning *unlikeness*, concerning *motion*, concerning *rest*, concerning *coming to be*, concerning *perishing*, even concerning *being* itself as well as *not being*.

In a single formula: Concerning whatever you may suppose, whether you suppose that it *is*, whether you suppose that it *is not*, or whether you suppose that it admits anything else, you must attend to [136C] the consequences relative to *it* and relative to each one of the others, whether (as you choose) relative to more or to all of them in the same manner. And once more, you must attend to the consequences for the others both relative to themselves and relative to whatever you may have chosen, whether you suppose that what you suppose *is* or that it *is not*. All this, if you intend to get complete exercise for authoritative discernment of reality.

S You talk of an incredible undertaking, Parmenides, and I don't understand it very well. Why don't you yourself choose some supposition and go through the procedure for me so that I might better understand?

P [136D] It's a large task, Socrates, which you set for someone of my age.

S How about you, Zeno? Why don't you go through the procedure for us?

Pythodorus said that Zeno smiled and said:

Zeno Socrates, we must have Parmenides himself for this. For what he speaks of is no slight task. Or do you not see the sort of undertaking that you set? Indeed, if there were more of us, it would be quite unfair to require it of him. It would be improper for him to hold forth on such matters before many persons, especially at his age [136E]. For the many could hardly understand that, without this wandering and passing through everything, it is impossible for the mind (*nous*) to meet with and possess the truth. And so, Parmenides, I join Socrates in enjoining you so that I, too, may hear after all this time.

When Zeno had said these things, Antiphon said that Pythodorus himself entreated Parmenides (as did Aristotle and the others) not to refuse and to give a demonstration of what he meant.

P I must yield to such persuasion. Even so, I find myself feeling like the Ibycian horse, [137A] old and in the race, about to start the chariot race, and from long experience trembling in fearful anticipation. Ibycus, comparing himself with that horse, speaks of himself as old and required to enter upon a love affair. And I think of myself, furnished as I am with memories and at my age, as very fearful at being required to swim through such a sea of arguments. Even so, I must be obliging, since, as Zeno says, there are just ourselves. Then how [137B] shall we begin, and what supposition shall we take first? Or do you wish, since you seem set upon playing out this enterprise, to start with myself and my own supposition, determining concerning the supposition of the one itself what must be the consequences *if one is* and *if one is not*?

Who then is to respond to me? The youngest? He would be the least prone to over-complication and the most likely to respond with what he believes. And at the same time there would be a bit of rest for me while he replies.

Aristoteles   [137C] I am at your service, Parmenides, for when you speak of the youngest, you mean me. Only ask, and I shall respond.

Parmenides, in the wake of his devastation of Socrates' response to Zeno, asks Socrates what he is now going to do about philosophy. In what, for once, is actual and not methodological bewilderment, Plato's mentor and chief protagonist replies that at the moment he simply does not know, thus setting the stage for Parmenides' diagnosis and treatment. And he is told that he has tried *too soon* to define 'Beautiful, Just, Good, and each one of the forms.'

I think that Parmenides has sufficient justification for the comment in the severe criticism that we have just gone through. Socrates' procedure of enquiry cannot treat 'sortal' forms (man, horse, etc.) within the same rational frame as Beautiful and Good. He cannot countenance forms for 'undignified' things like hair and mud, though he has no rationale for their exclusion other than the presumed honorific character of the forms. And he cannot provide a defensible account of what it is for something to have a share of a form.

But the justification for the comment is not simply negative. Parmenides goes on to say that what Socrates needs is *exercise* (gymnastike, γυμναστική). The needed exercise is described as 'seemingly unprofitable' and considered by most people to be 'mere talk.' It is further noted that the procedure of Zeno in his book is an example of such exercise. Then, a bit later, Parmenides is persuaded to provide another example using 'his own' supposition, viz., *If one is* (in addition to Zeno's *If many are*). The idea is that, after having such exercise (and, presumably, more, involving other suppositions), Socrates may be prepared to engage in the task of defining such things as Beautiful and Good. Even with my justification of the 'too soon' comment and even after review of so much of Zeno's example as Plato gives us and the long example provided by Parmenides, one may still be puzzled about how these are going to be a help to Socrates in making and justifying definitions.

It may provide some clarification to take note of an Aristotle reference to *gnoristike* (γνωριστική) in *Metaphysics* Gamma:

For sophistry and dialectic turn toward the same kind of thing as philosophy, but philosophy differs from the first in the nature of its capability and from the latter in its concern for the direction of life. Dialectic is tentative (*peirastike*, πειραστική) *precognition* (γνωριστική) in the concerns of philosophy. Sophistry is apparent, but not real, *precognition* in these matters. (1004b 22–7)

The passage is part of a metaphilosophical essay leading up to the statement of the fundamental logical principle and including the much-discussed principle of *pros hen ambiguity* (which G.E.L. Owen called the principle of *focal meaning*). Were there world enough and time, this could be the occasion of a serious examination of the connections between the *Parmenides* and Aristotle's treatments of *one* and *being* in the *Metaphysics* (primarily in B). There is surely not time, though I shall return to the matter somewhat less briefly in discussing the second supposition of the second part of the *Parmenides*.

For present purposes, it is important to note Aristotle's use of 'precognition' (γνωριστική) to refer to dialectic. My translation of *peirastike* as 'tentative' is probably misleading. 'Tentative' does not carry the sense of 'making trial of' anything, and I think that with the use of *peirastike* Aristotle thinks of dialectic as exercise that is used for the purpose of making trial of something. In the present context of the *Parmenides* it would seem that the exercise carried out by Parmenides on 'his own' supposition (*if one is*) makes trial of the supposition as allowing interpretation that will provide the intellectual frame for saying what can intelligibly be said and for the conduct of serious inquiry. It seems likely, therefore, that the *procedure* should provide means of responding to the severe criticism of Parmenides in the first part of the dialogue.

Aristotle's common use of 'dialectic' (in contrast to that in the above quotation from the *Metaphysics*) to refer to reasoning or enquiry based upon opinion is, of course, in marked contrast to Plato's honorific use of the term. Certainly, as Plato uses the term in the *Sophist* its practitioner is the true philosopher.

Stranger Shall we not say that the division by kinds and believing neither that the same form is different nor that the different is the same surely belongs to the science (knowledge, *episteme*, ἐπιστήμη) of dialectic?
Theaetetus Yes.
S Then he who is able to do this sufficiently perceives one form (*idea*) extending through many, each one lying apart (*choris*), and many different from one another, encompassed from without by one, and yet one united through many wholes into

one, and many completely apart and separate. This is the knowledge and ability to distinguish that by which several individually can or cannot come together with one another.
T It is indeed.
S But surely you will not give dialectical ability (*dialektikon*, διαλέκτικον) to any other but one who philosophizes purely and rightly. (*Sophist* 253 D1–E6.)

So understood, the practitioner of dialectic *is*, in his/her practice, the philosopher *par excellence*. It should be noted, however, that this passage is from the metaphysical heart of the *Sophist* and not from the Collection and Division attempts to define the sophist. Indeed, it is not from any part of that definitional attempt. It is, rather, from the effort to exhibit the structure of the five 'greatest forms' and, in context, to explain how *not-being is*.

Still in context, this *Sophist* passage is taken to be applicable to the effort to determine which *kinds* (*gene*, γένη) will 'associate' (*koinonein*, κοινωνεῖν) with which. Earlier in the same section, the Stranger uses the metaphor of *mingling* (*summignusthai*, συμμίγνυσθαι). After noting that this procedure might be followed for all the kinds (254C), he decides to select only the 'greatest kinds' (Being, Same, Different, Motion, and Rest) for the purpose at hand. Two features of this portion of the *Sophist* deserve special notice. First, the Stranger does not hesitate to call the investigation of *association* or *mingling* 'dialectic' and to suggest that in the search for the Sophist he may have stumbled upon the Philosopher. This comports, of course, with Aristotle's characterization of useful exercise as dialectic. Second, the careful use of *association* and *mingling* is rather more indicative of the investigation of *possibilities* than of any sort of effort to arrive at definitional or logical certainties or necessities. It is therefore rather more like the investigation of consequences (for some purposes, better, *compatibilities*) that I see the second part of the *Parmenides* as carrying on. I have claimed earlier in this book that Collection and Division is a procedure for arriving at definitions but not, strictly speaking, definitions of *forms*. What we are looking at here in the *Sophist* appears to reinforce my claim for the *Parmenides* that its second part lays out the intellectual underpinnings for the rational employment of Collection and Division.

What we are about to get into in the *Parmenides*, starting with the Platonic Version of the one supposition, is an attempt to articulate the logical (broad sense!) frame in terms of which genera/species orderings can be made intelligible and in terms of which there can be rational justification of the method of Collection and Division. The articulation of the frame is by means of what I earlier called *framework forms* (those used in the Zeno discourse). But the present concern has been with Parmenides' remark about Socrates' trying 'too soon' to get definitions. Full explanation of this talk of justifying the procedure of Collection and Division must wait at least until we have gone through supposition two. One more comment, however, may be relevant here.

Putting the matter somewhat differently, Parmenides is about to show, in the long illustration of the dialectical exercise, how it is that everything that we can say intelligibly can be said. The distinctions provided by exploitation of framework forms make possible exploration of the place of any given object or thing in the entire pattern of intelligibility. The illustration does this by, first, accounting for plurality and the possibilities for mathematical ordering of that plurality, then, with elaborate distinction-making, explaining how a thing can be – in different senses – both F and not F. 'Thing' here is a term to be used, depending upon context, either to mention an ostensible form or to mention a form-participant (named after the form) or, as we shall see, a number-participant. And both the thing-term and the replacement for F are to be seen as occupying places in the intelligible frame. (This is not, of course, a recipe for a definition, but part of the explanation of the framework for arriving at and justifying definitions.)

Zeno's Procedure (135D–37C)

When told that he needs exercise or training, Socrates asks what sort of exercise. And he is told exercise in the sort of practice he heard from Zeno. And again one wishes that Plato had incorporated all or even a part of Zeno's book in the *Parmenides*. From what we have in the dialogue, however, the general procedure is reasonably clear. Problems come with detail and point of the procedure. What one is to do is to take some *supposition* (*hypothesis*, ὑπόθεσις) and somehow determine its consequences. The one clear instance we have so far is the one with which the dialogue begins:

Supposition: Those that are are many.
Consequence: They are likes and unlikes.

But, as we saw on Zeno's reading, the attempted consequence is an impossibility, and one must conclude that it is not the case that those that are are many. What we shall be noting quite carefully in sequel is a renewed effort in the 'Platonic' interpretations of the one supposition to distinguish senses in which being likes and unlikes poses no problem. ('Renewed' because, of course, with the doctrine of having shares, Socrates has already attempted to escape the consequence of Zeno's argument.)

It is tempting to use this example of Zeno's practice not only as a key to the large *exercise* of the *Parmenides* but also as an aid in understanding what Aristotle is reacting to in his attempts to defeat the famous paradoxes in *Physics* VI. In the long exercise performed by Parmenides, which we are about to look at, the generating of consequences from *If one is* occurs by the use of several framework forms and animadversions on *whole* and *part*. Though detail must wait for the commentary on the large exercise, it is possible to suggest how some of the famous paradoxes of Zeno might have grown out of this sort of use of Zeno's supposition, *if many are*. Consider the following:

Supposition: Those that are are many.
Consequence: Those that are many have parts.
Consequence: Every part is such that it may have parts.
Consequence: Every part of a distance to be traversed may have parts.
Consequence: Every distance may have an unlimited number of parts.
Consequence: To traverse any distance every part must be traversed.
Consequence: It is impossible to traverse *any* distance.
Consequence: It is impossible for those that are to be many.

This is obviously merely a sketch of a sketch. I use it because it suggests how what Socrates takes to be the purport of Zeno's book might be made to fit the pattern of one of the Zeno arguments reported by Aristotle in *Physics* VI. Though it would be speculative to attempt to work out the details for all (or even one) of the Zeno arguments in *Physics*, I think it could be done and thus give some plausibility to the idea that Aristotle is drawing upon the same book as that referred to early in the *Parmenides*. I am not, however, trying to make a case for there being but one Zeno book.

Before giving Socrates much of any detail, Parmenides informs him that he did well to restrict his response to Zeno to forms and not to include *visibles* or visibles as such. Socrates did, of course, bring in visibles in speaking of those that have shares of forms, *but he brought them in only as having such shares*. He did not bring them in *simply* as visibles. For contrast, cf. Socrates' remark that hair, mud, dirt, etc. are 'just what we see them to be' and have no shares of forms. Indeed, Socrates' comment about how easy it is to show that 'things can be likes and unlikes' etc. *if* the forms are brought in requires that those having shares of forms belong in the picture. I think, therefore, that Parmenides' present remark about restriction to forms is not intended to exclude individuals *qua* having shares of forms from the recommended exercise. The exercise is not *strictly* devoted to forms as such, though the major emphasis will be on the structuring of the frame of intelligibility by framework forms.

Before listing a number of framework forms that are candidates for suppositions, Parmenides says that one departure from Zeno's practice is in order, namely, attending to the consequences of the supposition that whatever one supposes is *not* as well as the consequences of the supposition that it *is*. As we shall see, this is a matter of considerable moment and ties in with Plato's resolution of the *is not* problem in the *Sophist*. I think that Plato's interest here is making sure that intelligible senses are articulated not merely for sentences of the form 'X is F,' but also for sentences of the form 'X is not F.' In the *Sophist* terms the former can be understood as 'X has a share of the F itself,' the latter as 'X has a share of the Different-from-F itself' (where the Different-from-F is one of the 'parts' of Different).

For the understanding of the exercise to come, this point has obvious bearing on suppositions three and seven. Supposition three asks about the consequences for the 'others,' *if one is*. And Parmenides requires attending to the consequences for whatever one supposes and also for the *others*. The *others* are *others than one* (or, generally, *others than F*). If you please the *others* are *not-Fs*. In current terminology, F and *not-F* (or *different from F*) determine complement classes (though I have been careful not to use the contemporary notions of *class* or *extension* in the interpretation of Plato in this book). Everything in the universe is either F or *not-F*. Being F is being something definite, namely, F. Being *not-F* is being something quite indefinite. 'The horse is running' tells you what is running. 'The not-horse is running' does not – except for eliminating horses. Aristotle (*De Int.* 16a 30-4) quite properly calls '*not-F*' expressions 'indefinite (*aorista*, ἀόριστα) nouns (or *names*, ὀνόματα).' Supposition three exploits this indefiniteness, as does supposition seven. Supposition seven is even more indefinite. since both the subject *and* the predicate are indefinite. As Plato duly notes, sentences of the form, 'The *not-F* is *not-G*,' appear to say something, but there is no way of determining what.

Plato is also interested in duly noting that 'X is not F' not only does not deny the existence of X; it *requires* it. The presumption is that, though the 'is not F' requires the indefiniteness of 'different from F,' that indefiniteness does not affect the subject term. (Though the form of the supposition does affect the subject term in supposition seven as we have just noted above.) The same point is made in the *Sophist* when the Eleatic Stranger requires that Theaetetus *be* in order for *flying* or *different from flying* to hold for him. But we shall be detailing the relevant points in the commentary on the suppositions to follow. Here I wish merely to underline the point of requiring the consideration of the consequences of supposing that whatever one supposes *is not*.

Parmenides proceeds to list a number of pairs of framework forms that may be suitable candidates for suppositional 'exercise.' Before listing them, however, it will prove useful to note that before long the list of forms will be greatly reduced — reduced to three basic forms, namely, Being, Same, and Different. With that promised reduction in mind, I turn to the list of candidates, now referring them by using italic type.

In addition to *one* and *many*, he lists *likeness* and *unlikeness*, *motion* and *rest*, *coming to be* and *perishing*, and *being* and *not being* (136B). There is the presumption in his manner of statement that yet other pairs of opposites may be used in suppositional exercise. Right now, it is important to note another consideration, this concerning the so-called *others* (or, if you please, *differents*). Parmenides, in inviting attention to the finding of consequences for whatever is supposed relative to itself and to its opposite (assuming that whatever is supposed and those other than it are 'opposites'), invites attention to sentences with what is supposed as subject 'relative to itself' and sentences with whatever is supposed as subject 'relative to the others': thus for the supposition of *one*, the finding of consequences for the *one* relative to itself and relative to the *others* (than the *one*); for the supposition of *likeness*, the finding of consequences relative to itself and relative to the *others* (than *likeness*); and so on. In the example furnished by Parmenides, there is consideration of the consequences both for the *one* relative to itself and relative to the *others* and also for the *others* relative to themselves and relative to the *one*.

In chapter 2 I introduced the term *framework* for the entities that Parmenides said were in Zeno's exposition, entities to which Socrates readily granted the status of forms. I promised then to expand that introduction. We now have a list (to which others may be added). It is important to keep in mind that there is nothing like formal logic in any of Plato's writings, however skilful he may have been in recognizing what we should take to be logical implications and logical mistakes. Indeed, it was as late as the *Sophist* (262A–63C) that Plato came to explicit recognition of the distinction between terms and sentences (in the 'name/verb' or '*onoma/rema*' [ὄνομα ῥῆμα] distinction, using 'Theaetetus sits' and 'Theaetetus flies' as examples), though we shall shortly encounter use of that distinction in the Platonic versions of the supposition *if one is*.

The terms in the list of candidates for suppositional treatment by Parmenides, however, are standard terms of Platonic philosophical analysis and criticism. All of them admit of replacement by more specific terms that share their 'oppositional' features. Thus *runs* is a specific kind of *motion* that has, among others, *stands* or *sits* as specific kinds of *rest* that are in opposition to *runs*. *Being* and *not being* cover much ground. *Being* admits as a substitute virtually any predicate, whether (still using Strawson's terms) characterizing or sortal. *Not being* admits all of the 'opposites' of *being* terms, whether contraries or contradictories. (Note: There is every reason to believe that Plato – and Aristotle – accepted the negation of terms and did not work with the modern notion of negation as a sentential device.) It will be interesting, while we go through the great exercise for *if one is*, to note that all of Parmenides' list of suppositional candidates figure in the several drawings of 'consequences.'

As I have hinted earlier in this book, there is a rather remarkable turning of the tables on Zeno in the long exercise using Parmenides' supposition, *if one is*. In what I shall shortly be calling the 'Platonic' versions of the supposition, the 'consequences' generally have the form, the *one* (or X) is both F and *not* F (or F and G, where these are contraries). The effect, despite appearances, is vindication of the intelligibility (though not the truth) of commonsensical beliefs and sentences – unlike Zeno's destruction of that intelligibility. Ironically in what I shall be calling the 'Parmenidean' versions of the supposition, the 'consequences' generally have the form, the *one* (or X) is neither F nor *not* F (or neither F nor G where these are contraries). The price of accepting the Parmenidean versions is both the unintelligibility of saying anything and, as the *Sophist* makes clear, the unintelligibility of the Parmenidean claim that *one is*.

This may be the time to comment on a remark of Zeno's that I glossed over in the last chapter. Readers may recall that at 128D Zeno, in the course of denying that his treatise was intended to be pretentious, says that he was coming to Parmenides' aid 'against those who set upon him with caricatures to the effect that, *if one is*, many ludicrous conclusions follow as well as conclusions contrary to his contention.' What the statement seems to require is that those attacking Parmenides construed his supposition as allowing all manner of predications. Assuming, I think correctly, that Parmenides intention was simply to make a claim for the One, allowing no predication, Zeno could claim, as he does, that the assumption of the Many leads to contradiction. What I wish to emphasize is that the Zeno remark seems to require what I shall shortly claim, namely, that Parmenides' intention is to allow no predication.

As I noted a page or so back, the entities I have been calling 'framework' entities admit of 'reduction' to a smaller number. As we shall see in discussing the second supposition, Being, Same, and Different provide the means for the generation of all of the numbers (and shapes). As we shall note in chapter 9 on the *Timaeus*, Being, Same, and Different are the crucial grounds for the intelligibility of the universe. And, as we shall note in chapter 10 on the *Sophist*, the 'greatest forms' are Being, Same, Different, Motion, and Rest (with Motion and Rest defined in supposition two as *always in a different* and *always in the same*).

Reduction is, however, not quite the right term for what I am about. What I wish to note is that the *numbers* are produced from Being, Same, and Different in the second supposition and that with the numbers comes the notion of sequences and concatenations (some very complicated indeed). The *Timaeus* idea of the physical world's being due to the informing of the Receiver (*hypodoche*) by the intelligible numbers invites the notion that the entire temporal sequence in a given Great Year is the working out of an intelligible mathematical formula or, as I believe Plato would have put it, an intelligible number. (As we shall note in chapter 9, Plato thinks of the entire physical world as *limited* in extent and duration, though the latter is made up of an unlimited number of successive limited and identical Great Years, each encompassing the period from a given positioning of the heavenly bodies to their return to that same positioning.) The presumption is, of course, that there is nothing at all that is not derivative from the intelligible order and that, as I shall claim, the World Animal of the *Timaeus* is the source of whatever is or comes to be in the universe. This is a large order, and giving the full defence of the claim will have to wait until the last three chapters of the book. For the present issue, it is enough to suggest that the framework entities derive from the basic forms of intelligibility.

The Pattern of Suppositions in Parmenides' Example

Socrates is still a bit bewildered about the exercise and asks that Parmenides provide him with an example of the exercise. After some demonstration of reluctance to take on the task and exhortation by Zeno and others present, Parmenides agrees, using 'his own' supposition (*if one is*) and Aristoteles as a responder. The reluctance is presumably due to the length and difficulty of the task (swimming through 'a sea of arguments'). The sea of arguments is divided into eight unequal parts (with an addition put in after the second). Four of the eight parts are easily explained, namely, 1, 3, 5, and 7 below:

1 and 2: The consequences for the *one, if one is*.

48   The *Parmenides* and Plato's Late Philosophy

3 and 4: The consequences for the *others, if one is.*
5 and 6: The consequences for the *one, if one is not.*
7 and 8: The consequences for the *others, if one is not.*

As the left-hand numbering suggests, each of the four is paired, thus producing eight. Question: What determines the pairing? The key is found, I believe, in two quite different constructions to be placed upon *if one is*. On the first construction, '*is*' plays no independent role. As Parmenides says at the start of supposition two, it is as though the supposition just dealt with (in supposition one) were *if one one*. On this construction, therefore, though there is presumed *naming*, nothing is *said* of what is so named. ('Presumed,' because of the requirement in naming that there be *both* the *name* and the *named*, thus more than one. But of this much more later.) On the second construction, *is* plays at least a quasi-independent role and thus names (or *means*) something different from what is named by *one*. Put a bit over-simply, the first construction amounts to confirmation of Zeno's claim of 'no many' and literal application of what I have called Zeno's Stricture. (And, as we shall see, it supports Plato's account of Parmenides' doctrine in the *Sophist* and Aristotle's claim in *Physics* I.2 that 'Parmenides had not got so far as the sentence.') The second construction amounts to the recognition of sentential predication.[1]

I call the first construction of the one supposition the Parmenidean Version and the second construction the Platonic Version. The Parmenidean Version yields for all four of its consequence sets *neither/nor* consequences of the form 'The one is neither F nor G (where F and G are opposites of some sort),' though in the last supposition there is not even the 'appearance' of a one to be or 'appear' to be neither F nor G. I take this to be, at its simplest, a rather picturesque way of saying that on the Parmenidean Version there simply can be no sentential predication at all. The Platonic Version yields for all four of *its* consequence sets *both/and* consequences of the form 'The one is (or in supposition seven *appears to be*) both F and G (where F and G are opposites of some sort).' Though this would seem to be unacceptable, my contention is that, in every such case, Plato is at pains to distinguish *senses* or *respects* that mitigate the paradox or contradiction in saying that the one is both F and G. But note that the consequences for the Platonic Version do not require that for any given sentence or predication both it and its opposite are true; it requires rather the *intelligibility* of such opposites.

The order of presentation Plato gives us is as follows:

1. Parmenidean Version: The consequences for the one, *if one is.*

2. Platonic Version: The consequences for the one, *if one is*.
3. Platonic Version: The consequences for the others, *if one is*.
4. Parmenidean Version: The consequences for the others, *if one is*.
5. Platonic Version: The consequences for the one, *if one is not*.
6. Parmenidean Version: The consequences for the one, *if one is not*.
7. Platonic Version: The consequences for the others, *if one is not*.
8. Parmenidean Version: The consequences for the others, *if one is not*.

The single juxtaposition of two consequence sets on the Platonic Version in the case of 2 and 3 is explained, I believe, by Plato's need to establish a way of writing about the *others* that is not available on the Parmenidean Version. But this will be evident when we come to examine supposition three.

I noted earlier that there is an interlude (which I call the Coda) or, if you please, a separate consequence set sandwiched between suppositions two and three. It makes use of *both* the Parmenidean and the Platonic versions of *if one is*. The problem it addresses is, however, that of *change*. What Plato is worried about is successive stages in the change of X from being F to being G. There can be no time strictly speaking when X is both F and G (or both of some intermediate change). What Plato appears to opt for is a theory of catastrophic change with the *instant* or *the all of a sudden* lying between the successive stages. But the *instant* is not a time interval; it is rather a non-time in which X is characterized as being *neither F nor G*, hence the usage of the Parmenidean Version. But this is at the moment simply a hint of what can properly be discussed only in context.

I can, however, enlarge a bit on the hint by alluding to the first part of the *Theaetetus* (154C1–55C7). In the section leading up to Protagoras' 'secret doctrine' according to which what is perceived (and the perceiving) is a joint function of sense organ and some external motion, Socrates takes it as obvious that nothing can be both F and G (where these are opposites) at the same time. And he takes it as equally obvious that something can change from being F to being G. What he is working towards is, of course, taking note of the paradoxicality of the claim assigned to Protagoras that, for example, the same wind can, without undergoing a process of change, be correctly reported by different people as both hot and cold (152A–C).

As I have suggested earlier, what I see Plato doing in the remarkable exercise that is put in the mouth of Parmenides is to use the very procedure of Zeno (primarily by the recognition of the one that *is*) to defang the latter's defence of 'no many.' Juxtaposing the Parmenidean versions of the supposition with the Platonic versions, Plato can plausibly do honour to Parmenides and Zeno (crediting them with the procedure itself) while exposing their claims as indefensible and laying out his own deep-level solutions to a vexing nest of one-many problems. And his *Parmenides* is not made explicitly to refute the position of the historical Parmenides. It may even be that Plato wishes to suggest that, had Parmenides realized the problems of *one* and *is* (for which Parmenides is severely criticized in the *Sophist*), he (Parmenides) would have on his own reached the Platonic position. As I noted in chapter 1, and as I claim at the end of this book, I believe that the mature Plato thought of himself as in deep agreement with Parmenides' claim that *'it is the same that can be thought that can be.'*

Supposition One: A Parmenidean Version:
The Consequences for the One, *If One Is* (137C–42A)

As I have noted earlier, supposition one, as a Parmenidean Version of the one supposition, has only negative consequences, the reason being that the Parmenidean versions simply do not allow for any sort of predication. The *one* of the present supposition is not *F* (for any value of *F*), not because it is conjoined with the *different from F* (which would, of course, be Platonic), but because the Parmenidean reading will not allow any conjoining at all. The issue is precisely the one emphasized by the Eleatic Stranger in the *Sophist* when he notes that Parmenides, in saying that One *is* (thus allowing One and *is* to be different), engages in self-refutation.

The pattern for the remainder of the suppositions is set in this one. Part/whole plays a controlling role. Plato assumes that, unless ontological bedrock consists of wholes whose parts have no independent existence, we are stuck with the problems of the Parmenidean versions of the one supposition, that is, no predication. The motive here is that behind the name/verb (*onoma/rema*) doctrines of the *Sophist* (262D2–6) and Aristotle's *On Interpretation* (16a20–16b26). 'Intertwined' (*symplocated*) expressions are, as it were, wholes whose parts are themselves incapable of truth or falsity and have as references wholes whose parts must be capable of joining with other parts. If an affirmative intertwined expression is false, of course, Plato thinks of the reference as a whole, one of whose parts is a part of Different. Much more will be said of these matters later. For now, I need the notion that a *one that is* is a whole of parts, neither of which can *be* independently. And on the present supposition, given the Parmenidean reading, *there can be no such whole of parts*. (Note: with this paragraph I am ceasing the capitalization of 'one,' thus indicating rejection of the Neoplatonic emphasis on a 'super-essential One' and recognition of the term's use simply as a contrast term to 'many.')

Whole and Part, Shape (137C–38A)

Text:

Parmenides Very well. If one is, what else but that the one should not be many? Then there must be no part of it, nor can it be a whole. The part is, I presume, part of a whole. But what is the whole? Must it not be that of which no part is wanting? In both ways then the one would consist of parts: as being a whole and as having parts. Then in both ways [137D] the one would be many and not one. Yet it cannot be many but itself simply one. And so it will not be a whole nor will it have parts if the one is to be one. Accordingly, if it has no part, it can have no beginning, no end, and no middle. For these would as such be parts of it. Also, of course, an end or a beginning of anything is a limit. Thus the one is unlimited, if it has neither beginning nor end. And thus it is without shape, for [137E] it has a share of neither circular nor straight. Circular is, I presume, that of which the extremes must everywhere lie equally from the middle. And straight is that of which the middle must lie in a line with both extremes. Thus the one would have parts and be many if it were to have a share of either straight or circular shape. So it is neither straight nor circular since it has no parts.

What Plato needs in order to respond appropriately to Parmenides' critique in the first part of the dialogue and what in supposition two he opts for is a one that is also many. In supposition one, of course, the one cannot be many. Given that Plato's route to the one's being many in supposition two is its being (as a 'one-being') a whole of parts, Parmenides here, with no such 'one-being,' immediately moves from the opposition of one and many to the consequence that the one cannot be a whole of parts.

Assuming that anything with dimensions must have beginning, middle, and end and that these are or require having parts, the one of supposition one cannot have a dimension or dimensions. And having no dimensions, it can have no shape. Since beginning and end are treated as *limits*, the one, as having neither, is declared to be unlimited (*apeiron*). Interestingly, this is the sole affirmation (aside from the illegitimate use of 'one' as a presumed name in *Sophist* 244D7–10) that is made of the Parmenidean one, and it is, of course, an odd affirmation. It is rather like attempting to name the unnameable or to describe the indescribable. It relegates the One to the status of Aristotelian prime matter or the *Timaeus*' Receiver sans any dimensionality or even the errant cause.

The passage invites comparison with the attack in the *Sophist* on the his-

52   The *Parmenides* and Plato's Late Philosophy

torical Parmenides' description of the 'whole' as 'like the mass of a sphere' that is 'equally weighted' from the middle with nothing predominating. The attack is based, of course, on the requirement that such a sphere must have parts (*Sophist* 244E–45A).

Place, Motion, Rest (138A–39B)

Text:

Parmenides   And, being such, it would be nowhere, neither in another nor in itself. If it were in another, it would, I presume, be circularly encompassed by that in which it was, and it would be touched many times by many [parts] of the latter. But it is impossible for what is one and partless and having no share of circle to be touched many times by a circle. On the other hand, being in itself, it would be encompassed by none other than itself, since it would be [138B] in itself. For it is impossible for anything to be in something without being encompassed. Thus the encompassing would be one thing, the encompassed another. For, taken as a whole, the same thing cannot simultaneously undergo and do. And thus the one would not be one, but rather two. And thus the one is not anywhere, since it is neither in itself nor in another.

Now see whether, given this, it can either be at rest or in motion. Because, were the one in motion, it would be either carried about [138C] or changed. For these are the only motions. If the one were changed from itself, it would be impossible, I presume, for it still to be one. And so it is not in motion by being changed. But then is it carried about? No, for, if it were carried about in a circle, it would be carried about in the same place, or it would pass from one place to another. Carried about in a circle, it must be centred in a middle and its other parts carried around the middle. But what means can [138D] there be for that to which neither centre nor parts belongs to be carried in a circle about the center?

But then does it change place and come to be in one place at one time and in another at another time? Is it in motion in this way? But was it not shown to be impossible for it to be in anything? But then isn't it even more impossible for it to come to be [in anything]? If something comes to be in another, is it not necessary that it not yet be in that other while still coming to be and that it not be altogether outside that other, since it is even then coming to be in it? If, therefore, anything [138E] were to allow for this, it would only be something of which there would be parts. For some of it must be in that other while at the same time some of it would be outside. What has no parts cannot in any way as a whole and at once be neither inside nor outside something. But is it not much more impossible for that of which there are no parts and which is not a whole to come to be in anything at all, since it cannot come to be in it either part by part or as a whole?

So then it does not shift [139A] its place by moving somewhere or by coming to be in anything or by being carried around in the same, nor does it admit of change. Then the one must be in every way motionless. But we also said that it cannot be in anything. Then it is never in the same. Because it would already be in something by being in that which is the same. But, as it was neither in itself nor in another, could it be in the same? Then the one is never in the same. [139B] But what is never in the same neither maintains rest nor stands still.

And so it appears that the one neither stands still nor is in motion.

The one of the Parmenidean interpretation can hardly be in a place; for, as the context makes clear, to be in a place is to be surrounded by something, touching the surrounding thing everywhere or, at least, many times. And this, of course, requires that the one have parts. Even if it were in itself, assuming intelligibility for those words, it would have to encompass itself, thus touching itself many times. And again it would have to have parts. Plato evidently has in mind an account of place that is related to that of Aristotle in the *Physics*, where place is thought of as the innermost boundary of a containant (IV 212a20). He adds, however, the idea that a thing may contain itself, presumably, as having an outer surface or being a *whole*. And he notes that, as contain*ing* itself and being contain*ed*, the one would both do and undergo.

And the account of place is related to the accounts assumed here for motion and rest. To be in linear movement is constantly to be in a 'different,' that is, different place. But, if the one cannot be in place at all, it can hardly be constantly in different places. Even if it were moving as a sphere revolving on an axis, there must be a middle with other parts being carried around the middle, and we are back with parts again. If the one were in motion in the sense of being changed, then it would, in changing, cease to be itself and thus not be one. It is important to keep in mind here that *changing* in the sense in which something that changes continues to be itself has been ruled out by denying that it can be a whole of parts. (As we shall see, the one-being of the Platonic versions, as a whole of parts, can maintain the 'one' part while replacing the 'being' part.)

But the one cannot even be motionless or at rest; for, given that being at rest is being in the same, and given that the one cannot – on pain of being many – be *in* anything, it cannot even be at rest. So the one neither stands still nor is in motion.

Different and Same, Like and Unlike (139B–40B)

Text:

Parmenides And, surely, it will not be the same as a different or the same as itself, nor again can it be different from itself or a different. If it were somehow different from itself it would be different from one and would not be one. And again if it were the same as a different, it would [139C] be that and would not be itself. So that it would in this manner not be just what it is, namely, one, but different from one. Thus it will not be the same as a different or different from itself.

And it will not be different from a different so long as it is one. For it is not appropriate for one to be different from anything, but rather only for a different to be different from a different and from no other. Therefore, because it is one, it will not be different. But if not because of this, then not because of itself; if not because of itself, not itself. [The one] itself being in no way different will be different [139D] from nothing.

Nor indeed will it be the same as itself. The very nature of the one is surely not also the very nature of the same. Because it is surely not the case that when something comes to be the same that it thereby comes to be one. Coming to be the same as the many something necessarily comes to be many, but not one. But if the one and the same differ in no way, then, whenever something came to be same, it would always come to be one; whenever it came to be one, it would come to be same.

[139E] If, therefore, the one were to be the same as itself, it would not be one as [or in] itself; and thus being one it would not be one. But this is impossible. So it is impossible for the one to be different from a different or to be the same as itself.

Then the one must not be different from or the same as either a same or a different.

Nor would the one be like or unlike anything, whether itself or a different. Because that which admits the same in some way admits like. But the nature of the one was shown to be quite separate from the same.

[140A] And, surely, if the one were to admit anything quite separate from being one, it would admit being greater than one; and this is impossible. Then in no way can the one admit being the same either as another or as itself.

Then it cannot be like either itself or a different. Nor can the one admit being different. For in this case also it would admit being greater than one. [140B] What admits the different either from itself or another would be unlike itself or another, if what admits the same is like. The one, it seems, in no way admitting different is in no way unlike either itself or a different.

The one must therefore be neither like nor unlike either a different or itself.

The one cannot be the same as a different, for then it would not be itself at all. And it cannot be different from a different, for then it would be a different and not one. At bottom, in order to *be* a same or a different, whether as itself or a different or from itself or a different, the one would indeed have to *be* same or different. But then it would be required to be something other than itself. We are back, in this as in other parts of this supposition, with the original conundrum of Zeno, that is, that it is impossible, *strictu sensu*, for one thing literally to be another. And the Parmenidean versions would require this if there is to be any predication. So this and the other Parmenidean versions of the suppositions find nothing but paradox and contradiction in predication (where predication is not simple identity).

The move from same and different to like and unlike is simply mediated by the claim that 'same admits like' and 'different admits unlike.' I take these to mean that, if something is like another, it must be the same in some respect and, if unlike another, different in some respect. Thus the objection that the one cannot *be* same or different holds for its being like or unlike either itself or another. And once again there is an echo of the original Zeno argument, that is, in the linkage of same and like and different and unlike. And there is the further echo of Parmenides' criticism of Socrates' use of the paradigm/copy model for something's having a share of a form, in that Parmenides treats *being like* as requiring having a share of a common form in order to generate the regress.

Equal and Unequal, Older, Younger, of the Same Age (140B–41D)

Text:

Parmenides Being such, it would be neither equal nor unequal either to itself or to another. Being equal it would be of the same measures as that to which it would be equal. And being larger or smaller [140C] than those with which it would be commensurate, it would have more measures than the smaller and less measures than the larger. With respect to those with which it would not be commensurate, it would be of smaller or larger measures. But isn't it impossible for what has no share of the same to be either of the same measures or of any other sames whatsoever? And so, not being of the same measures, it would not be equal either to itself or to another. But whether it is of more measures or of less measures, it would be of just so many parts as measures. And [140D] thus once again it would not be one, but would be just so many as its measures. Even if it were of one measure, it would have become equal to that measure. But it was shown impossible for it to be equal to anything. Therefore it has no share of one measure, of many, or of few. And it cannot, it seems, be equal to itself or to another. And it cannot be larger or smaller than itself or a different.

[140E] Well then, does it seem that the one can be older or younger or of the same age than or as anything? It cannot because, having the same age as itself or another, it would have a share of equality or of likeness of time – of which we said the one has no share, either of likeness or of equality. And it has no share of unlikeness or of inequality. We also said that. Being such, [141A] how then could it be older, younger, or of the same age than or as anything? Then the one cannot be older, younger, or of the same age than or as either itself or another.

But then is it possible for the one to be in time at all, if it is to be such? Or isn't it necessary, if anything is to be in time, that it always come to be older than itself? And the older is always older than a younger? [141B] Then whatever comes to be older than itself also comes to be at the same time younger than itself, if it is to have anything than which to come to be older.

If a different differs from a different, it cannot come to be different from what is already different, but it must be different from what is already different, have come to be different from what has come to be different, or be about to be different from what is about to be different. But from what is coming to be different, it cannot have come to be different nor be about to be different nor be different; it must only come to be different [141C] (or not be different at all).

But, I presume, older is difference from younger and from no other. And so what comes to be older than itself must also at the same time come to be younger than itself. But it cannot come to be a longer or less time than itself, but rather it must come to be an equal time to itself. So also for being, having come to be, and being about to be.

And so it seems to be necessary that whatever is in time [141D] and has a share of time is of the same age as itself and at the same time is coming to be older and younger than itself. But the one admitted none of these.

Once again same and different are at the heart of the problem. Being equal to itself or another, it would be of the *same* (number of) measures. And thus the problem of how it can be *same* arises again. But, whether it is larger than, smaller than, equal to anything, whether commensurable or incommensurable, the one would be *of measures* and, of course, of as many parts as measures. But the one can have no parts. And, if it were of but one measure, it would be equal to that measure and thus the same. Thus there can be no measure of it at all.

The one cannot be of the same age as itself or another for the by now tedious *same* reason. Since it cannot be unlike or unequal for reasons given above, it cannot be of unlike or unequal age either with itself or another. If it cannot be of unequal age, then it cannot be older than itself (or a different).

Obviously for something to be older, younger, or the same age as itself or a different, it must be in time; and Parmenides assumes that time can be thought of as broken into intervals or measures. Thus, if something *is* the same age as a different, they *now* have equal measures of time. And so on for past and future tenses and for older and younger. He gives a parallel account of *coming-to-be* (*genesis*, γένεσις). Thus the age comparisons for both *being* (*einai*, εἶναι) and *coming to be* (*gignesthai*, γίγνεσθαι), for proper time interval comparison, must be appropriately tensed. And Parmenides relates *being* and *coming to be* in the following manner: if something *came to be*, it *was*; if something *has come to be*, it *is*; if something *is coming to be* or *is about to come to be*, it *will be*.

If something comes to be older, it comes to be older than itself in that the measures of time it comes to have are greater in number than the measures it had at whatever time is chosen for the beginning of the coming to be older. And it can come to be younger than something younger in that the proportion of time measures for each comes to be smaller. Thus something that is ten years old at the beginning of a new five-year period comes to be younger during that period than another that is five years old at the beginning. The age proportion at the beginning is 2:1; at the end is 3:2.

Adversions of this sort on age and time are developed in exhaustive detail in supposition two, where they are taken to have serious application. In the present supposition, because the Parmenidean one admits of no parts in any sense (indeed, of no qualification at all), they amount to no more than animadversions on the ways we and speakers of Attic Greek use (relative) age and temporal terms. And, of course, they suggest that Plato, in the second part of the *Parmenides*, has an interest in accommodating his philosophy to the general patterns of the sorts of things we assume that we can say intelligibly.

Time, Being, One, Name, Reasoning, Knowledge, Perception, Opinion (141D–42A)

Text:

Parmenides Thus it has no share of time, and is not in any time.
Well then, do not *was, has come to be*, and *was coming to be* appear to signify hav-

ing a share of time that has come to be at some time? [141E] And this: *will be, will be coming to be,* and *will come to be* – signifying having a share of the hereafter going to be? And *is* and *is coming to be* of the now obtaining?

Therefore if the one has no share of time in any way, it has not ever come to be, was not ever coming to be, and was not ever; it has not now come to be, is not now coming to be, and is not now; and it will not hereafter come to be, will not be hereafter coming to be, and will not be hereafter.

But there is no way for something to have a share of being (*ousia*) other than in one of these ways. Therefore the one in no way has a share of being.

And thus the one in no way is.

Thus it is not even such as to *be* one. For if, *qua* already being, it were, it would have a share of being. But it seems that the one neither is one nor is, if this reasoning [142A] is to be trusted. What is not – this not being – could anything be to or of it?

And thus there is no name of it, no reasoning concerning it, nor any knowledge of it, no sensation of it, no opinion of it.

Thus it is not named, or talked about, or opined about, or known (γιγνώσκεται), nor does any being have sensation of it. Is it possible then that these things obtain concerning the one?

Aristoteles   It doesn't seem so to me.

Not being older, younger, etc., the one is not in any time. Thus it neither was, was coming to be, is, is coming to be, will be, nor will be coming to be. And so in no way does the one have a share of being. Furthermore, it cannot even *be* one. And there can be no name for it, no reasoning concerning it, no knowledge or perception of it, no opinion concerning it. Aristoteles agrees that none of these can obtain for the one.

Final Comments

For all that is claimed in this first supposition, there is nothing especially significant in the supposition's being about the one or even *a* one. If there is but a single term – whatever the term – nothing connects. And even the notion of a term's signifying something becomes incoherent. To signify requires some sort of connection with a different; to say or think a term's signifying requires even more. One is reminded of the Stranger's challenge to Parmenidean naming at the *Sophist* 244D: 'If, on the one hand, he assumes that the name is different from the thing, he is surely speaking of two things ... Whereas, if he assumes that the name is the same as the thing, either he will have to say it is not the name of anything, or if he says it is the name of something, it will follow that the name is merely a name of a name and of nothing else whatsoever.'[2]

But we are about to look at supposition two, that is, the consequences for the one of the Platonic Version of the one supposition. And here the story is very different indeed. First, however, it will prove helpful to intersperse a short preparatory chapter that underlines the important and remarkable innovations of the Platonic Version.

4

Supposition Two as the Clue to the *Parmenides*

It would be a mistake to think that the upshot of going through the procedure for the Parmenidean Version of the affirmative one supposition is utterly negative and barren. There are at least two important results. First, what Parmenides has shown in going through Zeno's procedure is precisely what one would expect from what Plato took to be the doctrine of the historical Parmenides. Second, the form of the great exercise has been given the shape and arrangement that Plato wants us to understand before we move to the other versions of the one supposition. Let me discuss these in order.

As we have seen in looking at Zeno's defence of Parmenides' 'no-many' claim, Zeno's book is supposed to be an attempt to show that Parmenides' critics must accept even greater absurdities than those the critics attribute to Parmenides. What Parmenides has done in this first supposition is to exhibit, if you will, the other side of Zeno's coin. It exhibits what (at least on the Parmenidean Version) goes along with Parmenides' own supposition. In a way, it justifies Zeno's claim about greater absurdities, for there are apparently no out-and-out absurdities (contradictions) that go along with the supposition. I say 'apparently' because, as is echoed in the *Sophist*, the claim that *one is* is a self-refutation. It is interesting to note in retrospect how careful Plato was when, in the first part of the dialogue, he did not attribute the claim that *one is* to Parmenides. He simply says 'one' and, with Zeno in mind, says 'No many,' thus avoiding any hint of predication.

On the second point, it is worth keeping in mind Aristotle's description of *exercise* (*gymnastike*) as dialectical practice (*Metaphysics* Gamma), while working through the several consequence sets. The list of what can be and be said (or, in the case of the Parmenidean versions, cannot be or be said) stays fairly constant (with understandable exceptions) through the several consequence sets. As we shall shortly see, it looks as though Plato is trying in the *Platonic* versions to accommodate virtually everything that 'common sense' would recognize or the language would allow, especially after rather sophisticated distinction-making. It is probably more illuminating to think of the accommodation as the recognition of *logical* possibility. Indeed, if 'logical' is not construed narrowly, I think that what is at stake *is* logical possibility.

If this is right, then Parmenides' earlier comment that Socrates has attempted 'too soon' and 'before exercise' to produce definitions (135C) can be given some bite. Socrates needs practice in the exploration of logical possibility or, in Aristotle's characterization, dialectical practice. But it is not clear why the lack of such practice should have laid Socrates open to Parmenides' critique in the first part of the dialogue. And it is certainly not clear how the exposition of the possibilities of the first supposition can provide the needed practice.

It should be noted, however, that the definitions that Socrates has attempted 'too soon' are said to be definitions 'of the forms,' not definitions *simpliciter*. Given Socrates' earlier insistence that the forms are individually isolated from one another, there can be no definitions of forms by reference to other forms, for that would require removing the isolation. Even so, this might not prevent efforts to say, for example, what it is to be *F* in the case of *the F itself* (on the assumption that what is said 'names' the same thing as 'the *F* itself'). Given the apparent requirement of a definition to be something other than a mere synonym, even this would seem to require removing the isolation of the forms from each other. And we know from the *Sophist* mingling of the 'greatest forms' that Plato gives up the isolation. (That he does so in the *Parmenides* is shown in subsequent chapters.) But the point to be made here concerns the relevance of Parmenides' statement that Socrates needs 'exercise' before attempting to define the forms. The relevance of the exploration of logical possibility, as it turns out, is certainly present, but it takes a rather different form from what one might have thought. The relevance is almost immediately introduced with supposition two, and it takes the form of putting an end to Socrates' separation of the forms from one another.

This comes with the exploration of the consequences for the Platonic Version of the positive form of the one supposition. This version begins by making a momentous distinction. It distinguishes between construing the one supposition as 'If one one' (the Parmenidean Version) and construing it as 'if one *is*' (the Platonic version). And Plato moves immediately to construing the latter as requiring that the one *have a share of (metechei, μετέχει)* being. All of a sudden Plato presents us with an account of *having a share* that requires that neither *one* nor *is* can ever lack the other and that *having a share* be given a part/whole construction. And the account allows for a form's having a share of another form.

That the account needs to be taken seriously is clear not only from what follows in the *Parmenides* but also both from the *Sophist* passage that treats the Parmenidean claim that *one is* as tantamount to self-destruction and from the metaphysical heartland of the *Sophist* that introduces *koinonia* or *mixture* of the 'greatest' forms. We are thus put on notice that the Platonic Version of the supposition will be the exploration of the possibilities resident in a fundamental and foundational duality. And Socrates' exposure to *exercise* will be dialectical or logical exercise that immediately provides a resolution of the participation problem on which his earlier claims faltered.

Mention of the *Sophist* invites attention to a portion of the *Sophist* in which the Eleatic Stranger complains about a number of Presocratic philosophers who, as he puts the matter, 'have treated us like children' (242C). What they are alleged to have done is to say of several presumed basic entities that they 'are.' And Parmenides says of *one* that it 'is.' The Stranger's complaint is that, having so said, these several philosophers do not tell us what they have in mind by 'is' or 'are.' If they should respond to the complaint, they would merely repeat themselves. Were they to do so, he seems to think they would do what the beginning of the second supposition accuses the propounder of the first supposition of, viz., merely repeat (the relevant term or) 'one,' in effect muttering, 'if one one' (rather than saying, 'if one is').

A part of what I am getting at here is that I think it likely that this portion of the *Sophist* is of a piece with our present concern here at the outset of the second supposition, namely, how to understand what Parmenides calls 'his own' supposition. And I think it is quite clear that the Stranger in the *Sophist* finds Parmenides' failure to give an intelligible response to his question about the *is* in *one is* to be damning. Indeed, he obviously finds the claim that one *is* is self-refuting in that it requires more than one entity. That the *Sophist* passage is of a piece with the present concern in the *Parmenides* is in itself justification for taking what I have called the Parmenidean Version of the consequences for the supposition 'if one is,' as requiring that there be no predication.

There is more, and it involves questioning the status given the *one* in a great deal of interpretation of Plato, but most especially the interpretation of the Neoplatonists. What I wish to suggest is that the contrast between 'if many are' and 'if one is' is just what it appears to be, and no special significance is to be attached to 'one.' Zeno's concern with 'if many are' is to show that predication requires contradiction and is thus more 'ludicrous' than the consequences of 'if one is' where this is given a Parmenidean interpretation. As noted earlier, there is some point to Zeno's claim, for the Parmenidean interpretation of the first supposition does not as such lead to contradiction – if only because it does not allow predication at all. Adversion to the *Sophist*, however, leads to noting that the claim that *one is* is self-refuting, if it is said by a strict Parmenidean.

It is worth noting that what we have of the poem of the historical Parmenides simply does not use the term 'one' in its arguments and claims except in stating that 'thinking and the thought that *it is* are one and the same' (Fragment 8, 34). There is thus no ground in the poem for attaching a special significance to 'one.' For Plato's purposes in the *Parmenides*, the contrast between *many* and *one* is in the service of the procedure of determining 'consequences' from suppositions. In the interest of allowing for predication and the consequent interrelation of things, Plato in effect points out that Zeno's use of the procedure leads to claiming that predication is contradictory and that Parmenides' use of it leads to no predication at all. Now, in supposition two, he uses the procedure in the interest of allowing for predication and interrelatedness. So to use the procedure, he needs to make the same sort of move that he makes in the *Sophist* in demanding that the partisans of many or of one explain the *is* or *are* that they append to their claims for a many or a one, thus the insistence upon the second supposition's one that *is*. As might be anticipated we shall be back at this matter again in chapter 10 on the *Theaetetus* and the *Sophist*.

It may be important to note that Aristotle's characterization of dialectic as 'trial exercise in the concerns of philosophy' (*Metaphysics* Gamma, 1004b 25–6) strongly suggests that such 'exercise' was a regular activity in some group, perhaps the late Academy (while Plato was still alive) or among Aristotle's followers. Though Aristotle in various places makes it clear that he rejects Plato's forms and, along with that rejection, any need for *participation* or *having a share*, it is equally clear that he castigates Parmenides for not distinguishing between a subject and what 'holds for' it.[1] And, as we shall see, there are several features of the late Platonic philosophy that he picks up and uses in his own way, for example, the notion of negative terms as unlimited or boundless (*aorista*, ἀόριστα).

Still on the matter of Socrates' having tried 'too soon' to produce various definitions, I want to look ahead to an important matter that will get its primary airing when other late dialogues are formally discussed. What I want to take notice of is Socrates' remarkable announcement in the *Philebus* that he has run onto a procedure of enquiry that is consistent with the 'road' that he has 'always loved' but that has 'often left him deserted and bewildered' (16B6–7). And he describes that procedure as one 'through which all the discoveries of craft (*techne*, τέχνη) or art have been brought to clarity' (16C2–3). He proceeds to the well-known statement of a 'gift of the gods to men' brought by a 'Prometheus,' namely, the procedure of Collection (*synagoge*, συναγωγή) and Division (*diairesis*, διαίρεσις). Without for the moment attempting to offer detail of that procedure, let me note that its product is genera/species trees and thus definition by location in such trees.

On the face of it, this *Philebus* passage looks like Socrates' announcement that he has gone through whatever was required to enable him to come up with proper definitions. Indeed, the comment that the 'road' he has loved has often left him 'deserted and bewildered' could well be a reference to his bewilderment after Parmenides' questions in the first part of the *Parmenides*. I shall try in the *Philebus* chapter to make the case for this and at the same time for several other features of Socrates' role in that dialogue.

It is important to note here that in all of the uses and descriptions of Collection and Division in the *Sophist*, the *Statesman*, and the *Philebus*, there is no overt indication by Plato that the procedure is *as such* one for the investigation of the forms, though it is clearly related to and, I believe, presupposes the intelligible frame of the forms (or the forms plus the numbers). The *Philebus* passage, quoted above, finds the procedure crucial to the several discoveries made in or by the *crafts*. And the examples given in the *Philebus* are drawn from what Plato would take to be *crafts* (*technai*).

Going through the numerous examples provided in the three dialogues noted above certainly reinforces the impression that the procedure is somewhat less exacting and demanding than Plato would require for investigation of his eternal forms. Many of them appear almost frivolous, though each can be read as productive of some sort of genus/species tree and thus of a definition that just might be useful. And many serious Plato scholars who have taken Collection and Division as enquiry into the forms as such have been at a loss to make coherent sense out of the parade of possible definitions in both the *Sophist* and the *Statesman*.

What are we to make of this situation? As suggested above, I think that we are to take Parmenides at his word and recognize the 'exercise' as just what he says it is. It is not a procedure for arriving at satisfactory definitions; it is, rather, one for arriving at rational presupposition or underpinning for definitions by using the procedure of Collection and Division. And it is that in at least two ways. First, the Platonic versions, in their exhibition of consequences by separating out a variety of term-distinctions, give a rather complicated indication of factors that must be taken into account in arriving at and defending definitions. Second, the Platonic versions, in their recognition of the basic interrelatedness of everything, invite exhibition of the varieties of interrelatedness, for example, sentential, genera/species, and qualifying.

Even so, Collection and Division, though productive of defensible definitions, is not as such exploration of the forms. It rather presupposes the forms and, I must add, the numbers in the sense that the forms and numbers, as providing the intelligible structure of everything, underlie and make possible for human beings the use of the procedure of Collection and Division. I say 'for human beings' because only human beings, with their need for and dependence on perception as well as their souls' innate concepts and the use of language, have need for Collection and Division.

As one might suppose, this last point is rather complicated and requires attention to Plato's mature accounts of perception. Before turning to perception as such, however, let me lay out quite baldly the crucial features of what I take to be Plato's late ontology, leaving serious defence of that position until the chapters on the other late dialogues. I think that ontological bedrock for late Plato is a rather small set of forms that ground the intelligibility and structure of everything else. These are Being, Same, and Different. From these, as supposition two makes clear in its generation of the numbers, the numbers are derived, thus an incredible array of possibilities. The numbers inform the Receiver (*hypodoche*, ὑποδοχή) of the *Timaeus*. This, in turn, provides for a huge spatial and temporal array that constitutes what can be properly thought of as the physical world. It is limited both in size and temporal extent, though it is temporally without end due to an unending succession of 'Great Years.' This application of limit assures that the physical world is (not simply any possible world but is) as well-formed as it can be and conforms to the Philebus requirements of beauty, symmetry, and proportion.

Soul, of course, enters the picture, accounting for change and motion. The soul of the World Animal (of the *Timaeus*) presumably accounts for the rational pattern of changes in the physical world. Individual souls, primarily those of human beings, account for the motions of individual animals. But human beings, since they are earthbound and in constant need of sustenance, need means of getting around and thus apprehending their environment. So perception appears to be a necessity for such individuals. In the *Timaeus* Plato treats perception as the soul's apprehension of the world around it by physical changes in the body's sense organs that are brought about by interaction with the physical environment. Those changes in the organs are accompanied by sensations that are, in turn, used by the soul to represent the world around the body (and, as well, states of the body).

'Sensation' invites attention to an ambiguity that Attic Greek exposes with the distinction between *aisthesis* (αἴσθησις) and *aistheton* (αἴσθητον), roughly, 'sensing' and 'sensed.' But commonly *aisthesis* invites translation as 'perception.' Unfortunately, recent philosophy muddies the waters. A number of major figures have taken 'sensing' to be distinguished from 'perceiving' and having as its 'object' a *sensum* or *sense-datum*. And they have taken 'perceiving' as having *things* as its objects, *things* that are indicated by but not identified with the objects of sensing. I say 'unfortunately' for several reasons, but the relevant one at present is that this doctrine of perceiving is easily confused with what I take to be Plato's.

What I take Plato to be contending, as noted earlier, is that *aisthesis* is to be treated as perception and is an activity of soul that uses the deliverances of sense (that is, *aestheta*) and its own conceptual abilities to represent various physical things, including bodily states. The great illusion of *aisthesis* is what H.H. Price called 'perceptual acceptance' of *aistheta* as actual features of physical things.[2] Also as noted earlier, doing so leads to the acceptance of things that are and are not and thus to the illusory world of sense. What is important at present, however, is that Plato does not distinguish, as many recent philosophers have, between *sensing* and *perception*. Thus there is not for Plato any such egregious activity as *sensing a sensum* or *sense-datum*. We do not escape from the errors of perception into the certainties of sensing, though we can, as Plato makes clear in Book VI of the *Republic*, come to correct for the errors of naïve perception.

The Platonic situation is akin to the contemporary one where one must distinguish between perceptual consciousness and the physical/physiological facts of perception. For Plato what there is to be perceived is the mathematized physical world, and this is for the present purpose akin to the world of contemporary theoretical physics. And for Plato as for our present situation, even if we know that what we are really perceiving is Plato's mathematized physical world or the world of modern science, we are still, as it were, stuck with the necessity of unchanged perceptual consciousness. Things still are naïvely perceived as red or green, C-sharp or loud, sour or sweet, etc. even though we know that this is misleading and that, in a world without perception, there would be none of these qualifications.

For Plato as well as for us in our present situation, we can and do get on pretty well even in complete ignorance of Plato's mathematized physical world or that of modern physics. We have and he had a language that was centuries of human experience in the making and that provides for a variety of distinctions between 'appearance' and 'reality.' In *using* the language for daily life we come to anticipate and expect colour changes in various circumstances, different reports from people whom we take to be 'colour-blind,' and the like for all of the senses. Given standard procedures for craft-practice that are enshrined in the language, there is a variety of 'got it rights/got it wrongs' that are commonly taken for granted. Given equally standard procedures for getting on with one another, distinctions between what one thinks is right and what is 'really' right are also built into the language. All of this is quite aside from the issues that led to and are articulated by Plato's basic ontology and by modern science.

What these considerations lead to is the recognition that Plato's use of Collection and Division is a procedure that, though it presupposes the basic ontology, does not in practice require knowledge of that ontology. In order to engage in it successfully one needs to be able to move around in a reasonably good language and to be able to exercise the native concepts of the soul (that is, Being, Same, Different, and some numbers – the concepts noted in the *Theaetetus* 185–6). In this way one may practice Collection and Division successfully and in accordance with the description of it in the *Philebus*, thereby acquiring genera/species style definitions that are on a par with those arrived at in the several examples of the procedure given in the late dialogues.

Two important points emerge from all this. First, if it were not for the mathematical physical world and the underlying forms, there would be no reason to believe that the operation of the innate concepts of the soul and consequent sophistication of language over time would be a procedure with any (causal) grounding in the fundamental nature of the world. Second, assuming the sophistication of the language and the consequent ability of its distinctions to allow one who uses it to make sense, the 'both/and' possibilities of the Platonic versions of the supposition of the one provide a training ground for one who would use the procedure of Collection and Division to produce useful and defensible definitions.

To return to the as yet undiscussed text of supposition two, any definition of motion must accommodate the possibility that a thing may be both in motion and at rest at the same time. Any definition of aging must accommodate the possibility that a given thing may come to be and be both older and younger than itself. And so on. This should become clearer as we move through the consequences for the one on the Platonic Version of the one supposition. Perhaps more important for some purposes, in the examples of Collection and Division given in the *Philebus*, is the ordering of sensations

68 The *Parmenides* and Plato's Late Philosophy

by the causal influence of the underlying order of numbers and forms. For example, that ordering is reflected in the musician's collecting the harmonic and rhythmic species under genera and in the provision of definitional explanations of them (even though, much later in the *Philebus*, Socrates claims that the musician in practice engages in empirical guesswork). Similarly, in the *Philebus* the collection of human sounds and their division into kinds is credited to a remarkable Egyptian (though, once again, we have an empirical scheme that owes its possibility to the underlying structure).

And, of course, without the interrelatedness of everything that the Platonic versions adumbrate, there could be no metaphysical validity to the empirical/linguistic procedures of Collection and Division. In this connection it may be worth noting as well that the *Philebus* is really concerned with the *human* good and must therefore find it in the possibilities available to human beings who live all their lives subject to the restrictions of sense (but who, fortunately for Plato, are capable of understanding the nature of the *real* order and the very special pleasures associated with that understanding). Socrates' interlocutor, Protarchus, points out forcefully that human beings are not gods and that it is the good for the former that is at stake in the dialogue.

But enough for now about Collection and Division. We must return to supposition two and its remarkable unfolding. I have noted several times that this supposition is a Platonic version and thus a 'both/and' one. Even so, the first few pages of that unfolding give no attention at all to 'both/and' consequences. They are devoted entirely to taking notice of the one that *is* as explaining having a share(s) by virtue of joining in a 'one-being' and the duality consequence that there is never a one without a being and vice versa and then proceeding to the generation of the numbers.

As we shall see in the detailed commentary, the duality of the one-being at the most fundamental level provides an indefinitely replicative dyad, thus the progressive series of 2, 4, 8, 16, etc. – put simply, a 'two machine.' With the recognition that *one* and *being* must be *different* from one another, thus adding *difference* and, with it, there is a 'three machine,' replicating in the series of 3, 9, 27, etc. With the two series and the combined results of the two machine and the three machine, all of the numbers are generated – to infinity.

Plato, like Euclid after him, takes a number to be a *multitude* (*plethos*, $\pi\lambda\tilde{\eta}\vartheta o\varsigma$) and the parts of a number to be its factors (numbers that *measure* it). The parts of 12, for example, are 2, 3, 4, and 6. Twelve is thus (in the terms used both by Plato and Euclid) even, 2-times 6 and 6-times 2 (even-times even), 3-times 4 (odd-times even), and 4-times 3 (even-times odd).

Most of the larger numbers are, of course, much more complicated factorially. Reflection on the possibilities of the scheme leads one to think of incredible complications. Indeed, as I argue in the commentary, there is sufficient complication to provide a mathematical ground for the most complicated things and their changes in time.

In supposition two Plato moves immediately from numbers to geometric shapes. Euclid appears to follow him in this, for the *Elements* (Books V and VII) treats numbers and geometric shapes in almost exactly parallel ways. What we seem to have here in supposition two, with the derivation of the numbers and geometric shapes from the one-being, each of whose parts is the same as itself and different from the other, is at least partial fulfilment of the *Republic*'s promise to move from geometric knowledge (*dianoia*, διάνοια) to the non-hypothetical knowledge on which the former depends (*noesis*, νόησις), though there is no mention of the Form of the Good. I shall argue later that what we have is also the key to understanding the fundamental ontology of the *Philebus*.

Without attempting detailed justification of these comments about the *Republic* and the *Philebus*, however, it is clear enough from this summary of the first part of supposition two that Plato takes seriously this generation of the numbers/shapes from *one*, *being*, *same*, and *different* and means for it to play a major role in the *Parmenides*. And I have argued earlier in this chapter for its playing a foundational role in the justification of the procedure of Collection and Division and for that procedure's providing the sort of definitions that Parmenides thinks that Socrates needs. Before returning to the *Parmenides* text, it will help, I believe, to expand a bit on the linkage of this account of the numbers with the mathematizing activity of the demiurge in the *Timaeus*.

The *Timaeus* first constructs the heavens, assuring us of its regularity and rationality, invoking only the forms of Being, Same, and Different (35A2–B4). Later (48E ff), in what is called a new beginning, Timaeus says that, in addition to the eternal and its perceptible copy, he needs a third, namely, the Receiver (*hypodoche*, ὑποδοχή), a special non-thing that has no nature of its own but is infinitely capable of taking on features. As I read these passages and those following concerning the mathematizing activity of the demiurge, that mathematizing activity is the informing of the Receiver by what, in the *Parmenides*, are taken to be the numbers. Given the close association, if not identity, of the numbers and the shapes, this informing results in the mature Plato's physical world. And the physical world is both spatial and perceptible. Indeed, space and place are functions of the informing of the Receiver; the Receiver is not in itself spatial.

I shall not at this point enter the lists of *Timaeus* interpretation to offer a detailed defence of the above, though that will be done in chapter 9, on the *Timaeus*. What I wish to point out, however, is that it *is* textually defensible and that it accords remarkably with what the *Parmenides* seems to require and, as well, that it helps a great deal with the interpretation of the *Philebus*. Two final notes on this matter. The *Timaeus* requires a spatially finite universe and a temporally infinite universe (with successive 'Great Years'). And the latter part of the *Timaeus* gives a somewhat detailed account of perception, explaining it to be the result of a physical process and to involve causally produced sensations. Both of these have been remarked on earlier in this chapter.

After the generation of the numbers (and shapes), supposition two proceeds immediately to a rather large set of 'both/and' consequences. These are all explicable in context, with appropriate distinctions made to reconcile apparent contradictories or contraries. All of them have to do with predications made of subjects, whether of those subjects in relation to (*pros*, πρός) themselves or in relation to 'others.' As noted earlier, supposition three is concerned with predications made of the 'others' as subject(s). The whole scheme of the Platonic versions (including the negative ones) has to do with the interchanges of the 'one' (a definite subject) and the 'others' (indefinite subjects) as subjects and the 'both/and' predications that can be made of them. This is the scheme of the Parmenidean versions also, but, with no possibility of predication, they are uniformly dismal.

On the face of it and even with a relatively superficial reading of the *Parmenides*, there is a *prima facie* claim for taking supposition two as the key to the *Parmenides*. First, it begins with the rather startling announcement that we are to take the supposition 'one is' as equivalent to 'one has a share of Being,' thus inviting us to believe that it contains a solution to the most vexing problem of the first part of the dialogue. Second, this invitation occurs along with characterization of the first supposition as not allowing for predication. Third, it goes on almost immediately to a rather elaborate construction of the means of generating all of the numbers. And that process itself suggests attention to Aristotle's *Metaphysics* A and Book VII of Euclid's *Elements*. Fourth, it is far and away the longest of the suppositions and contains elaborate efforts to mitigate the apparent paradoxes of its consequences with carefully wrought distinctions. If one adds the evidence I have adduced from the other late dialogues, there seems little question that supposition two is indeed the key to understanding the second part of the *Parmenides*.

5

Supposition Two, Part One (142B–48D)

Platonic Version: The Consequences for the One, *If One Is* (142B–48D)

The One That *Is* (142B–43A)

Text:

Parmenides   [142B] Would you have us then take up the supposition again from the beginning to see if something of a different sort might appear to us in going through it again? We say then, if one is, the consequences concerning this, whatever they happen to be, must be conceded, do we not? Attend now from the beginning. If one is, can it be and yet not have a share of being (*ousia*)? Then there must also be the being (*ousia*) of the one that is not the same as the one. For, unless that being were of it [the one], that [142C] [the one] would not have a share of it [being], and saying *one is* would be like saying *one one*. But the supposition from which we must now see what must follow is not *if one one*, but rather *if one is*. Isn't it? And does not *is* signify something other than *one*? Therefore, when someone says (for short) that *one is*, what is said would be nothing other than that *the one has a share of being* (*ousia*).

Let us say again, *if one is*, what will follow. Consider whether this supposition must not signify that the one is such that it [142D] must have parts? In this way. If *is* is said of the one being, and *one* is said of the being one, and the being and the one are not the same, but are of that same of which we made our supposition, that is, the one being, then isn't it necessary for the one being to be a whole of which the one and the being (*einai*) are generated as constituents (*moria*)? Should we speak of either of these constituents as a constituent simpliciter, or must we speak of the constituent as constituent-of-the-whole?
Aristoteles   Of the whole.
P   And whatever is to be one is therefore a whole and has a constituent. Well then, can either [142E] of these constituents of the one being, the one or the being, take

leave of the other, whether the one of the being constituent or the being of the one constituent? Then once again either of the constituents, the one and the being, must have the other, and the smallest constituent comes to be anew from two constituents, thus endlessly according to the same formula: Whatever constituent comes to be must always have the two constituents. The one must always have the being, and the being must always have the one. So that it must always be generated [143A] as two and must never be one.

We turn from the consequences for the one on the supposition that we have only a single term ('if one' – the Parmenidean Version) to the supposition that we have two terms ('if one *is*' – the Platonic Version). As we have noted before, this is a highly abstract way of expressing the truism that everything whatsoever *is*. Indeed, it *is* incoherent to make an ostensible reference to something and then to deny that it in any manner *is*, if only that it is being ostensibly referred to or that someone is aware of it. Again, as was noted earlier, Plato himself charges Parmenides with just this sort of incoherence in the *Sophist*.

But in the present context it is more important to note the requirement that anything whatsoever *is*, whether what it is is gotten at by a characterizing or a sortal term. In material mode of speech what this amounts to is the claim that everything is paired with something else. And, as noted earlier, what we have is the semantic distinction between *meaning* and *truth*, the distinction between a *term* and a *state of affairs* (actual or possible).

We should not assume that, *as terms*, there are *subject* terms and *predicate* terms. I think that what Plato has in mind here is rather like Aristotle's logical requirement that terms as such are interchangeable, so that a given term, *F*, may be either a predicate or a subject term without any syntactical or logical violation. To put this matter rather baldly and to link it to our immediate text, to be a *one* or to be a *being* is not a matter of simple meaning but rather of place in a *one-being*. I hasten to note, however, that to secure proper reversibility of terms proper syntactical changes must be made to ensure subject/predicate fit.

I may remark, parenthetically, that this is aided by the Greek language, which rather easily allows for nominalization of verbs (and verb forms) and for verbalization of nouns (and adjectives). The matter of tenses will come up later in our discussion of supposition two.

Plato, in the 'one is' expression, finds duality but not dualism everywhere. With the insistence that neither the one nor the being can forsake the other, he has the basis for a *matrix* that offers the possibility of the abstract generation of a geometric progression. Before turning to that generation it should be noted that Parmenides three times in quick succession uses the verb that was so troublesome in the first part of the dialogue, namely, 'have a share of' (*metechein*, μετέχειν). When he says that 'one is' simply says shortly 'one has a share of being,' we seem suddenly to have an answer to the participation problem. That is: *To say that one has a share of being is simply to say that the one-being involved has being as an inseparable part.* We shall see in the next section that there is the same ground for saying that being has a share of one. And to reinforce what was said a paragraph back, we may note that there will be no restriction on what may fill the role of the *one* part.

But Parmenides moves immediately to what for late Plato is a momentous matter, namely, the generation of numbers. He does so by taking the *one-being* as a matrix for the generation of a series. It will simplify exposition for much of what follows later to symbolize *one* by 'F' and *is* by 'G.' Keeping in mind that there is never an F without a G and vice versa and recognizing the completely unrestricted character of both, we readily get the following:

        F G

    F G   F G

F G   F G   F G   F G

and so on – a series that proceeds as 2, 4, 8, 16, 32, etc. The 'etc.' is mirrored in the text by the expression 'unlimited multitude.'

In the above F G would be two made up of F and G. (But, importantly, it is a 'one-being' matrix for 'generating' other numbers.) As the text notes, each part, F and G, taken just by itself is one, and they are together two. The numbers generated from F G would be, of course, 4 and 8 and so on. The reason for this 'generation' (or 'coming to be') is the inseparability of *one* and *being*. Though the term used (*gignomai*, γίγνομαι) is the same as that used by Plato and others to speak of 'coming to be' in temporal change, the use of it here is a standard one of Greek mathematicians for the generation of various mathematical series.

Part of the justification for treating the one-being as a matrix is in the text at 142E, 3 ff: 'Then once again either of the constituents, the one and the being, must have the other, and the smallest constituent comes to be anew from two constituents, thus endlessly according to the same formula: Whatever constituent comes to be must always have the two constituents.

The one must always have the being, and the being must always have the one. So that it must always be generated as two and must never be one.' I have noted earlier and will note again that Aristotle in *Metaphysics* A (987b 29–34) speaks of Plato's generation of the numbers from a *matrix* (*ekmageion*, ἐκμαγεῖον), a matrix that he identifies with the *dyad*. And, of course, the one-being appears to be the special sort of two that such a dyad would be. But it is too soon to make trial of that well-known Aristotle text. Serious discussion of it occurs in the appendix in connection with Kenneth Sayre's *Plato's Late Ontology*.

As we shall shortly see, there will be reason for a progression by threes to supplement the progression by twos, and we shall turn to the reason and the progression shortly. For now and for convenience of reference in what follows I shall refer to the progression by twos as using the 'two machine' and the progression by threes as using 'the three machine' (terms suggested by my Ohio State colleague, Stewart Shapiro).

Before moving on, however, it will be useful to make some introductory comments about the Greek conception of number, using Euclid as the prime source for the comments.

Those of us who grew up with a modern conception of the foundations of arithmetic are likely to take 0 and *successor* as primitive, include mathematical induction, and rely on the apparatus of recursive definition for the definitions of the several arithmetic operations (addition, multiplication, etc.). And we are likely to think of numbers as sets of sets. Finally, we are likely to think of foundations of arithmetic procedure just outlined as producing a calculus. So doing, we distinguish between an 'interpreted' and an 'uninterpreted' calculus, treating the latter as having in itself no semantical significance. Our approach is quite different from that of Euclid and the other Greek mathematicians. Just how different and the import of the difference will emerge as we go along.

Euclid takes numbers to be 'multitudes' of 'units' and proceeds to an articulation of the features of those multitudes. The basic intuitive notions for him are *whole* and *part*, where the parts of a given number (*multitude*) are its factors, and the determination and adumbration of a number's factors are fully analogous to the determination and adumbration of the 'measures' of a line. Thus, if line A measures line B, A will go into B so many times without remainder, thus being, as it were, a factor of B. Euclid's concerns with numbers are reflected in his definitions of odd, even, prime, prime to another, even-times even, even-times odd, odd-times odd, odd-times even, plane, solid, and individual and serial proportions (*Elements*, Book VII). These are illustrated with marginalia consisting of linear, planar, and solid figures and 'proofs' involving reference to lines, planes, or solids, thus continuing the geometrical analogue.

Given Euclid's example, it should be no surprise that Plato a little later in the present supposition makes an easy transition from numbers to figures, and I shall attend to it in due time. I note here, however, that this will prove a major theme in the late philosophy of Plato. That theme is most obvious in the *Timaeus* where there is conspicuous 'construction' of the four 'elements' from half-equilateral and half-isosceles triangles (54B–55C).

As I have noted several times, the late Platonic dialogues rely heavily on the notion of a vast mathematical combinatorics that flows from the basic principles of intelligibility ('the greatest forms' of the *Sophist*). This mathematical model provides the model for the demiurge's mathematizing of the visible world in the *Timaeus* and the articulation of what, in the *Philebus*, Plato speaks of as the *limit* (τὸ πέρας). What we are just getting into in the *Parmenides* is the only explanation of that combinatorics that exists in Plato's published writings (though it may have figured heavily in the lost lecture *On the Good* as we shall see in the appendix discussion of Sayre's *Plato's Late Ontology*).

Although I am confident that the generation of the numbers must proceed along the lines I have been laying out, it is impossible, of course, to be certain that the sort of detail I am offering is precisely that Plato has in mind. I would, moreover, remind the reader that we are dealing with a completely abstract combinatorial scheme. It is not, however, 'abstracted' from empirically presented items, and there is no such 'abstraction' in Plato. It is, rather, an attempt to exhibit a combinatorial scheme sufficient to justify the certainties of arithmetic and geometry. And it is made possible by the assumption of the fundamental connectedness of things.

The Generation of the Numbers (143A–44E)

Text:

Parmenides Well then, attend a bit further. We say that the one has a share of being; therefore it is. And for this reason the one being was exhibited as many. What of this? The one itself, which we say has a share of being, if, in thought, we were to grasp it just by itself without that of which we say it has a share, would this itself be exhibited as one or as many?
Aristoteles As one, I believe.
P [143B] Now let's see. Is it not necessary for the being of it to be a different and for it to be a different, since the one is not being, but, considered as one, has a share

of being? So, if the being is a different, and the one is a different, it is not by virtue of one that the one is different from being nor by virtue of being that the being is other than the one, but by virtue of the different or other that they are differents from one another. So that the different is not the same as either the one or the being.

[143C] What of this? If we should select from among these, whether, say, the being and the different, the being and the one, or the one and the different, do we not in each selection select a pair that is rightly to be called *both*?

A How is that?

P As follows. There is mentioning being? There is also mentioning one? Then have we not spoken of each of the two? Now, when I mention being and also one, have I not thereby mentioned both? So, if I speak of being and also different or different and also one and so on, do I not in each case speak of both? [143D] And whatever is rightly to be called both – is it possible for it to be both and yet not be two? Whatever may be two – is there any way by which each of the two would not be one? Therefore, since singly they combine in pairs, each of them must also be one. If each of these is one, when any sort of one is added to any sort of pair, do they not all come to be three? Are not three odd and two even? And what of this? There being two [143E] must there not be twice, and there being three must there not be thrice, since it holds for two to be twice one and for three to be thrice one?

And what of this? There being two and twice, must there not also be twice two? And there being three and thrice, must there not also be thrice three? And this? There being three and twice as well as two and thrice, must there not also be twice three and thrice two? Then there would be even-times evens, [144A] odd-times odds, odd-times evens, and even-times odds. If then these obtain and in this manner, do you think there can be any number left over that is not included? So, if one is, there must also be number.

But, there being number, there must be many, indeed, an unlimited multitude of beings. Or is it not the case that number is generated as unlimited in multitude and as having a share of being? So, if every number has a share of being, must not each constituent of number have a share of being? [144B] And thus being is distributed through all of the many beings and stands aside from none of the beings, neither the smallest nor the largest. Isn't it absurd even to raise the question? For how could being really stand aside from the beings?

It is therefore maximally cut up into the smallest, the largest, and all manner of beings; and it is the most partitioned of all. Indeed, the parts of being are without [144C] limit. Then the parts of being are most multitudinous. But what of this? Is there any of them that is a part of being that is not yet one part? Rather, I think, if it is, then it must always – so long as it is – be some one, and it cannot be no one. Then the one is in addition to and alongside each and every part of being, not abandoning a smaller or larger or any other part.

But then is one [144D] in many places at once as a whole? Consider that.
A   I am considering and see that it is impossible.
P   Then, if it is not a whole, it is divided into parts. For there is no way that it can attach at the same time to all the parts of being otherwise than as divided into parts. And what is cut up into parts must surely be as numerous as its parts. Then we did not speak truly just now when we said that being has been distributed into most multitudinous parts. For it is distributed into no more than the one, [144E] but equally many, it seems, as the one. For the being is not lacking to the one nor is the one lacking to being, but the two are always equally present throughout everything. Then the one, itself cut up by the being, is many, indeed, unlimited in multitude.

Thus, not only is the being one many, but also the one itself, divided up by the being, is necessarily many.

In a mild echo of the Largeness argument of the first part of the dialogue, Parmenides suggests that if, 'in thought,' we were to think of the one without the being constituent, it would appear simply as one and not many. Given this thought experiment, it is clear that the one in and by itself is *different from* being. So a new player is on the scene, namely *different* (*heteron*, ἕτερον).

Different, as most readers will recognize, plays a key role in the *Sophist*, a role that makes its first Platonic appearance in the *Parmenides*, though not so clearly at this point. Its obvious role in the *Parmenides* is in the notion of the consequences for the *others* (or, if you please, *differents*). That role, in common with the role of *different* in the *Sophist*, is the origin of Aristotle's notion (in *On Interpretation*) of the *indefinite term* (*onoma aoriston*, ὄνομα ἀόριστον 16a32).

At least part of the role of *different* in the *Sophist* is to solve the problem of 'notness,' that is, to find some sort of reference for *what is not* (257B3–58B7). Plato finds it in *different* and its 'parts.' The parts of different are indicated by such expressions as 'different-from-F,' 'different-from-G,' etc. To say that something is not F is to say that it has a share of 'different-from-F.' And this allows for negative terms, as 'the not-F,' understood as 'the different-from-F.' Such terms are indefinite indeed. F or not-F can be used to refer to absolutely everything, for not-F refers to everything in the world that fails to be F. Thus the *Sophist* solution to the notness problem carries with it the liability of indefinite reference. (Whether for Plato's purposes this is a liability is another matter, and we shall see advantages in it in considering the consequences for the 'others' and the negative suppositions.)

For the present passage the introduction of *different* is crucial, for it gives Plato what I earlier called 'the three machine.' What we now have are one, different, and being. Since the one is different from the being, they are differents, differents always coming in pairs (a different being different from a different). In terms of the parts of different, we have at least *different-from-one* and *different-from-being*. And we know that for any one we may choose (for example, man) there is an indefinite number of *differents-from-one*, similarly, *mutatis mutandis*, for any being we may choose (for example, walks).

Plato lists three possibilities for any given one being, namely, 'the being and the different, the being and the one, or the one and the different.' Letting * stand for the different and continuing with F and G, we can express the production of three one beings in the following manner:

F G

F * F G * G

Since the different may occupy either the 'one' place or the 'being' place, the generated three are really all dyads, though the pattern shows the generation in that each of the components appears twice and only twice. Given that all three of the generated one beings are dyads, it is clear that the three machine could be used on each one of them, thus producing 9 one beings, then 27, and so on indefinitely. And we have seen the operation of the two machine, producing the sequence 2, 4, 8, 16, etc.

With both the two and the three machines, we get, of course, 2, 3, 4, 9, 16, 27, etc. If, moreover, we combine the machines, so as to get, as Plato suggests, thrice 2 and twice 3, etc., much gets filled in. With these suggestions, we get 6. And working with both 'machines,' we can generate numbers that are odd, even, even-times even, even-times odd, odd-times odd, and odd-times even. The list will not be exclusive, for some numbers will be both odd-times even and even-times odd, as well as, of course, odd and odd-times odd and even and even-times even. Working out the additional possibilities for even-times even and odd-times odd, it is possible to get all the numbers except the primes. Of these last more shortly.

Interestingly, in the famous passage in Aristotle's *Metaphysics* A 987b 23–34, to which allusion was made earlier, Aristotle speaks of Plato's using a matrix (ἐκμαγεῖον) to generate the numbers and claims that, in so doing, Plato fails to get the primes. And so it would be if the two machine and the three machine are not joined in a single step. But consider that joining:

FG FG

FG   FG   F*FG*G

Here the first one-being is subjected to the two machine and the second to the three machine. The result is five. By a similar procedure, one could start with three one-beings, subject the first two to the two machine and the third to the three machine and get seven. With similar ingenuity, it would be possible to generate all of the primes.

Parmenides' claim in the passage is that the procedure generates *all* of the numbers where, of course, this is an indefinite multitude. There is nothing in the passage or elsewhere in the *Parmenides* to back up my procedure for generating the primes. There is only the claim that, with the two machine and the three machine, *all* of the numbers get generated: odd, even, even-times even, even-times odd, odd-times even, and odd-times odd. Nothing is said of primes, primes to each other, or proportions. I think it is clear enough, however, that Plato takes this first part of supposition two as a sufficient account of the generation of numbers.

This much said, some comments are in order. First and rather simply, it may be worth noting again that 'generation' (*gignesthai*, γίγνεσθαι) is the standard term in Greek mathematics for constructions and derivations of series. There is no implication of the standard Platonic sense of 'becoming' as contrasted with 'being.' Second and more important, recognizing that Plato has in mind a vast combinatorics a part or all of which may be the model for some such embodiment as that described in the *Timaeus* or what he has in mind in using 'the limit' in the *Philebus*, the internal ordering of parts of numbers is significant. It makes a great deal of difference, for example, whether the 12 that is part of a certain number is even-times even as 6 times 2 or as 2 times 6 and, *a fortiori*, if it is even-times odd or odd-times even. With this consideration in mind, the possibilities for detailed specification of an embodiment get quite remarkable.

Third, and important as suggesting an explanation of a much-discussed passage in Aristotle's *Metaphysics* A, all of the numbers except primes and two and three are made up of other numbers in individually differing arrangements. In the simplest example, 6 is either 2 times 3 or 3 times 2. In this manner they are each 'many alike,' as Aristotle suggests 'the mathematicals' (*ta mathematika*, τὰ μαθηματικά) are at 987b17. Numbers, as we have been treating them here, make up a non-sensible and 'eternal' combinatorics and might well be thought of as between (*metaxu*, μεταξύ) the forms and sensible – which is how Aristotle characterizes Plato's 'mathematicals.'

(More will be said about *sensibles* later, but let me here give a clear indication of the account to be given. I think that Plato's explanation of the *causal* origin of sensibles in the *Timaeus* takes the physical solids (tetrahedra, cubes, octahedra, and icosahedra) to impinge in various ways on the sense organs, and he takes the several sensibles to arise from such impingements. So considered, sensibles have a causal origin but no causal progeny, unless one counts memory images [as influencing souls to act] among the causes. 'Impinge' must be taken *cum grano salis*, for there is no ground for attributing to Plato any sort of materialist causality of bumping and grinding, despite his speaking with the vulgar in parts of the *Timaeus*.)

Parmenides, having shown that number, as generated, is an 'unlimited multitude,' proceeds to point out that this requires being and one to be unlimited multitudes, since each is a constituent of every number and its parts.

Why is Parmenides at pains to begin the working out of consequences for supposition two with the generation of the numbers? Because, I believe, Plato has in mind the notion that numbers in the sense discussed earlier and as derivative from the principles of intelligibility provide a sufficiently articulated model for the complexities of the physical universe and a paradigm for a part-whole understanding of participation (*methexis*, μέθεξις). I think it likely, if not obvious, that, when the demiurge of the *Timaeus* works his compromise with Necessity, he mathematizes the Receiver in accordance with this model. I think it also likely that Plato in the chapter in the *Philebus* (27B7–10) has this model in mind in speaking of the Limit (*to peras*, τὸ πέρας).

Quite aside from the motive of getting the articulation of his later ontology going, the opening part of the treatment of the Platonic Version of supposition two is the natural place for Plato to lay out his account of the numbers. Indeed, it places remarkable emphasis upon the difference between the Parmenidean and the Platonic versions of the supposition. And it introduces the generation of the numbers along with what must be taken as the fundamental forms, namely, Being, Same, and Different. Since what appear to be definitions of the other two 'greatest forms' of the *Sophist*, namely, Motion and Rest, will follow shortly, Plato provides remarkable intellectual continuity both with the *Sophist* and the *Timaeus*.

If, as in Euclid, one thinks of both geometers and arithmeticians as able to illustrate the interrelated diversity with sensible diagrams (and Euclid's *Elements* provides diagrams equally for magnitudes and numbers), one may think of geometry and arithmetic in the manner of the Divided Line's account of geometry in the *Republic*. The knowledge of geometers and arithmeticians (treated in *Republic* as *dianoia*) is, relative to the knowledge of dialecticians (treated in the *Republic* as *noesis*), hypothetical and admits of illustration by diagrams. On the present account the knowledge of the dialectician would appear to be that of the unconditioned one-being and its accompanying Same and Different. (More will be said of this matter later in the commentary. It is worth commenting that, as early as chapter 1, I pointed out that the Doubly Divided Line appears to anticipate this second part of *Parmenides*.)

I have noted that, in accordance with the first use of 'have a share of' (*metechein*, μετέχειν) in supposition two, where the one is said to have a share of being, the sense of 'have a share of' seems to be something like 'is joined in a one-being with.' But it is more perspicuous, I believe, to put this in part-whole terms; thus our exemplary one has a share of being in that it is part of a whole that includes being. Indeed, there are many uses of 'have a share of' in the several suppositions. What they seem to have in common is the part-whole pattern, though this needs some explanation. I turn to a first run at that explanation, 'first run' because the full sense of some features of the explanation can become clear only later.

First, F has a share of G if F is joined in a one-being with G (the sense mentioned in the above paragraph). Second, F has a share of G if G is a number and F is a factor of G. Third, X has a share of F if it is patterned in accordance with F. Fourth (and related), X has a share of G if X has a share of F, and F has a share of G. F and G range over forms or numbers, and X ranges over changeable things. X in this is a bit misleading, for, as I read the late Plato, there can be no X that fails to have a share of an F. (There are no 'bare particulars,' and a proper name always 'is' some F or other *necessarily*.)

In supposition one Parmenides uses the 'have a share' expression many times, always, of course, to negative effect. Given the negative result of the examination of 'have a share' in the first part of the dialogue and the advice to Socrates that he practice the procedure of Zeno, this is at first blush surprising. I think, however, that the repeated use of the expression in the first supposition is deliberate and prepares the reader for its use almost immediately in supposition two where 'the one is' is treated as simply another way of saying 'the one has a share of being.'

It will be noticed that this account, though it is a part/whole account, avoids a major liability of Socrates' first attempt to defend the notion of having shares in the first part of the dialogue, namely, that according to which a thing may have the whole form as its share. The problem there was the unity of the form, since more than one thing having a share of it seemed to require that the form be separated from itself. On the present account there would seem to be nothing to prevent a form or a number from being a constituent in any number of wholes or from being a whole having any number of constituents.

What we have looked at so far in supposition two is in effect theoretical backdrop for everything to come. We have not yet seen in supposition two any effort to show how the *one* can be both F and G where these are either contraries or contradictories. But the most obvious contrast between the Parmenidean and Platonic versions of the suppositions is the ubiquity of 'neither/nor' in the first and that of 'both/and' in the second. We are now about to work through the 'both/and' effort of supposition two, where, it will be remembered, we are concerned with the 'consequences' for the *one*. As we shall see, in every case, the *one* is saved from the bad effects of contrary or contradictory characterization by distinguishing various senses of being F or G.

Whole, Part, Limit, Unlimit, Beginning, Middle, End, Shape, in Itself, in Another (144E-46A)

Text:

Parmenides Also, because the constituents are constituents of a whole, the one must be limited by the whole. Or are the constituents [145A] not encompassed by the whole? But what encompasses must be a limit. Thus the one being is, I suppose, one and many, whole and constituents, limited and unlimited in multitude. So, since it is limited, must it not have extremes?

What of this? If it is a whole, must it not have beginning, middle, and end? Or can something be a whole without these three? And, if any of these were to withdraw, will it still wish to be a whole? And so it seems that the one must have a beginning, [145B] an end, and a middle. But surely the middle lies equally far from the extremes. For it would not otherwise be a middle. Being such, the one must, it seems, have a share of some shape, whether straight, circular, or some a mixture of both.

This obtaining, will it not be in itself and in another? Each of the parts, I presume, is in the whole and none is outside the whole. And all of the parts are encompassed [145C] by the whole? And surely the one is all of its parts, neither more nor less than all of them.

Is not the one also the whole? If then all of the parts happened to be in a whole, the one is all of the parts, and the one is itself the whole, and all the parts are encompassed by whole, the one would be encompassed by the one. And in this manner the one itself would be in itself.

But again the whole is not in the parts, neither in all of them nor in [145D] any of them. For, if it were in all of them, it would necessarily be in one of them. For not being in some one of them, it could not be in all of them. If this is a certain one of the all and the whole is not in this one, how will one yet be in all of them? Nor, indeed, is it in any of the parts. If the whole were in some part, the greater would be in the less, which is impossible. But not being in many or one or all of the parts, must not the whole be in some different or not be anywhere [145E] at all?

Being nowhere, it would be nothing, but, being a whole, since it is not in itself, must it not be in an other? *Qua* whole, therefore, the one is in an other. *Qua* all of the parts, it is in itself. And in this manner the one must be both in itself and in a different. Being of such a nature, must not the one be both in motion and at rest? It is at rest, I presume, if it [146A] is in itself. For being in one and not going out from it, it would be in the same, namely, in itself. That which is constantly in the same must constantly be at rest.

But what of this? That which is constantly in a different, on the other hand, must never be in the same and, never being in the same, not be at rest, and, not being at rest, must be in motion. So the one, being constantly in itself and in a different, must constantly be in motion and also at rest.

Taking *F* and *G* to be opposites (that is, contraries or contradictories), one can think of Parmenides as initiating a series of observations, comments, and arguments leading to claims of the form 'the one is both *F* and *G*.' Though some interpreters have taken these to be simply paradoxes, there is, I believe, good reason to attend carefully to the distinctions made in order to see how the distinctions enable one to reduce or relieve the apparent paradoxes. Parmenides proceeds in a manner that almost certainly apes that of Zeno. But, where Zeno uses 'is or must be both *F* and *G*' destructively, Parmenides, in the Platonic versions of the one supposition, is intent on making distinctions that remove the paradoxes. The distinctions make it clear that there is nothing in all of this that requires denying the truism that nothing is or can be at the same time and in the same respect both *F* and *G*, where *F* and *G* are opposites. Plato is thus, in effect, making a detailed response to Zeno in the latter's own terms.

One might well ask what the point of so doing might be. I answered this question earlier, but we are now into the primary process of the second part of the dialogue and thus into text that supports my answer. What Plato is attempting to exhibit is that the fundamental intelligible framework of the world, properly understood, supports the distinctions we need for getting on in the world and conducting disciplined enquiry. Those distinctions need not be, as they seem to be in Parmenides' poem, relegated to the 'Way of Seeming.' To sound another earlier note, the exhibition of the intelligibility of such distinctions can be seen as the sort of 'exercise' (cf. Aristotle's talk of *exercise* [*gymnastike*] as dialectic practice) needed by the young Socrates as preparation for making definitions and thus conducting serious enquiry. Indeed, what appears to be going on lays the ground for intellectual justification of the procedures of Collection and Division, procedures praised and practiced in the *Sophist*, the *Statesman*, and the *Philebus*. (We have noted, however, that Collection and Division is not *as such* about the forms, though it provides a model for much of human intellectual activity.)

Parmenides begins by pointing out that the parts of the one, by being parts of a whole, are limited by the one *qua* whole. Drawing upon earlier conclusions as well as this one, he then claims that the one is both one and many, whole and constituents (parts), and limited and unlimited in multitude. Paraphrasing, one might say that it is possible (that is, not contradictory) to claim of a given one (say, Socrates) that he is one (as being one man) and many (as having parts or constituents). And, of course, it is possible to distinguish a thing from the sum of its parts. Finally, it is possible for a thing to be limited, that is, having limits. And we have just recently shown that the one can be unlimited in multitude.

Given a linear number, it surely can be thought of as having limits and thus necessarily having beginning, middle, and end. Euclid's *arithmetical* books do not deal with curves or circles, but, in principle, it should be possible to have circular and even spherical numbers as well as square and cubical numbers. The idea of the one's (as productive of the numbers and related to lengths and shapes) having a share of some shape or other appears virtually intuitive. If one thinks of a thing as having a share of a number, there is little problem in taking it to be in itself and in some other. In itself, as containing all its parts; in another, as contained (especially since it is neither in all nor any of its parts).

The subsequent definitions of motion and rest are worth more extensive comment. The idea that to be in motion is 'constantly to be in a different' is intuitively plausible as is the complementary idea that to be at rest is 'constantly to be in the same.' A simple example should make this clear. A person who is walking presumably maintains his/her identity as a person, that is, is constantly in the same (parts are contained by the whole). While walking, however, that person is constantly in a different, that is, constantly in a different place. Thus through a given stretch of time one and the same thing can be both at rest and in motion.

There are problems in connection with the unidirectionality of time. (And we shall shortly be looking at sections of supposition two that make a great deal of time and unidirectionality.) Clearly, in the timeless world of forms (and numbers) there can be no temporal progression. But, if any movement in the world is to be intelligible, it must have a share of a motion number; and, if it is to be in time, that motion must be irreversible. The *Timaeus*, while emphasizing that circularity is the appropriate motion for the gods, produces the rationally ordered circular movements that account for day and night, seasons, years, etc. – and even the Great Year. The before and after of such movement, while everlastingly repetitive, provides the sidereal clock by which other motions are measured.

Noting the interconnection between the physical motions described in the *Timaeus* and numbers containing formulae for motions, one can think of the interrelated and harmonic motions of the heavens as the physical embodiment of a complex and ordered (set of) number(s) and thus as indeed 'a moving image of eternity.' It is possible to take the complex and ordered set of form-numbers as rather like an hypostatized algebraic formula that provides the specifications for a Great Year (that is, the period between a particular state of the physical heavens with all its detail and a return to precisely that particular state). Time specifications for motions not incorporated in that formula could be relativized to that formula. Though those specifications would vary somewhat (given that many are the results of the activities of infersior souls), the unidirectionality of motions so specified relative to those of the specifications for the Great Year could in principle be made clear. Given unidirectionality within a Great Year, a successor Great Year could in principle be specified by reference to inferior motions that 'carry over' into another Great Year. Whether that is how Plato actually thought of the unidirectionality of time for successor Great Years is, I believe, unclear. What is important in all this is, of course, the plausible characterization of time and motion in the forms and numbers, one that illuminates the *Timaeus* phrase 'a moving image of eternity' and that could account for the unidirectionality of inferior physical motions.

I cannot resist some comment on the *Sophist* introduction of Motion and Rest after the gods' rejection of taking knowing as *doing* and being known as *undergoing*, since they require change in the forms. What the Eleatic Stranger seems to be doing in including Motion and Rest among the forms is taking both to be, *qua* forms, unchangeable (and thus at rest).

It is clear, however, that the 'gods' think of *knowing*, *qua* doing, as a kind of motion (and of being known as an undergoing) and thus as a doing or activity of soul. They reject this account of *knowing* as requiring change in the forms and (probably) as thereby subverting *knowing* (*Sophist* 248A7–E4). Immediately following their rejection, the Stranger cries out that soul, life, and knowing cannot be left out of the All. As we shall see in chapter 10 on the *Sophist*, the justification of the outcry lies in the notion of the World Animal in the *Timaeus*. Part of that justification may be anticipated now, especially since it does not explicitly involve the *Timaeus* and will assist in the commentary on the *Parmenides*.

The *Cratylus* (389D4–90E4) appears to take quite seriously the notion of there being *name-forms*.[1] Doing so, one may think of such name-forms as relative to (*pros*, πρός) the forms of which they are name-forms. In this manner *The name of the F itself itself* would be a form and would be relative to *The F itself*. The 'Slave/Master' argument of the *Parmenides*, Part I, takes the several *sciences* (knowledges) in similar manner to be forms and to be relative to (πρός) their subject-matters (related forms). What I wish to suggest in this connection is that a person who has a given piece of knowledge has a share of the relevant knowledge-form. Even as the share of a name-form that a person has would be a concept that has articulations appropriately connected with those of other concepts in a given language, so also a share of a knowledge-form would be a more elaborate set of conceptual articulations (associated with a given language). The acquisition of such concepts and conceptual articulations would be a matter of learning and critical practice over a period of time (and they could be lost with failing memory). Such dispositional and episodic knowings would obviously be motions in human beings. But they would not be motions that change the relevant forms and thus subvert their claims to be knowledge. And their being 'of' their subject-matter forms would be a reflection of the relation (*pros ti*, πρὸς τι) between the knowledge-forms and the related forms. In the light of the mathematical patterns we have been discussing, it is tempting to think of what I have been calling 'name-forms' as themselves mathematical patterns that mirror and are *pros* yet other patterns. But the temptation is, of course, more than a little speculative.

Returning to our *Parmenides* text, the notion of being 'constantly' (*aei*) in another or in the same is a bit puzzling. At the level of forms there would seem to be needed for motion a number that incorporates a continuous function such that a physical incorporation of it would present a smooth continuity. Since rest would be intelligible only relative to some motion or other, a number would seem to be needed that links a continuous function with a degenerate case or a discontinuous function. As we shall see in the Coda to supposition two, Plato insists that there is no time interval in which a motion takes place, that is, that it cannot be the case that a moving thing is both in and not in a given other or, what in context comes to the same, is simultaneously and in the same respect in two 'different' others. This would, I believe, require that Plato in some sense hold, *contra* Aristotle, that there is an actual infinite.

Given the notion of physical embodiments or sharing in forms for motion, there would have to be actual infinites among the numbers – thus giving added punch to Plato's earlier insistence in this supposition that the numbers are infinite or indefinite in number. And here one has something like Leibniz' claim that, in the noumenal world, there is nothing to prevent there being another item between any given two items. In the physical embodiment there could, of course, also be an actual infinite, though it may be true that our apprehension of a physical motion is always the apprehension of successive discrete states of that motion and that we express that apprehension by appeal to time intervals. But more on these topics in later parts of the commentary.

As Aristotle notes in his responses to Zeno in *Physics*, it is as possible to use a measure (*metron*) for temporal sequences as it is to use a measure for spatial magnitudes. Thus a given change from F to G can be thought to have a measure (say, a moment) such that it may 'take' ten minutes. Even as a line may have an indefinite number of finer-grained measures (say, metre, dekametre, centimetre, etc.) so a given change may have an indefinite number of finer-grained measures that asymptotically approach 0. To say that a thing that changes from F to G in ten minutes is 'always in a different' is simply to recognize continuity in change. And, though the form or number structure for such a specific change would be incredibly complex, there is nothing in principle to prevent there being such a structure. The idea here is akin to Leibniz' insistence that there can be no curve, however irregular, that cannot be captured in an algebraic equation.

A final comment on motion concerns the Coda to supposition two. If we suppose that a particular body is moving and thus occupying different places, we cannot assume that there is a time interval in which it is in two different places. The Coda is quite emphatic in insisting that there can be no time interval in which anything is changing from F to G where these are opposites. The Coda thus endorses what I shall call 'catastrophic' change, though this is compatible with the infinite divisibility of time. But we shall be at this issue and more in discussing the Coda.

Same, Different, Part, Whole, Like, Unlike (146A-48D)

Text:

Parmenides   And again it must be the same as itself and different [146B] from itself, and in the same way be the same as and different from the others, if the foregoing is to hold. Everything is, I believe, related to everything as follows. It is either the same or different. If it is neither the same nor different, it must be part of that to which it is related, or it must be related to it as whole to part. Well then, is the one part of itself?

Aristoteles   In no way.

P   Then it would not by being a part relative to itself be a whole relative to itself as part of itself. But then is the one different from one? Then it cannot be different from itself. If then it is neither different from nor whole nor part relative to itself, must it not be the same as itself?

But what of this? Must it not by being in a different [place] from itself while being in the same, namely, itself, be different from itself if it is also to be in a different [place]? Indeed, this was shown to be the case for the one – being both in itself and at the same time in a different. Then, as it seems, [146D] the one would be – by virtue of the same – different from itself.

Well then, if something is different from something, will it not be different from a different? But are not all such as are not one differents from the one, and is not the one a different from those that are not one? Then the one must be a different from the others.

Look then. Are not the same itself and the different itself opposites of each other? Then will the same ever consent to be in the different or the different to be in the same? Then if the different will never be in the same, there is no one of the beings in which the different is at any time. [146E] For if it were in something at any time, then during that time the different would be in the same. Isn't that the case? But, since the different is never in the same, it would never be in any of the beings. Thus the different would be neither in those that are not one nor in the one.

Then it cannot be by virtue of the different that the one would not be different from those that are not one or those that are not one would be differents from the one.

Nor would it be by virtue of themselves that they would be differents from one another, since they have no share [147A] of the different. If it is not by virtue of themselves nor by virtue of the different that they are differents, will not their being differents from one another elude us in every way?

But then those that are not one do not have shares of the one. For they would then not be not one, but would in some way be one. And those that are not one would not be a number. For, having number, they would not in every way not be one.

What of this? Are those that are not one then constituents of the one? Or would those that are not one in this way have shares of the one?

A   They would have shares.

P   If in every way it is one and those are not one, [147B] then the one could not be a constituent of those that are not one nor could it be a whole with them as constituents. Nor, again, could those that are not one be constituents of the one nor wholes with the one as constituent. But we said that those that are not constituents or wholes or differents from one another must be the same as one another.

Shall we then say that the one in relation to those which are not one is related as same to sames? It seems then that the one is different from the others and from itself and also the same as them and itself.

[147C] Well then, is the one both like and unlike itself and the others? Since it was shown to be different from the others, the others must also be differents from it. Then is it different from the others just as the others are also differents from it – neither more nor less? Then if neither more nor less, in like degree?

Then *qua* admitting different from the others and the others in the same way admitting different from it, in just that way the one would admit being the same as the others and the others the same as the one.

A   [147D] What do you mean?

P   This. Do you not use each name as a name for something? Well then, can you use the same name many times or only once? If you use it once, you speak of that of which it is the name, but, if you use it many times, do you not speak of it? Is it not rather that, whether you utter the same name once or many times, you must surely be always speaking of the same? And *different* is a name for something? [147E] Then, when you utter it, whether once or many times, you use the name for an other and name nothing other than that of which it is the name.

When we say that the others are different from the one and the one different from the others, in saying *different* twice it is not thereby applied to some other, but we always speak of that nature of which it is the name. Thus, in that the one is a different [148A] from the others and the others different from the one, admitting the different they are affected by the same and not other. But the one would then be affected by the same as the others. What is affected by the same is like, is it not?

In so far as the one admits different from the others, as being affected by the same everything would be like everything else. For everything is a different from everything else. But the like is the opposite of the unlike. So also the different is opposite of the same. But it was also shown that the one is the same as [148B] the others. Admitting being the same as the others is opposite of admitting being different from the others.

And in so far as it is different, it was shown to be like. Then in so far as it is the same, it will be unlike as admitting an affection that is opposite to the like affection. And the different, I presume, made it like. Then the same will make it unlike; otherwise it will not be opposite to the different.

[148C] Thus the one will be both like and unlike the others – in that it is different, like; in that it is the same, unlike. But something else also holds. In so far as it admits the same, it does not admit another sort; not admitting another sort, it is not unlike; not unlike, it is like. But in so far as it admits other, it is of another sort; being of another sort, it is unlike.

Thus because it is the same as the others and because it is a different from the others, for both and each of these reasons, the one must be both like [148D] and unlike the others. Likewise with regard to itself, since it was shown to be both a different from itself and the same as itself, for both and each of these reasons, the one will be both like and unlike.

The text continues with showing how something can be both the same as and different both from itself and from the others. The first section is rather simple.

With respect to itself and everything else, a thing is either the same or different, or, failing either of these, it is either part or whole. Case 1: It cannot be a (proper) part of itself, nor can it be a whole with itself as a (proper) part. And it can hardly be different from itself. So it must be the same as itself. Case 2: But, as we saw earlier, it is in a different while simultaneously in the same (itself). But, by virtue of the latter, it must be different from itself. Case 3: If something is different it must be different from a different. By definition the others are differents from it (the one). So it must be different from the others. Case 4: Note that the different will never be in the same. Note also that everything is the same (as itself). So the different cannot be in anything. Those that are not one (the others) cannot be differents from anything, and they cannot have shares of the one (for then they would in some way be one). So they cannot be a number and thus cannot be constituents of the one nor it of them. Nothing is left but that the one is the same as the others.

So the one is different from the others and from itself and also the same as the others and itself. The one is also shown to be like and unlike itself and the others.

Case 1: In so far as both the one and the others are different, they are both differents and thus like. In this way the one and the others are the same. (When Aristoteles questions the claim, Parmenides points out that 'different' or any other such term names the same whether used once or many times.) And affected by the same, the one and the others are like one another. Indeed, since everything is different from everything else, everything is like everything else. Case 2: As being the same by virtue of the different and, given the opposition of differents, by virtue of the same the one and the others are different and thus unlike.

Parmenides proceeds to draw the apparently paradoxical conclusion: The one is different (and thus unlike) both itself and the others by virtue of the same; and it is the same (and thus like) both itself and the others by virtue of the different.

One might legitimately raise the question, Why is Parmenides made to say to the young Socrates that he has tried too soon to define a number of terms and thus needs practice in Zeno's procedure? How is the procedure we have gone through so far supposed to be helpful?

If I am correct in assuming that Zeno's procedure is what Socrates at the beginning of the dialogue takes it to be, that procedure takes the form of *modus tollendo tollens*. And it takes the antecedent to be some form of affirmation of 'many' and the consequent to be unacceptable if not contradictory. It is quite possible that the Zeno treatise goes through a series of arguments like the ones we have seen in supposition two (leaving the generation of the numbers to one side) – but all resulting in denial of 'many.'

What we have seen so far in supposition two is a set of 'both/and' conclusions that are, on the surface, paradoxical. But the text is careful to make distinctions that remove the paradoxes or seeming contradictions. We shall see this sort of procedure followed in all of the Platonic versions of the 'one supposition' (and a similar procedure for all of the Parmenidean versions reaching 'neither/nor' conclusions). I think it is clear enough that the exfoliation of the *one which is* into the numbers is seriously intended and that it renders plausible the part-whole understanding of 'having a share.' This accomplishes two things. First, it shows how the intermingling of the forms is possible, thus correcting Socrates' claim in responding to Zeno that the forms cannot intermingle. Second, it is responsive to Socrates' inability to respond to Parmenides' early questioning concerning what forms there are, that is, 'sortal' or 'thing' forms and forms for hair, mud, etc. With the *one that is* there is no distressing distinction between sortal and characterizing forms (or numbers). And the thrust of the moves made in the second supposition is that there is nothing that fails to be a form, a number, or a changeable that has a share of a number or a form. It may be, however, that 'changeables' (including those that persist through other changes) should be construed as *instancings* of numbers and thus sharing the structures of the relevant (eternal) numbers. Finally, it may be worth noting at this early stage of the exposition of the suppositions that practice in recognizing and making subtle distinctions that undermine the Zenonian contentions should make Socrates less naïve in responding to Zeno and others like him.

6

Supposition Two: Part Two (148D–55E)

Platonic Version: The Consequences for the One, *If One Is* **(148D–55E)**

Touching and Not Touching (148D–49D)

Text:

Parmenides   Now what of this? Consider how it goes in the matter of the one's touching and not touching itself and the others. The one was shown, I believe, to be in itself as a whole. And the one was also shown to be in the others. Then in so far as it is in the others [148E] it would touch the others. In so far as it is in itself it would be precluded from touching the others; but, being in itself, it would touch itself. So the one would both touch itself and the others.

But what of this? Must not anything that is to touch something lie next to that which it is to touch and occupy the location next after that of what it touches? So that, if the one is to touch itself, it must lie immediately next to itself, occupying the place adjoining that in which it is. Now if it were two, the one might do [149A] this and might come to be in two places at once. But, so long as it is one, it will not. Then there is the same necessity for the one not to be two as for it not to touch itself.

But neither will it touch the others. Because, as we said, what is to touch must be separate from and next to that which it is to touch, and there is not to be a third between them. Then there must be two at least, if there is to be a touching.

If there should be two and a third comes to be in succession, there will be [149B] three but two touchings. Thus whenever one comes to be added, one touching comes to be added, and it follows that the touchings are less by one than the multitude of numbers. For by that amount that the first two exceeds the touchings the number is larger than the touchings; in an equal amount every succeeding number exceeds all of the touchings. Since the remainder [149C] is kept, whenever a one is added to the number, one is also added to the touchings.

Therefore whatever the number of the beings is, the touchings are less by one. If there is one only and not two, there would not be a touching.

We said that the others than the one are not one and do not have shares of it, since they are others. Then number is not in the others, since the one is not in them. So the others are not one, nor are they two, nor do they have the name of [149D] any other number.

Then the one is just one and cannot be two. And there is no touching without two beings. And so the one does not touch the others, nor do the others touch the one, since there is no touching.

Thus on all of these counts the one touches and does not touch both the others and itself.

Almost all of the remainder of supposition two is devoted to issues of *space* and *time*. The present section lays emphasis on space and thus on *touches* or *contacts*.

The relevance of the issues of space and time is to be seen clearly in several important sections of the *Timaeus*. As readers of that dialogue will know and as I have earlier noted, Plato there speaks of a mathematization of the so-called Receptacle (better, *Receiver, hypodoche, ὑποδοχή*), producing a large and complex spatial array of tetrahedra (fire), cubes (earth), octahedra (air), and icosahedra (water). As noted earlier, these are in themselves imperceptible and, as consisting of faces made up of half-equilateral and half right-angle triangles, capable of an unlimited variety of sizes, conjoinings, disjoinings, and transformations into one another. All the bodies in the universe are thought to be made up of them, and the great sphere of the universe is taken to be completely filled with them (no void). On the largest scale they are set constantly in motion by the rotation of the great sphere. On a number of other scales they are set in motion by the souls that animate them. (As I shall shortly note, this talk of being set in motion by the rotation of the great sphere needs some emendation.)

This is, of course, in marked contrast to Parmenides' 'all' or 'whole,' which Plato in the *Sophist* says is 'everywhere like the mass of a well-rounded sphere, equally matched in every way from the middle. For there must be neither something greater or something smaller here or there' (244E2–8). The Eleatic Stranger is made to go on and say that it is impossible for anything so characterized to be strictly and in itself one. But this is familiar territory for Plato scholars. What the present section of *Par-*

menides claims is that the one that *is* is capable of the multiplicity that a mass of shapes in contact with one another must have.

In that mass there may be any number of wholes composed of parts that are contained by yet other wholes and that contain their parts. Once this sort of interpretative line is seen, the animadversions of this section on 'touching' fall into place and, indeed, seem rather obvious.

Several interpreters of the *Timaeus* have been led to speak of Plato's 'atomism.' This is, at best, misleading, especially so if it really invites comparison with Democritus or Leucippus. But the issue is a vexed one. In the *Timaeus* Plato writes quite freely of causal interactions between and among his elementary bodies, all of them involving contact or 'touching.' One would like to think, however, that, in the manner of Plotinus, Plato has it that all genuine causes are directly or remotely the work of the universal power of rationality (subject only to the peculiar 'necessities' of space and time). In favour of this are two considerations. First, there is no evidence in Plato of a serious mechanics of contact causation, in particular, no evidence of inertial motion. Second, as Aristotle rather sarcastically notes, the 'solids' of the *Timaeus* appear to be made up of two-dimensional sides that are capable of leaving a given 'solid' and regrouping with other such sides to form yet another 'solid.' It is likely, however, that, despite the apparent *Timaeus* talk of contact causality, Plato is speaking with the vulgar where it will do no harm to his intention of showing how the mathematization of the receptacle can serve the purposes of the demiurge. What I think he really intends is for his mathematized receptacle to be a spatializing of the Receiver that maximally embodies via the numbers the rational pattern of the forms.

The association with the atomists is mistaken because Plato did not take his mathematical elements to be any sort of crude matter or stuff. And Aristotle's criticism of the construction of solids from two-dimensional figures is likewise irrelevant because what results from the mathematizing of the Receiver is a three-dimensional array of geometric figures. Aristotle is clearly taking the solids to be in principle perceptible solids that are filled with or made of some stuff or other, and he takes their solidity to be impossible to construct from non-solid, two-dimensional shapes. It is also a mistake to think that the imperceptibility of Plato's mathematical elements is a matter of their being too small to see or feel. Quite the contrary, they are in principle imperceptible (except as constructs that are capable of causally accounting for our experience of sensibles) and thus quite unlike the 'atoms' of Leucippus and Democritus.

One more matter before returning to the *Parmenides* text. This lies in the *Timaeus'* explanation of perception. As various interpreters have noted, there is in the *Parmenides* (except in supposition seven, which is quasi-humorous and will be dealt with in due time) no serious attention paid to perception and the standard perceptibles. Thus adversion to the *Timaeus* is in order. It will help, as well, to take some note of the 'secret doctrine' of the *Theaetetus* (155E3–57C3).

In the *Timaeus*, Plato offers physical accounts of the causal conditions of sensible experience. The several accounts of visibles, audibles, tangibles, 'smellables,' and 'tastables' link (in more or less complicated ways) the 'impingements' of the different elements (tetrahedra, cubes, etc.) on the sense organs with the comings-to-be of the various sensible experiences. The various colours, sounds, odours, etc. *as experienced* are neither Platonic elements nor combinations of such elements, though they are, of course, correlated with the different kinds of 'impingements' of those elements. Indeed, as I have suggested in an earlier chapter, with the 'impingements' of these on the body's sense organs, there come to be sensory apprehensions, that is, the soul's use of sensibles (aistheta, αἴσθητα). Thus our 'immediate' sensible apprehensions are representations of things as qualified by causally derivative sensibles.

Thus Plato gives us a common sense world that on the side of (what Aristotle would call) the special sensibles are misleadingly linked to the 'real' physical world. (Although, with proper attention to the manifold variations of sense apprehensions and sensibles and with use of the soul's concepts of Being, Same, and Different, they give clues to that physical world.) On the side of (what Aristotle would call) the common sensibles, it gives us shapes and numerical differentiation. And Plato accounts for the variation of the sensible shapes by adverting to rulers and his geometric account of perspective (later rendered formal by Euclid in his geometric *Optics*). In the *Republic* and in the *Philebus* especially, Plato praises carpenters for their use of measuring devices and thus for their correction of perspectival illusion. (I have placed 'impingements' within quotation marks because I think Plato's talk in the *Timaeus* of the 'tearing action' of tetrahedra, the rigidifying of rays coming from the eye, etc., is concession to vulgar accounts of collision and impact. But I shall be at this theme again in chapter 9 on the *Timaeus*.)

I think that it is worthwhile to advert to these perceptual matters (a) to explain their absence from and irrelevance to the *Parmenides* text and (b) to explain how the austere *Parmenides* text can be related to matters that have been of central concern to modern philosophers. It may be worth commenting as well that we may think of Plato with these perceptual doctrines as showing that the 'way of appearance' (which the historical Parmenides advises us to shun), however deceptive, is fully compatible with the way of being (taking it as the subject-matter of most of the second part of the *Parmenides*). I may note, finally, that, with the misleading character of the sensibles and with his association of them with pleasure and pain, Plato at once acknowledges their necessity in human learning and, as in the *Philebus*, accords them the lowest status in his ontological hierarchy.

Given that this Platonic version of the one supposition is, as I have claimed, a turning of the tables on Zeno, how might we attempt to reconstruct some Zeno arguments concerning contact or touching? Consider the following possibility:

If many are, they must both touch and not touch one another. But this is impossible. So no many.

If two things are to touch, there must be no interval between them. But, if there is no interval, they are not two, but just one. If there is an interval, there is no touching, and, if another is assumed to occupy the interval, we are back with the original argument. Hence there is no touching. But the assumption is that they touch. But they cannot both touch and not touch.

If I am right about the physical world of the *Timaeus*, this argument would be ineffective against Plato. If the physical world is the mathematized Receiver and it is thus an immense array of shapes, there would presumably be no gaps in it at all. Indeed, Plato claims in the *Timaeus* that it is completely filled in, having no void (58A 5–7). Given no gaps and the vast mathematical array, there could well be an immense three-dimensional array of solids with an equally immense set of common borders or edges. The matter of which such solids are next to which would be a purely mathematical one, and the impossibility of common borders without single entities would be rendered harmless and based on a misconception.

In the next chapter, taking up the matter of change, we are going to find Plato insisting that there is no stretch of time in which a thing which is changing from F to G (where these are incompatible) is both F and G. There is rather a non-interval, which he calls the 'instant' (*exaiphnes*, ἐξαίφνης) 'between' being F and being G. Given what Aristotle would call an 'actual infinite,' Plato could allow for such apparently catastrophic change to be a smooth transition. I am inclined to think that concern about common borders and the maintenance of difference could, with invocation of an actual infinite, be taken care of in a similar fashion. Plato does not, however, say anything further about the matter except what appears here and in the *Timaeus* text. I shall add a bit to the discussion in chapter 9 on the *Timaeus*.

Parmenides starts the present text by alluding to an earlier pair of claims: in so far as the one is in itself, it touches itself; in so far as it is in the others, it touches the others. It will be recalled that the first of these depends upon a sharp distinction between the one as a *whole* and the one as *all its parts* (a distinction that I have not given our hypothetical Zeno, supported in this by the denial of the whole/part distinction for the Parmenidean one of supposition one). There are, however, clear senses in which a thing is not just its parts. One is the obvious organic sense: most things are not just their materials. Another derives from the construction of the numbers. And a reasonably complex number, as we saw, is not just its factors: it is its factors joined together in a particular way so as to make just that number. Yet another and related sense is provided by the earlier talk of a whole *encompassing* its parts, a terminology that, I believe, tolerates talk of touching.

So the one touches itself as whole touches parts. And, as encompassed by an other or others, it touches them, construing these as other ones. And these must be taken to be wholes, or there is danger of denying that the one and the others are really more than one.

But, Parmenides goes on in the text, what touches another must lie immediately next to what it touches, and the one as a whole does not do so relative to its parts. So, in this sense, the one does not touch itself.

And the one cannot touch the others, for, taking the other or others to be non-ones, it or they are not one or any other number. Given that it takes two to touch, the one thus cannot touch the others.

And so on. It may be worth noting that we have here a 'both/and' set of conclusions where the components are not contraries, but rather contradictories. The reason is, of course, that there is no obvious contrary for touching or contact.

Equal, Unequal, Larger, Smaller (149D–51E)

Text:

Parmenides Now then, is it both equal to and unequal to both itself and the others? If the one were larger than or smaller than the others or, [149E] again, the others were larger than or smaller than the one, would it still be the case that the one, by virtue of being one, and the others, by virtue of being others than the one, would be larger or smaller than one another – that is, by virtue of their own natures? If, on the other hand, in addition to having their own natures, they were to have equality one to another, they would then be equals to one another. If the others were to have Largeness, and the one were to have Smallness, or if the one were to have Largeness, and the others were to have Smallness, to whichever form Largeness were added, it would be larger, to whichever Smallness were added, it would be smaller.

But then must there not be these two forms, Largeness and Smallness? If not, they could not be opposites of each other, nor could they come to be [150A] in the beings. If then Smallness came to be in the one, it would be in the whole of it or in part of it. What if it should come to be in the whole of it? Would it not either be stretched out equally through the whole of it or surround it?

Must not Smallness then, being equally stretched through the one, be equal to it, from surrounding it, be larger? But is it possible for Smallness to be equal to or larger than something and thus function as Largeness or Equality, [150B] not performing its own functions? Then Smallness cannot be in the whole one, but, if at all, in part of it.

But then it cannot be in all of a part. It it were to be so, it would do just as it did in the case of the whole. Smallness would be equal to or larger than whatever it came to be in. Then Smallness will be in none of the beings, since it can come to be neither in the part nor in the whole. Nor will anything be small except Smallness itself.

And then Largeness will not be in the one. For, if it were, then something [150C] other than Largeness would be larger, to wit, that in which the Largeness would be, since there would be no small in it, which Largeness must exceed if it is to be large. But this is impossible, since Smallness is nowhere in a one. But Largeness itself is larger than no other than Smallness itself, nor is Smallness smaller than any other than Largeness itself.

And then the others are neither larger than or smaller than the one, since they have neither Largeness or Smallness. Nor is either Largeness or Smallness, taken [150D] relative to the one, able to exceed or be exceeded, but only taken relative to one another. Nor can the one be larger than or smaller than these two or the others, since it has neither Largeness nor Smallness.

If, then, the one is neither larger nor smaller than the others, it must not exceed or be exceeded by them. What neither exceeds nor is exceeded must surely be of equal extent and, if of equal extent, equal. [150E] And indeed the same must hold for it considered relative to itself. Since in itself it has neither Largeness nor Smallness, it cannot exceed or be exceeded by itself, but, being of equal extent, it must be equal to itself. And so the one must be equal to itself and to the others.

Being in itself, it must surround itself from outside, and, surrounding itself, it must be larger [151A] than itself and, as surrounded, it must be smaller. And in this way the one would be larger and smaller than itself.

And is this not also necessary: that there is nothing outside of the one and the others? Yet whatever is must always be somewhere. Whatever is in anything will be in a larger, since it is smaller? Otherwise a different would not be in a different. Since there is no different apart from the others and the one, and these must be in something, is it not by the same token necessary that they be in one another, the others in the one and the one in the others [151B] – or be nowhere at all?

Because, therefore, the one is in the others, the others would be larger than the one, since they surround it. And the one would be smaller than the others, since it is surrounded. Because the others are in the one, the one by the same reasoning would be larger, and the others smaller than the one.

And so the one is equal to, larger than, and smaller than itself and the others.

And since it is larger than, smaller than, and equal to, it would be of equal, more, and less measures to and than itself [151C] and the others; and, since of measures, of parts.

Thus, being of equal, more, and less measures, it would be less and more in number than itself and also equal to itself and the others for the same reason. It must be of more measures than whatever it is larger than and, if of measures, also of parts. And the same holds for whatever it is smaller than. Likewise for the same reason for whatever it is equal to. Since it is larger than, smaller than, and equal to itself, it would [151D] be of equal, more, and less measures to or than itself; since of measures, of parts as well.

Since it is of equal measures with itself, it would be an equal with itself. Since it is of more and less measures, it is a larger or smaller number than itself.

And does not the same reasoning hold for the one relative to the others? Because it is shown to be larger than they, it must also be a larger number than they. Because smaller, a smaller number. Because equal in Largeness, also an equal multitude to them. So once again, it seems, the [151E] one will be an equal, a larger, and a smaller number to and than itself and the others.

This section is the most puzzling part of the Platonic Version of the consequences for the one on the supposition that *one is*. In dealing with smaller, larger, etc. it does continue the general pattern of the Parmenidean Version. But that version is comparatively simple, given that, according to it, there is no predication. And, of course, there are echoes here of the arguments of the first part of the dialogue having to do with large and small, including the use of abstract singular terms (that is, Largeness, Smallness, Equality). Again, we are all familiar with the apparent paradoxes of large and small that, unless qualified (by, for example, large for a flea), allow the same thing at the same time to be both large and small. There is as well the condition that allows a thing at one time to be large (relative to some other thing) and, at a later time, to be small (given increase in that other thing). I do not think that all of these are relevant to the present section, but we and Plato's ancient audience have them in mind when large or small is at issue.

The stress in the opening comment on the *natures* of the one and the others is significant. About all we have so far on the *nature* of the one as such is that it is a whole of parts. (And we shall see that the others on the Platonic Version of the affirmative one supposition can be, in a sense, a whole of parts.) That does not, of course, preclude some individual one, say, a horse, from having a more determinate nature (specified by genus and differentia and arrived at by Collection and Division). What the opening comment asks us to consider is the possibility of *adding to the nature* of the one (or the others) the *nature* Smallness, Largeness, or Equality.

It seems clear enough that nothing could be whatever it is said to be and, in so being, fail to exhibit or be qualified in accordance with its nature. A triangle cannot fail to be a plane figure, nor can it fail to have three sides. Its nature allows it to be any colour, any size, in any location, etc. But it cannot be one dimensional or two-sided. What Parmenides seems to be asking us to do is to consider the one (or the others) with, say, Smallness as part of its *nature*. It cannot be the one and fail to be small. It's an odd idea, but, taken seriously, such a one would be small through and through, as it were. Even as it is a whole through and through containing its parts, so it would be small through and through. With Smallness as part of its nature, the one would *qua* small be equal to itself and *qua* small would surround itself (*qua* parts), thus being larger than itself by virtue of Smallness.

It must be emphasized that Parmenides is not simply considering the possibility that the one is small (or large or equal). He is considering the possibility (if it is a real possibility) that the one is equal or large by virtue of having Smallness as part of its nature. And if Smallness is part of its nature and the earlier claims concerning the one's containing and also being its parts hold, this is a live possibility.

But then Parmenides insists that it is impossible for 'Smallness to be equal to something or larger than something and to do those of Largeness or Equality, but not do those of itself' (literal translation). I have translated this in the text as 'function as Largeness or Equality, but not function as itself.' I think the sense of this claim is that anything that has Smallness as part of its nature and is by virtue of this both equal to and larger than something else has Smallness functioning as Equality and Largeness rather than functioning as itself. And this is impossible. So Smallness cannot be in the 'whole' one, that is, cannot be part of the one's nature. For the same reasons Smallness cannot be part of the nature of any of the parts of the one. So, says Parmenides, 'Smallness will be in none of the beings ... nor will anything be small except smallness itself.' This last reads in Greek as πλὴν αὐτῆς σμικρότητος. It would, at least in just this passage, be convenient to read this as 'without Smallness itself,' for this would obviate the problem of assuming that Smallness is small.

But the very next statement of Parmenides appears to take Largeness as itself large and to assume that there must be a small in the one for Largeness to exceed if it is to be large. With no Smallness in the one, there cannot be Largeness in it either. There seems therefore no getting around Parmenides' taking Smallness to be small and Largeness to be large. There is, however, the demand that the *pros ti* or relational character of both large and small be recognized – no large without a small and vice versa. And this provokes the insight that neither Largeness nor Smallness can really be part of a thing's *nature*. Were either to be the case, that thing's nature would be impossible, the point being that either requires both.

Since neither Largeness nor Smallness is in any of the beings, the one, being neither larger nor smaller than itself or the others, must, says the argument, be equal to itself and to the others.

At 151A the earlier argument that treats the one as both in and containing itself is used to claim that the one is both larger and smaller than itself. (And this is quite different from that of the possibility of Smallness or Largeness as added to the nature of the one.) The text then goes on to show the possibility of one's being both contained by and containing the others, thus being both larger and smaller. It then concludes with the statement that the one is equal to, larger than, and smaller than itself and the others.

Parmenides moves on to asserting that, if the one is equal to, larger than, and smaller than itself and the others, it must have an equal, greater, and smaller number of measures (and parts) to and than itself and the others. Standing by itself this statement about numbers of measures is a palpable absurdity. Indeed, the claim that being equal, larger, and smaller requires an equal, larger, and smaller number of measures is also absurd. For, unless qualifications are added, the same thing can be both larger than and smaller than another, but it cannot be both of more and less measures than another.

The ostensible reason for bringing in the *natures* of Equality, Smallness, and Largeness is to enable Parmenides to conclude that, failing to possess either Largeness or Smallness, the one must be equal both to itself and to the others. The containing and contained argument used to establish larger and smaller for the one does not lead to being able to claim the equality of the one to itself and to the others, and the main exposition needs that claim for the conclusion that the one is larger than, smaller than, and equal to itself and to the others.

Giving Parmenides (Plato) the comprehensive 'both/and' conclusion he evidently wants for continuing the pattern of the Platonic Version of the supposition, the idea of Largeness or Smallness as part of the nature of something remains somewhat startling. It lacks the specificity one wants in a definition. Even so, given the sort of genus/species tree one would get by division, it could have the sort of specificity one might get in combination with an appropriate genus or species. For example, one may have *mammal* as a genus or species and then add *large*, thus satisfying the specificity requirement with, in effect, *large for a mammal*. For cases like *triangle*, however, it could not function (as I noted earlier in this section) as a proper differentia.

Time (151E–55C)

Text:

Parmenides Well then, does the one also have a share of time? Is it and does it come to be younger and also older than itself and the others and as well neither younger nor older than itself and the others, if it has a share of time?

Since one is, then somehow being holds for it. But is *is* anything other than having a share of being [152A] with time present, just as *was* is communion of being with time past and *will be* is communion of being with what is to come? Then the one has a share of time, since it has a share of being as well. And thus of time as it moves forward?

So the one is always coming to be older than itself, since it advances temporally.

Now don't we remember what is older comes to be older than what is coming to be younger? And so, since the one comes to be older than itself, it would be [152B] coming to be older than itself coming to be younger.

In this manner it comes to be both older and younger than itself. And is it thus not older when it is at a temporal *now*, coming to be between *was* and *will be*? Or can it, while being carried along from the *heretofore* to the *hereafter*, step over the *now*?

Then must it not cease from *coming to be* older [152C] when it reaches the *now* and is not coming to be but actually *is* at that time older? For, while it advances, it cannot be seized by the now. For what advances touches both – the *now* and the *hereafter* – letting go the *now*, seizing upon the *hereafter*, coming to be between both the *hereafter* and the *now*.

But if nothing that comes to be can elude the *now*, then, when it is at the *now*, it must cease from [152D] coming to be and then *be* whatever it happened to be coming to be. And thus the one, when, in coming to be older, it happens upon the *now*, would cease from coming to be and then *be* older.

It is then older than that than which it was coming to be older, and it was coming to be older than itself. And is the older older than a younger?
Aristoteles It is.
P   And thus the one is then younger than itself, when, coming to be older, it happens upon the *now*.

[152E] But the *now* is present to the one throughout all of its being (εἶναι). For it is always now whenever it is. And thus the one always is and is coming to be older and younger than itself.

But is it or does it come to be for a longer [period of] time than itself or for an equal time? But whatever comes to be or is for an equal time has the same age. And what has the same age is neither older nor younger. Therefore the one, coming to be and being an equal age as itself is and comes to be neither older nor younger than itself.

But what about the others?
A   I cannot say.
P   [153A] But surely you have this to say, that the others than the one, since they are differents and not a different, are more [in number] than the one. If they were a different, they would be one. But, being differents, they are more than one and must have multitude. And, being a multitude, they must have shares of a number larger than one. And of number shall we say that the larger or the smaller come to be or have come to be earlier?
A   The smaller.
P   Then the smallest must be first. And this is the one, isn't it? [153B] Then the one has come to be first of all those having number. And all of the others have number, if they are others and not an other.

Since, I believe, the one came to be first it came to be before the others and the others came to be later. And those that have come to be later must be younger than what came to be first. And thus the others would be younger than the one, and the one would be older than the others. Now what about this? Can the one have come to be contrary to its nature, or is that impossible?
A   It's impossible.
P   But the one was shown to have parts, and, having parts, a beginning, an end, and a middle. And surely the beginning comes to be first of all, whether of the one or of any of the others, and after the beginning all the others right up to the end? And we would say that all the others are constituents of the whole and one and that it has come to be one and whole simultaneously with the end.

The end, I think, comes to be last. And the one by nature [153D] comes to be simultaneously with it. So that, if the one cannot come to be contrary to its nature, it would, having come to be simultaneously with the end, be so natured as to come to be last of the others.

Then the one is younger than the others, and the others are older than the one.

But what of this? Must not a beginning or any other part of the one whatsoever, if it is to be a part and not parts, be one – since it is a part?

And so the one must come to be simultaneously with the first that comes to be, simultaneously [153E] with the second, and leave behind none of the others as they come to be including whichever may be added to whatever others, until, reaching the last, it has come to be a whole one. It cannot leave behind the first, the last, or any others in its coming to be.

Then the one must have the same age as all the others. So that, if the one itself is so natured as not to be contrary to its nature, it could not be such as to have come to be either before or after the others, but simultaneously [154A] with them. And by this reasoning the one would be neither older nor younger than the others and the others neither older nor younger than the one. But by the earlier reasoning it would be both older and younger, and in the same way the others would be both older and younger.

And so, with this obtaining for it, it is and has come to be. But once again, what about its coming to be both older and younger than the others and the others than the one coming to be older and younger than the one *and* coming to be neither older nor younger? Does the same obtain concerning coming to be as concerning being or does something different?

A   I cannot [154B] say.

P   But I can say this much. Even if a different is older than a different, it cannot come to be older still, or it cannot come to be more widely separated in age than it was at the outset. Nor, again, can a younger come to be younger still. For, if equals are added to unequals, temporal or any other sort of equals and unequals, the difference between them will always be equal to that which obtained at first.

But then what is older than what is younger or younger than what is older cannot come [154C] to be older or younger, since they differ in age by an equal. If one of them is and has come to be older, and the other is and has come to be younger, neither is coming to be so.

And thus the one, being older or younger than the other beings, does not ever come to be older or younger than they.

Now let's see whether they come to be older or younger in this way. In that the one was shown to be older than the others and they older than the one. [154D] When the one is older than the others, it has come to be for a longer time than the others. Consider once more. If we add an equal time to a greater or smaller time, then will the greater differ from the less by an equal or a smaller proportion?

A   By a smaller.

P   Then whatever difference there was in age between the one and the others at first will not obtain hereafter, but with the adding of an equal time, the one will constantly be less separated in age from the others than before. Or not? And must not whatever is less separated [154E] in age than before relative to something come to be younger than before relative to those than which it was older before?

A It will come to be younger.

P If it comes to be younger, must not those others in turn come to be older than before relative to the one? So what came to be younger comes to be older relative to what came to be earlier and is older is never older, but constantly comes to be older than it. For the one advances towards the younger, the other towards the older. [155A] The older, as well, comes to be younger than the younger in the same way. Both move towards the opposites and come to be the opposites of each other – the younger older than the older, the older younger than the younger. But they do not come to be such in the end. For, if they were to do so, they would no longer come to be, but, rather, would be. As things stand, they come to be older and younger than one another. The one comes to be younger than the others because, as we saw, it is older and came to be earlier. [155B] The others come to be older than the one because they came to be later. On this accounting the same would obtain for the others as well relative to the one, since we saw them to be older than it and to have come to be earlier.

Therefore, in that nothing comes to be older or younger than its different in age, since they are always separated from one another by an equal number, the one cannot come to be older or younger than the others, nor the others than the one. But, in that those that have come to be earlier than those later and those that have come to be later than those earlier must [155C] be separated by a constantly different constituent, it is necessary that they come to be older and younger than one another, the others than the one, the one than the others.

On all of these accountings, the one is and comes to be both older and younger than itself and the others and also is and comes to be neither older nor younger than itself and the others.

Since the one has a share of time and of coming [155D] to be both older and younger, must it not always have a share of the *then*, the *hereafter*, and the *now* – since it has a share of time?

Then the one was, is, will be, came to be, comes to be, and will come to be.

Timaeus 37D3–9 reads:

The nature of the (paradigm) Animal was to be eternal. And it was impossible to attach this completely to the generated universe. But he purposed to make a sort of moving likeness of eternity. And in the course of putting the heaven in order, he made an eternal likeness (moving according to number) of what eternally maintains itself in (the) one – this being what we call time. For days, nights, months, and years – of which there were none before the coming to be of the heaven – he brought about their coming to be in combination with the heaven. All of these are parts of time. The *was*, the *will be* are generated forms of time, which we forget in applying them incorrectly to the eternal being. For we say that it was, is, or will be, when, speaking truly, 'is' alone is appropriate. 'Was' and 'will be' are obviously to be said of coming to be in time. For they are motions, but it does not belong to that which is always the same and changeless to come to be older or younger in time nor ever to come to be or have come to be now or hereafter to come to be, nor generally such things as coming to be has attached to those that move in the arena of sensation, but these forms of time have come to be – mimicking eternal things moving according to number in circles.

With the *Timaeus* passage in mind, it is clear that the present section of the *Parmenides* applies only or primarily to changeable things that have shares of forms or numbers. And it would seem that having a share of time must consist of having a share of some number or other, presumably one that is either a determiner of the great sidereal clock or is coordinated with the great clock. So far as the great clock is concerned, determination of time is related always to a given Great Year, where a Great Year is the interval between all of the heavenly bodies' being in a given position and their return to that original position. Plato has little or nothing to say about the persistence of non-heavenly bodies and their changes through or beyond Great Years except that the proper measure of their changes is the great clock.

For a given one – among the changeable things – to have a share of *being* is in this context to *be* something or other, running, tall, or whatever, in connection with time past, present, or future (or a combination of them). Parmenides' first moves are clear enough. Each one of us, as s/he grows older, is coming to be older than s/he was and, with the stretch of time getting larger, is coming to be younger (relative to a position reached). But Parmenides goes on to speak of 'the temporal now.' Partly he is making the simple point that, when something that is coming to be reaches the *now*, then, as at the now, it ceases to come to be and *is* whatever it was coming to be. And this allows the conclusion that the one is not only coming to be older and younger, but also when reaching a *now*, *is* older and younger than itself.

The only other helpful information we get about the *now* is that it is constantly present throughout a thing's being, for it is constantly now whenever that thing is F or G or whatever. This suggests, of course, that the *now* is a non-stretch of time between what was and what will be. And, as I have suggested and we shall see in the next chapter, this comports well with the idea of there being no time stretch in which something that is changing from *F* to *G* is both *F* and *G*, that is, the idea of catastrophic change. There is not, as well, anything in the present section to suggest that a thing may not remain the same in one respect through a stretch of time during which it changes in another respect – an idea we attended to earlier in discussing how it is that a thing might simultaneously be in motion and at rest. It may be worth mentioning in this connection the anti-Heraclitean claim in the *Theaetetus* that it is impossible for everything to be in *every* kind of motion (*Theaetetus* 182C4–33D).

It is tempting to think that the *now* of this passage should not be equated with the *all of a sudden* (*exaiphnes*, τὸ ἐξαίφνης), the non-time 'during' which Plato (in the Coda) says that change occurs. The passage suggests a fairly non-technical use of 'now,' which may be taken as 'lasting' a little while. It is not likely, however, that it is a proper ancestor of the so-called 'specious present' that, in Augustine and others, appears to be a condition of awareness that bridges between an immediate past and an immediate future. What Plato is working on in this passage is, of course, a means of giving closure to a process of coming-to-be by invoking an *is* (or, if you please, an *is now*).

The conclusion that anything that comes to be through a stretch of time has come to be through that same stretch and is thus of the same age as itself is easy. As having come to be and thus *being* at a now, it not only comes to be the same age, but is the same age. So once again, having made the appropriate distinctions, there is nothing paradoxical about saying that the one comes to be and is both older, younger, and of the same age as itself.

Though I stressed in the previous chapter the ancient Greek foundation of arithmetic by determination of the parts of number rather than the modern apparatus of successor, recursive definition, and mathematical induction, there is no doubt that the ancient Greeks counted things in standard fashion. Parmenides uses this simple fact in his first comments concerning the *others*. He points out that the others are *others*, thus more than one. In counting, the first (one) comes before the later numbers (and note that Parmenides speaks of the numbers larger than one, thus implying that one is a number – contrary to what I claimed earlier [and what is commonly claimed] concerning the Greek concept of number). And since in temporal series the first comes before the others, the one must be older and the others younger.

Probably the best one can give this argument is that, taking the *others* as later items in a temporal series, obviously the one or first comes first. If one can accept this *and* the idea that the first item *persists*, it could be taken as older and the others as younger. It will hardly do to suggest that the counting order requires that the first in the count of several things must be temporally first. Even so, if one can accept these egregious possibilities, it will follow that the one is older than the others and that they are younger.

The next move is perhaps a bit more plausible. It relies on the earlier claim that the one has beginning, middle, and end, giving this a temporal rendering. And it construes the others as temporal parts of the one, parts encompassed by the one as a whole. Since the temporal one comes to be as a whole only at the end, it is treated as later than the others and thus younger. Finally, the temporal parts of the one are each treated as coming to be as one, thus numbering the same as the temporal others. So the one is the same age as the others.

The final portions of the present text carry on the fairly obvious implications of time separation. Even if X comes to be and is both older and younger than and equal in age to Y and older and younger than and equal in age to itself, the separation in age gets neither greater nor less, so the older, younger, and equal claims do not hold. It is thus reasonably clear that all of these paradoxical time considerations require the making of distinctions that render them logically harmless.

Conclusion of the Supposition (155D)

Text:

Parmenides And then there would be something which was, is, and will be of it. And there must be knowledge, opinion, and perception *of* it, since we are even now making all of these claims about it. And there is a name and also a sentence for it; and it is named and spoken of. And whatever happens to obtain for the others obtains as well for the one.

This last short section of the Platonic Version of supposition two summarizes and restates what has been said about the one's having a share of time and thus being in the temporal order. As such, it serves as a brief introduction to what I call the Coda, itself a rather short portion of the dialogue that makes use of both the Parmenidean and the Platonic affirmative versions, exploring some consequences for the one. As I noted earlier, its primary business is to give a rationale for a Platonic account of motion or change. Before turning to it, I must say something about the very last part of this section.

It will be remembered that towards the end of the first part of the dialogue, Parmenides is made to comment that if someone were to claim that the forms, if there are any, cannot even be known, he would be extremely hard to refute. Indeed, Parmenides claims that refutation could occur only with the making of a long and intricate argument. It is thus a bit shocking to read here the simple claim that 'there must be knowledge, opinion, and perception *of* it (the one), since we are even now making all of these claims about it.' We have, of course, encountered an earlier statement that the one cannot even be known (at the end of the Parmenidean Version of the first affirmative supposition). *There*, of course, the problem was utter inability to *say* or think anything at all.

Oddly enough, we have been through a somewhat long and intricate set of arguments, first, to claim that, on the Platonic Version, having a share is perfectly intelligible, then, to exhibit the foundations of arithmetic/geometry, and, finally, to show that (with the proper distinctions) a great many logically possible things can be said about the one (or any subject). With these in mind, it may be indeed that Parmenides can justify the claim that the one can be known, opined about, and perceived. That justification is not given here, though the logical possibility of the claim may be taken as evident.

We shall, of course, be at this matter again in later chapters.

7

The 'Coda' and the Remaining Affirmative Suppositions (155E–60B)

The Coda: Change and the Instantaneous (155E–57B)

Text:

Parmenides Once more and for a third time let us proceed with the account. If the one is such as we have described it, being both one and many, neither one nor many, and having a share of time, is it not necessary that it, because it is, then have a share of being, because it is not, then not have a share of being? Well then, when it has a share, can it then not have a share, or, when it does not have a share, can it then have a share?

Thus it has a share at one time and does not have a share at another. Only in this way can it both have and not have a share of the same. [156A] Is there not therefore a time when it comes to have a share of being and when it ceases from having a share of it? How is it possible for it to have the same at one time and not to have it at another unless it should at some time receive it and let it go?

Aristoteles It is not at all possible.

P And do you not then call coming to have a share of being coming to be? And is not ceasing from being perishing? The one then, as it appears, seizing and letting go being, comes to be [156B] and perishes. Since it is one and many and comes to be and perishes, must it not then, when it comes to be one, perish as many, when it comes to be many, perish as one? When it comes to be one or when it comes to be many, is it not necessary for it be separated or combined? And, when it comes to be unlike or like, to be make like or made unlike? And, when it comes to be greater, less, or equal, must it not be increased, diminished, or equalized? [156E] When, being in motion, it comes to rest and when, being at rest, it changes to being in motion, it must itself not be in one time. It is simply not possible for it to admit being earlier at rest and later in motion or earlier in motion and later at rest without undergoing change.

But there is not a time in which something can be at once neither in motion nor at rest. Nor can anything change without the changing going on. But then when does it change? For it does not change while it is at rest nor when it is in motion nor [156D] while in a time.

Is there, then, this extraordinary thing, in which it must be when it is changing?
A What sort of extraordinary thing?
P The instantaneous. For *instantaneous* would seem to signify the sort of thing from which something changes to an opposite. For something does not change from resting while still at rest, not does it change from motion while still in motion. But the very nature of instantaneous is something extraordinary placed between motion and rest that is not in [156E] time to which and from which something in motion changes to being at rest or something at rest changes to being in motion.

And so the one, since it is at rest and in motion changes to one or the other. Only under these conditions would it do both. Changing, it changes instantaneously, and when it changes, it must not be in time, and it must neither be in motion nor at rest then.

And is this not the case for the other changings? When something changes from being to perishing or from not being to coming to be, does it not come to be then between various motions and restings, and then neither is nor is not and neither comes to be nor perishes.

By this same reasoning, in going from one to many or from many to one, it is neither one nor many and is neither being separated or combined. [157B] And, in going from like to unlike or from unlike to like, it is neither like nor unlike and neither coming to be like nor coming to be unlike. And in going from small to large or to equal or any other of the opposites, it must be neither small nor large nor equal, nor increasing or diminishing or coming to be equal.

In truth the one must admit all of these, if it is.

'Once more and for a third time' clearly requires that what we have been given the first two times are what I have called the Parmenidean and Platonic versions of the drawing of consequences for the one on the supposition that the one is. What we have here in the Coda is a tongue-in-cheek combining of the Parmenidean and Platonic versions. I say tongue-in-cheek because no real comfort is about to be given to the Parmenidean and Zenonian claims of the early pages of the dialogue.

The major task of the Coda, as I have noted earlier, is to give a logically satisfactory account of coming-to-be or change; and what is to be avoided, in so doing, is having to accept the consequence that a changing or moving thing is at the same time and in the same respect both F and G (where G is either a contrary or contradictory of F). What Parmenides is made to contend is that there is no time in which any changing thing is both F and G. And, *pari passu*, he claims that there is a non-time in which a changing thing is neither F nor G (thus linking with supposition one). This 'non-time' he calls the 'instantaneous' (*to exaiphnes*, τὸ ἐξαίφνης) and he places it between a thing's being F and its being G. The presumption is that a stretch of time during which something is successively, say, F, G, and H (and thus 'is' both F and G) may be divided indefinitely, but there is no division of time during which this thing is both F and G (or whichever pair of opposed successor states). The theory being defended is, as I noted earlier, a theory of catastrophic change. I hasten to point out, however, that, if one understands the *Parmenides* Plato (as I do) to be holding a doctrine of a genuine mathematical infinite, there are grounds for taking him to have the means for handling issues of continuity. Even so, the Coda is devoted to denying that there can be a time during which a changing thing is both F and G.

It is worth noting that the Coda begins not only with reference to the Parmenidean and the Platonic versions of the supposition that one is but also with the straightforward comment that *the one has a share of time*. This would be possible, of course, only on the Platonic Version, for, as we have seen, it is simply denied on the Parmenidean Version. This is worthy of note because it clearly indicates that what is really at work in the Coda is the Platonic Version and that the Parmenidean Version is invoked simply for describing a non-time 'during' which a change occurs. This is the only use of a 'neither/nor' consequence in the Coda.

There is what many have taken to be a puzzling passage in the *Theaetetus* (154E–57D) that deals with the idea of something's being both F and G without undergoing a process of change. The passage ends with a presumed Protagorean account of sense perception according to which one and the same thing can be correctly reported to be both F and G at the same time. Though I think that Plato does not find the account uncongenial so far as the facts (not Protagoras' theory!) of sense perception as such are concerned, he is intransigent in claiming that nothing really does come to be G from having been F without undergoing a process of change. The passage, with its reference to six dice that are at the same time more than four and less than twelve, obviously requires relational (*pros*, πρός) predication and thus does not fit the simple F and G pattern. So also does the reference to Socrates, who does not change size, but comes to be smaller after being larger than Theaetetus.

Like a kindred claim in the *Phaedo* (102B3–103A1) this one needs the recognition of relational predication.

Though Plato's *Timaeus* account of sense perception (which, like the Protagorean account of the *Theaetetus*, can be used to explain the subjectivity of sense perception) is rather complicated, it also at bottom needs the recognition of relational predication. Colours (or sounds, etc.) as presented in perceptual situations are the causal results of interaction between sense organs and external stimuli (Platonic regular solids in motion), thus causally relational. Since either the sense organs of two perceivers may be different or the external conditions may be relevantly different, the naïve perceptions reported by the two may be quite different and even incompatible. Thus, in the *Theaetetus* example, the 'same' wind may appear to be warm to one perceiver and cool to another. Given that the *object* of a perception is a feature of the physical world, however, Plato, unlike Protagoras, does not endorse the doctrine that perception as such is never mistaken. Since the seeing/seen (perceiving/perceived, *aisthesis/ aistheton*, αἴσθησις/αἴσθητον) distinction is intentionally relational, seeings can be and commonly are mistaken.

Saving the first sort of naïve relational predication (which is properly reported using the vocabulary of *seeming* and *appearing*), claims about the nature of things perceived are subject to the requirement that something not be F and G at the same time. And genuine perceptual judgments about things in the world are equally subject to the requirement. But I have touched on this matter earlier and will do so again. And the point remains that nothing can come to be G from having been F without undergoing a process of change.

The doctrine of the 'all of a sudden' or the 'instantaneous,' the non-time between contrary or contradictory states of something, plays a background role, I believe, in Aristotle's doctrine of change or coming-to-be in the *Physics*. Aristotle, of course, is insistent that nothing is both F and G (where these are contraries or contradictories) through a given stretch of time. What every Aristotle student knows, however, is that Aristotle has a doctrine of *potentiality* according to which a given thing may in the same stretch of time be actually F and potentially G. And, with his worries about continuity in mind, Aristotle accepts a potential infinite but denies an actual infinite. There is no indication here (or, so far as I can tell, in other texts) that Plato did not accept catastrophic change. Given Plato's insistence upon the numbers' having no limit, however, (as well as 'beings' and 'ones') in supposition two, it is likely that he was not troubled by accepting an actual infinite. Indeed, a hypostatized mathematical formula for a given thing may contain an infinite number of states to be actualized in the informing of the Receiver in a finite stretch of time.

So far, however, the text has presented us only with what can be construed as states of a given thing where, with a bit of intellectual stretching, those states can be thought of as contraries. This ignores the distinction between sortal and characterizing terms and invites the sort of problem presented to Socrates early in the dialogue by asking whether there are forms for man, etc. The next part of the text raises that problem.

The latter (156E–57B) part of the Coda adds nothing in principle to what has gone before. It does, however, at the end of 156E and the start of 157A, raise for the first time the issue of the coming to be and perishing of individual things. 'When something changes from being to perishing or from not being to coming to be, does it not come to be then between various motions and restings, and then neither is nor is not and neither comes to be nor perishes?' Interestingly, the text has no clear subject for 'changes' (though one might assume 'the one' from the immediately previous passage). However that may be, Parmenides seems to be speaking of the coming to be and the perishing of individual things. The reference to 'various motions and restings' suggests that, in perishing, a thing (say, a human being) gradually degenerates and, as well, that there may be a gradual integration leading to the coming to be of a thing. The very next passage reinforces some such idea with its reference to separation and combination.

As I have noted earlier, the general account of having shares of in this latter part of the dialogue makes a place for substances or individual things. And it will be recalled that Socrates had no answer for Parmenides when questioned earlier about them. In the present general account, one may think of a thing as articulated in accordance with a certain number and that there may be a number for man, horse, or whatever. With just the number and the structured copy in the changing world, there is no Third Man issue of the sort we noted in the first part of the dialogue.

So we have an application of the primary claim of the Coda that holds not only for changes of various sorts but also for varying degrees of the coming to be and passing away of things. If they are thought of as coming to be by gradual approximations to thing numbers, every such approximation would be such that none is at the instant of coming to be an approximation either in the prior or the posterior state. And the same sort of account is to be given, *mutatis mutandis*, of passings-away.

All this seems to be the plain sense of the present text. The remainder of the Coda presents no interpretative problems if what has been previously said is on the right track.

Platonic Version: The Consequences for the Others, If One Is (157B–59B)

Negative Terms as Subjects (157B–E)

Text:

Parmenides Must we not then attend to what it is fitting for the others to undergo, if one is? Then we are to say what those other than the one must undergo. Well then, since they are others than the one, the others are not the one. For [157C] then they would not be others than the one. The others are not in every way lacking the one, but rather in a way have shares of it.

Because the others are others than the one as having constituents. For, if they did not have constituents, they would be completely one. Constituents, we say, are of that which must be a whole. But then the whole must be a one composed of many of which the constituents are constituents. For each of the constituents must be a constituent, not of a many, but rather of a whole.

If there were to be such a thing as a constituent of a many, [157D] and if it were itself among them, it would be a constituent of itself (which is impossible) and of each one of the others, since it must be *of* all of them. For, not being a constituent of one, it would be a constituent of all the others except that one, and thus be a constituent of each one of the many. And, being of no one of all of them, it would not be a constituent of any. And it would be impossible for it to be a constituent or anything else.

And thus the constituent is not a constituent of many or of all, but rather of a single form or one, which we call a whole, [157E] a completed one that has come to be from all, and it is of this that the constituent must be a constituent. If, therefore, the others have constituents, they must have a share of the whole and of one. And so the others than the one must be a completed whole that has constituents.

We move now from discussing the consequences for the one to the consequences for the others. As I have noted earlier, the others are non-*F*s, the predecessors of Aristotle's indefinites. So what we are turning to could be thought of as recognizing the sense of sentences that make use of expressions of the form 'non-*F*' as a term in the subject place. Plato uses the Greek term *allos* (ἄλλος), though the term *heteros* (ἕτερος) is, for the present purposes, a synonym. As I have noted earlier, readers who are familiar with the *Sophist* will recall Plato's use of *different* in the solution of the problem of not-being. Quickly put, that solution requires interpreting sentences of the form '*X* is not *F*' as '*X* has a share of the Different from *F*,' and taking Different from *F*, Different from *G*, and so on as the 'parts' of

Different. I am, of course, taking 'non-F' as referring to the Different from F, thus to everything that is not F.

The first logic book I read was a so-called 'idealistic' logic first published in the 1920s and was a detailed presentation of 'Aristotelian logic' with not a whisper about modern symbolic logic. And it not only allowed but insisted upon the use of what Aristotle called 'indefinite' (ἀόριστα) terms, thus, for example, allowing 'immediate inference' from 'Some F are not G' to 'Some F are non-G' and 'Some non-G are F.' I mention this book only to note how recent is the general rejection of negative terms. Nowadays, virtually all logic texts treat 'not' as a sentential 'connective' and disallow the sort of immediate inference noted above.

What we are looking at in the present section are the consequences for the *others*, thus what can be appropriately said with non-F terms as subjects. (Their use as predicates, as one might expect, is explored in the Platonic versions of the supposition that one is not.) The effort in this supposition is thus parallel to that of supposition two, since it is what I have called a Platonic version of the supposition 'If one is.' We should thus expect Parmenides to give a parallel treatment.

Before turning to text commentary proper, it may be useful to reiterate the fact that what is at stake in the early part of this version of the one supposition is the justification of allowing subject-place non-F terms to refer to genuine, if peculiar, entities. In contemporary terms, this comes to allowing sentences of the form '(the, every) non-F is G' to be well-formed.

Parmenides starts by pointing out that the others, as having constituents (and thus being a whole), must have a share of the one. And he goes on to claim that each of the constituents or parts of the others (if each is really to be *each*) must be one as having a share of the one. Once again, what this comes to is recognition of the reference of negative terms in the subject-place.

I think the most plausible interpretation of these comments would take the *others* as what the *Sophist* calls the 'Different.' And the constituents or parts are what the *Sophist* calls the 'parts of the Different.' These would have the form 'the Different from F,' 'the Different from G,' etc. (if you please, non-F, non-G, etc.).

I am uncertain whether we should construe the 'others' as encompassing constituents in the way the Different of the *Sophist* is said to have parts where these are 'Different from F,' 'Different from G,' etc. or to construe each of such others as having constituents. In the latter case there would be the whole set of items that are Different from F, Different from G, etc. In either event the constituents would be constituents of a whole and in this manner each would have a share of the one. It should be remembered in this connection that everything in the world is or is not F, whatever F may be. And something that is not F may be G, H, or whatever. Thus there is no limit except F to what something that is not F may be. And this is precisely Aristotle's reason for calling a term of the form 'not-F' *indefinite* (ἀόριστον).

Linguistically we are looking at sentences of the form 'not-F is G.' And, of course, though these may be construed as logically acceptable, they are strange sentences indeed where, unless restricted in some way, they are almost totally nebulous. In spite of this remarkable limitation, Plato proceeds to find in this supposition parallels to the 'both/and' consequences of supposition two.

It may be worth noting that supposition three, though a Platonic Version supposition, does not include anything concerning the generation of the numbers and that the generation of numbers section of supposition two includes none of the 'both/and' pattern of the remaining sections. (Nor, by the way, does the concluding section of supposition two concerning knowledge and opinion.)

157E–59B

Text:

Parmenides   And the same account holds as well for each of the constituents. For each must have a share of [158A] the one. For if each of them is a constituent, and 'each' presumably signifies being one, it is separated off from the others being just by itself, since it is an each. Because it is other than the one, it must have a share of the one. Otherwise, it would not have a share; it would itself *be* one. Obviously it is impossible for anything to *be* one except the one itself. So it is necessary for both the whole and the constituent to have shares of the one. For the whole must be a one of which the constituents are constituents. And, as well, each constituent of the whole must be one in order to be a [158B] constituent of a whole.

And must not those having shares of the one be differents from the one by virtue of having shares? And the differents from the one must be many. For, if the others than the one were neither one nor more than one, they would not be at all.

Since those having shares of the one constituent and of the one whole are more than one, must not those coming to have shares of the one then be *themselves* unlimited in multitude? Look at it this way. Is it not the case that those that come to have a share of the one come to have a share of it when they neither are one nor have a share of the one?

[158C] They are multitudes in which the one is not. What then? If we wished, in

The 'Coda' and the Remaining Affirmative Suppositions   119

thought, to separate off from them the fewest we possibly could, would not this which is separated off, since it would not have shares of the one, be a multitude and not one? And thus always, when we consider just by itself the *different* nature of the form, so much as we shall ever see of it will be unlimited in multitude.

And then, just when [158D] each of the constituents comes to be a constituent, in doing so the constituents have a limit relative to one another and relative to the whole, and the whole has a limit relative to the constituents.

It follows that for the others than the one, from the intermingling of the one and themselves, as it turns out, something different comes to be in them which gives them a limit relative to one another. Their own nature gives them – just by themselves – an unlimitedness. Then the others than the one, whether taken as wholes or as constituents, are unlimited but they have shares of limit.

[158E] Are they also likes and unlikes of one another and also of themselves? In that they are all in their own nature unlimited, admitting the same, they would be in the same. And in that they all have shares of limit, they would all be in the same, as admitting the same.

In that they are limited and admit unlimiteds, they would admit qualifications which are opposites [159A] of one another. And opposites must be maximal unlikes.

Thus, with regard to each qualification, they would be likes both of themselves and of one another; with regard to both, they would be maximal opposites and maximal unlikes.

And so the others themselves must be both likes and unlikes of themselves and of one another.

And given that they are sames and differents from one another, in motion and at rest, it will not be difficult to show that those other than the one admit all of the opposite qualifications, since [159B] it has been shown that they admit them.

And so, if we may pass over these as evident, let us again consider, whether, if one is, then the others than the one are not to be characterized in this manner only.

It seems clear enough that the others *qua* whole and each of 'its' constituents, not *being* one (if you please, as *non-ones*), are in themselves unlimited multitudes. *Different*, as I have noted, collects such constituents as non-*F*, non-*G*, etc. The number of such constituents is unspecifiable. So also is the number of items collected under each of the constituents. A non-horse, for example, is anything in the universe except a horse. And such sentences as 'The non-horse is moving' have virtually unspecifiable subjects. This can be made more graphic if one notes that Greek allows the nominalization of all manner of adjectives and participles.

Since the others and their parts all have shares of the one and are different from one another, though unlimited in themselves, they have, relative to one another, limits. Thus, for example, non-*horse* is limited relative to, say, non-*chicken*. Though a non-horse may be a non-chicken, it cannot be the case that every non-horse is a non-chicken and vice versa. And this obtains for every pair of the parts of the others. So they are both unlimited and limited.

They are like each other as being qualified by being limited (or, for that matter, unlimited). But, in so far as limited and unlimited are opposites and thus qualified by opposites, they must be unlike each other. So they must be likes and unlikes both of themselves and one another.

Late in 159A Parmenides notes that since 'they are sames and differents from one another, in motion and at rest, it will not be difficult to show that those other than the one admit all of the opposite qualifications, since it has been shown that they admit them.' Their being in motion and at rest probably would be shown (if Parmenides had done so) by means of the definitions (from supposition two) of *motion* and *rest* (constantly in an other and constantly in the same). 'All of the opposite qualifications' is, of course, a reference to the procedure followed out in the consequences for the one on the Platonic Version of the one supposition.

Parmenidean Version: The Consequences for the Others, If One Is (159B–60B)

The Others as Non-Subjects

Text:

Parmenides Then let us say from the beginning, if one is, what must hold for the others than the one.
Must not then the one be separate from the others and the others separate from the one? Because, I presume, there is no different besides these that is other than the one and other than the others. [159C] For everything has been spoken of, when the one and the others have been mentioned. There is therefore no additional different from these in which the one and the others might be, as in the same. Thus the one and the others can never be in the same.

And so are they separate? And we say that what is really one does not have constituents. Therefore the one cannot be in the others as a whole, nor can constituents of it, if it is both separate from the others and also does not have constituents. [159D] Then in no way can the others have shares of the one, since they have no shares of a part of it or of it as whole.

The 'Coda' and the Remaining Affirmative Suppositions 121

Then in no way are the others one, nor do they have any one in themselves.

And thus the others are not many. For each of them would be one constituent of a whole if they were many. As matters stand, the others than the one are neither one, nor many, neither whole nor constituents, since they in no way have shares of the one. Therefore also the others are not two or three nor are these in them, [159E] since they are in every way lacking in the one.

Thus the others themselves are neither likes nor unlikes to the one, nor is likeness or unlikeness in them. If they were likes and unlikes or if they had likeness and unlikeness in them, the others than the one would, I presume, have in them two forms that are opposites of each other. But it must be impossible for those to have shares of two things that cannot have shares of one. And thus the others are neither likes nor unlikes nor both. [160A] For if they were likes or unlikes, they would have shares of a single *different* form; if they were both, they would have shares of opposites. And these were shown to be impossible.

Thus they are neither sames nor differents, neither in motion nor at rest, neither coming to be nor perishing, neither larger nor smaller nor equal. Nor do they admit any other such. For, if the others were to survive admitting any such, they would have shares in one, two, three, odd, or even – those of which it was shown to be impossible for them to have shares, [160B] since they are in every way completely lacking in the one.

Thus, if one is, the one is both all things and not (even) one both relative to itself and, in the same way, relative to the others.

This is the last of the affirmative suppositions, and it is, of course, a Parmenidean Version. Having reached this point, I think it appropriate to make a final comment about the order of the suppositions. There are, of course, eight of them plus the Coda. Two are Parmenidean versions and two are Platonic versions of 'if one is.' And there are two Parmenidean and two Platonic versions of 'if one is not.' Plato starts with the consequences for the one for the Parmenidean Version of 'if one is' and then moves to the Platonic Version. As we have seen, the Coda makes use of both of these. Plato moves directly from it to the consequences for the others on the Platonic Version of 'if one is' and moves then to the consequences now being considered. The parallel ordering of the consequences for 'if one is not' alternate the Platonic and Parmenidean versions starting with the consequences for the one on the Platonic Version.

Having Parmenides start with the Parmenidean Version of 'if one is' seems appropriate enough, for Plato clearly thinks that the consequences drawn are applicable to the doctrine of the historical Parmenides. Moving to the Platonic Version next provides a startling contrast and, despite the implied condemnation of Parmenides and Zeno, really does put Plato on record as indebted to Parmenides. Both of these lead into and are presupposed by the Coda. Since both the Coda and the Platonic Version of the consequences for the one are naturally completed by the Platonic version of the consequences for the others, it seems appropriate to move to it next and to conclude the affirmative versions with the Parmenidean Version.

Starting the alternation of the Platonic and Parmenidean Versions for 'if one is not' with the Platonic version gets Plato on record with a number of important insights. Ending the dialogue with the aridity of the Parmenidean version of the consequences for the others again seems appropriate enough. Plato is obviously impressed and influenced by Parmenides and Zeno and their procedure, but he is no disciple. The unstated expression of debt (for the affirmation of the need for eternal things and for their interconnection and for the procedure of the 'exercise') and the critique of Parmenides go far in explaining Plato's praise of Parmenides in the *Theaetetus* and *Sophist* as well as the severe critique in the latter.

But it is time to get to commentary on the consequences for the others on the Parmenidean Version of 'if one is.'

Notice the early appearance of 'separate' (*choris*, χωρίς). It is used for the first time since the first part of the dialogue. And it will be remembered that major emphasis was placed upon Socrates' inability to bridge the gap between the forms and those that are 'in us.' Indeed, it was this inability that led to the conclusions of the 'Slave/Master' argument that the gods can neither know us nor be our masters.

Here the one and the others are said to be *separate* from one another, so profoundly so that there is no *different* by means of which they might be said to be the same (that is, by having shares of a *different*). In an echo of the first Parmenidean supposition, it is noted that the others cannot have constituents, thus cannot be a whole, and thus cannot be in the others either as a whole or as constituents of the one. Then the others cannot have shares of the one. Thus they cannot be one, nor can they be many, since each of them cannot be one constituent of a whole. So they are neither one nor many, neither whole nor constituents and are every way lacking in the one.

But let me put what is at issue here rather more simply and graphically. We saw in the first supposition that a single term or entity that, *qua* a Parmenidean one, admits of no characterization whatsoever; it cannot even *be*. This fourth supposition, concerned with *others* that are *separate from* each other and anything else, yields the same sort of conclusion for each of them. Indeed, to speak of *them* is misleading, for nothing implying a number can be said of them. But even this condition must be dropped. Keeping in mind that this fourth supposition needs to take the others as *subjects* and given the Parmenidean constraint, there is nothing of which anything can be *said*.

Final Comment (160B)

Text:

Parmenides Thus, if one is, the one is both all things and not (even) one both relative to itself and, in the same way, relative to the others.

The final comment by Parmenides is, of course, intended to be an abbreviated summation of the affirmative suppositions. Unlike the summation at the end of the dialogue, it appears to omit suppositions three and four, which take the others as logical subjects. Heindorf's conjecture would, however, replace τὰ ἄλλα with τἆλλα, καὶ τἆλλα in the comment. This would change the reading from '... relative to the others' to '... relative to the others, and the others in the same way,' thus rather simply including suppositions three and four.

8

The 'One' and the 'Others' on Both Versions of *If One Is Not* (160B–66C)

Platonic Version: The Consequences for the One, *If One Is Not* (160B–63B)

The major effort of this supposition is to show how negative predication is possible, thus doing away with the claim that negative predication destroys the possibility of saying *anything*. The effort is parallel to the effort of the *Sophist* to show how false belief is possible. Both the present effort and that of the *Sophist* require construing negative predication as a special form of positive predication, a form having the liability of treating negative predicates as *indefinites* (*aorista*).

160B-61A

Text:

Parmenides Well then, must we not, after this, consider what must go along with the supposition that the one is not? What can this supposition be, *If one is not?* Does it straight off differ from this one, *If not one is not?* Does it merely differ, or is saying [160C] *If not one is not* the complete opposite of saying *If one is not?*
Aristoteles It's the complete opposite.
P What if someone were to say, *If Largeness is not* or *If Smallness is not* or any other such, would he not make it clear straight off that in each case he says of some different that it is not? In the present case would he not make it clear, when he says, *If one is not*, that what it is that is not is different from the others. And do we not know what he says?
  First, then, he speaks of something known, then of a different from the others, when he says *one*, whether he adds to it that *it is* [160D] or *that it is not*. For noth-

ing is known the less by saying that it is not or that it differs from the others. Isn't that so?

Then we must say from the beginning, *If one is not*, what must be the case. First, this must hold for it, evidently, that there is knowledge of it, or there would not be knowing what is said when one says, *If one is not*.

And are not the others differents from it, for, otherwise, it would not be spoken of as different from the others. Then there is difference in it in addition to knowledge of it. [160E] For one does not speak of the difference of the others when one says that the one is different from the others, but rather of *its* difference.

And the one that is not has a share of *the that*, *the a* (or *an* or *a certain*), *the this, relative to this, these,* and all other such. For the one could not be spoken of, nor could the differents from the one, nor could anything relative to the one or of it, nor could anything be spoken of, if it did not have a share of *the a* (or *an* or *a certain*) or of these others.

It is not possible for the one to *be* if it is not, but [161A] nothing prevents it from having shares of several. Indeed, it must if it is to be *that* one and not some other that is not. If neither the one nor *that* is not, but the speech is of some other, it must be that nothing at all is being said. But if *that* one and not some other is laid down as not being, then it is necessary for it to have a share of *the that* and of many others.

In this Platonic version of consequences for the one on the negative supposition, we are dealing with sentences of the form '*F* is not *G*' or 'the one is not *G*.' It is important to keep in mind that for Plato as for Aristotle negation is negation of *terms*, not sentences. Thus the sentence form is not to be read as 'it is not the case that *F* is *G*' but rather as '*F* is not-*G*.' (That both Plato and Aristotle recognize the possibility of affirming or denying either a positive or a negative sentence is a different matter.) Though there is here no question of not-being as such, there remains the liability in the case of '*F* is not-*G*' that the predicate term is *indefinite*, a liability that is not the same as that of the supposition three, in which the subject term is indefinite.

In asserting early on that 'if not-one is not' is the 'complete opposite' of 'if one is not,' Plato tempts one to read the former as 'if it is not the case that one is not.' Aside from the fact noted above that Plato does *not* use not as a connective, the context makes it clear that the proper reading for the 'opposite' is 'if not-one is not.' 'Not-one' is, of course, equivalent to 'others,' and these are by the rules we have been working with *differents* from the one. Parmenides uses the example of Largeness and Smallness and their *difference* to make it clear that what makes for the 'complete opposite' is the difference between the one and the others.

He proceeds to claim that there must be knowledge of the one that is not 'or there would not be knowing what is said when one says, "'if one is not."' The point here is, I believe, the same as that made in the *Sophist* when the Stranger notes that in saying 'Theaetetus sits' nothing is said unless 'Theaetetus' names something ('A sentence in order to be a sentence must be *of* something; not being of something, it is impossible' 262 E). And he notes that, whether we say that the one (the subject) is different or that it is not, the one (the subject) must be 'known.' We must be cautious about taking the use of 'knowledge' too seriously. It does not here distinguish between knowledge and, say, opinion. Its purpose is to indicate strongly that we know what a negative sentence is about, given that it has a proper subject.

Parmenides proceeds to the apparently curious point that on the present supposition, in addition to knowledge of the one that is not, there is *difference*, where the difference is not difference from the others, but *its* (that is, that of the one) difference. I think that what is being emphasized here, as the subsequent context strongly suggests, is that a sentence of the form '*X* is different from *G*' ('*X* is not *G*') is true when and only when a specific difference holds for *X* or, if you please, by virtue of a specific difference. *X* has a share of the Different from *G*, rather than Different from *H*, etc. This would hold, of course, even though the predicate is indefinite.

The points made so far are reinforced by the next very interesting comments. Parmenides declares that, because the one that is not may properly be conjoined with specifying terms, it 'has a share of' the *that*, the *a* (or *an* or *a certain*), the *this, relative to this, these* and 'all other such.' Of a sudden, Parmenides makes a number of matters relatively clear. On the Platonic versions of 'if one is' or 'if one is not' (at least those working out the consequences for the one) there must indeed be a definite subject term. And there cannot be a definite subject term if the subject is taken to be an *other*, that is, a non-*one* or a non-*F*. Though, for example, 'that (or the or a certain) non-*F*' may *appear* to be a definite subject term, the indefiniteness of 'non-*F*' prevents it from *being* definite. So, Parmenides says, 'nothing at all is being said.'

This matter is somewhat complicated, however, for, as we saw in discussing supposition three, it is possible that something can be said when the subject term is indefinite and the predicate term is not. It will help at this point to advert to the *Sophist* with its understanding of not-*G* as Different from *G*, where, as the Stranger puts it, Different from *G* is one of the *parts* of the Different itself. There is no ordering of the parts of Different; each stands alone, as it were. Any grammatical sentence of the form 'The non-*F* is non-*G*' (which says 'The Different from *F* is Different from *G*') can express no connection whatsoever. Even granting the use of the definite article, nothing is being said, for the Different from *F* cannot have a share of the Different from *G*. When we come to supposition seven we shall find Plato making use of the language of *appearing* in talking about such grammatical sentences just for the reason that the apparent sentence is not really a sentence that says anything.

Both Plato and Aristotle make the point that for a proper sentence one needs a *name* (*onoma*, ὄνομα) and a *verb* (*rema*, ῥῆμα) for connectedness or 'interweaving.' The problem with our two parts of Different is that there is no interweaving; it is as though one simply listed two names. And any attempt to construe a connecting *is* as an identity leads to the genuine impossibility that one item is literally the same as or identical with some other item.

Let me make another comment about the matter of having shares of the *that*, the *a certain*, and so on. First, though it would have been relevant earlier, Plato waits until supposition five to introduce the idea that a subject term can appropriately be joined with *that*, etc. Why? Probably because he did not need it earlier. Supposition two presents no problem concerning the subject term. Second, one may be concerned about his using the expression 'have a share of' in connection with these qualifications of the subject term. Why does he do it? I think that the reason is that a predication is covertly involved. Thus, 'That horse is running' obviously allows one to infer 'That is a horse and it is running,' where *is a horse* can be predicated of *that*. 'A certain (or a particular) horse is running' allows 'There is a (particular) horse and it is running.' In later chapters I shall say more on the matter of existential claims for the late Plato; meanwhile let me here suggest that, based on the idea of *having a share of a certain*, Plato is claiming that 'horse' (or whatever term) has an individual reference. And, generally, I think, Plato treats failure of what we should take to be an existential claim as failure of reference.

A final comment on the matter of subject terms. With Bertrand Russell's well-known distinction between names and definite descriptions and its link with modern logic and 'existence' issues, the doctrine of 'connotation free' proper names was widely accepted in Anglo-American philosophy. Given this fact, there has been a temptation to interpret Plato in the light of Russell's distinction, a temptation that goes along with that to translate some of Plato's uses of the Greek 'to be' (*einai*, εἶναι) as 'exists.' The textual evidence seems to be, however, that Plato readily accepted the interchangeability of proper names and definite descriptions and found the latter rather more useful philosophically than the former. Descriptions

128   The *Parmenides* and Plato's Late Philosophy

involving the use of general terms provide a connection with the rational structure of the world. As the first part of the *Parmenides* states, various things around us are 'named after' the forms. There is thus reason to believe that, with the second part in mind, various general terms of a perspicuous language are to be associated with the numbers and/or forms in the rational structure of the world.

As noted earlier, Plato seems to take care of existence problems either with reference or failure of reference or with negative predication. The adjunction of the several demonstratives to general terms takes care of reference to individuals while maintaining the connection with the rational structure.

161A-E

Text:

Parmenides   And then Unlikeness is in it relative to the others. For the others, being differents from the one, must also be differents in kind. Are not differents in kind others in kind? And are not others in kind [161B] unlikes? If then they are unlikes of the one, it is clear that the unlikes must be unlikes of an unlike. Then there would be Unlikeness in the one, relative to which the others are unlikes of it.

But if Unlikeness of the others is in it, then is it not necessary for likeness of itself to be in it? If Unlikeness of one is in the one, the speech would not be concerning the sort of thing that the one is, and the supposition would not be concerning one, but rather concerning an other than one. [161C] But that can't be. So it is necessary for likeness of it to be in the one itself.

And it is not equal to the others either. For, if it were equal, it would thereby also be like them in respect of Equality. But these are both impossible, if one is not. Then, since it is not equal to the others, is it not necessary for the others not to be equals to it? And not equals are unequals. And unequals are unequals to an unequal. The one then has a share of Inequality [161D] relative to which the others are unequals to it.

But nevertheless Largeness and Smallness are of inequality. But then are Largeness and Smallness in such a one?
Aristoteles   That's likely.
P   Largeness and Smallness always are most dismissive of one another. But then there is always something between them. Would you say that anything other than Equality is between them? Then Equality is in whatever Largeness and Smallness are in, since it is between the two. [161E] Then, as it seems, in the one that is not there is sharing in Equality as well as Largeness and Smallness.

This section of the text leads directly up to the claim that, if a one is not, then it in some way *is*. Though the argument is rather involuted and much turns on *relatives to* (*pros ti's*) that are symmetrical, that is, such that what they are relatives to are, in the same way, relatives to them. For example, an *unlike* is relative to an *unlike* where the latter is relative in the same way to the former.

The argument here parallels the argument in 149D ff. in supposition two, both making use of abstract singular terms and dealing with Equality, Largeness, and Smallness. It will be remembered that supposition two's argument took abstract singulars as indicative of the *nature* of the one. The present section starts with Unlikeness relative to the others. And surely the one must be in nature unlike the non-ones that are the *others*. And it seems plausible enough that Likeness relative to itself is in the one as part of its nature. Indeed, as Parmenides notes, if it had Unlikeness relative to itself, it would not be the one but rather an *other*.

The claim that the one is not equal to the others rests on the idea that, if it were, it would violate its nature as having Unlikeness to the others, for it would then be like the others in a certain respect. So the one and the others are unequals to each other, and thus the one is capable of Largeness and Smallness. And what is so capable must be capable of being equal. So the one that is not 'has a share of Equality as well as Largeness and Smallness.'

Despite its rather strange sound, all of this seems to be in order. If F is not-G, even with the negative predication, F remains by hypothesis quite unlike any not-F. And F cannot be unlike itself, or the supposition would be about (have as a subject term) an *other*. And that would not do. So F must be like itself. Nor can F be equal to the not-F's, for then it would be like them in a given respect. If it can be unequal to others, it must be capable of Largeness and Smallness. And, if so, *mirabile dictu*, it must also be capable of Equality.

What this seems to come to is the following. A subject term of a negative predication is to be allowed the predication *possibilities* of being larger than, smaller than, and equal both to itself and to the others. In the general spirit of the *Parmenides'* exploration of the one supposition, there is nothing in negative predication of the one that precludes its admission of these predications.

When Parmenides says that Unlikeness relative to the others is *in* the one that is not, he explicitly does not use the adjective *unlike*. That Unlikeness relative to the others is in it is taken to be a necessary condition of being the one that is not. And it is a sufficient condition of its being unlike the others. The supposition 'if one is not' builds in, as it were, Unlikeness, for *Un*likeness entails Different from G. The one that is non-G, construing non-G as different from G, must, as being the one that is which not, have Different from G as an essential feature.

Parmenides goes on to note that, if Unlikeness *relative to one* were in the one, the supposition would not be 'if one is not,' but rather 'if non-one is not.' Given that Likeness or Unlikeness must be in it relative to itself (and it cannot have Unlikeness relative to itself), it follows that the one that is not must have Likeness relative to itself in it. And here we have an opening wedge for being allowed to say that the one that *is* not is something or other since Likeness relative to itself is a sufficient condition for affirmative predication.

Given these entailments from negative predication to positive predication, Parmenides concludes that the one 'must also have in some way a share of being.' In the next section, as we shall see, Parmenides attempts to explain precisely in what way it has a share of being.

161E-63B

Text:

Parmenides   And it must also have, in some way, a share of being. What holds for it must be as we say it is. For, if it were not the case, then we would not be speaking the truth when we say that the one is not. But, if it is the truth, it is clear that what we say is the case. Isn't that so? Since we assert that we speak the truth, we must [162A] assert also that we are speaking what is the case.

Therefore, as it seems, the one that is not, is. For if, since it is not, it were somehow to give up being to not being, straightway it would be.

So it must, since it is not, have the being of not being as a fetter, if it is not to be, just as being has the not being that is not as a fetter – so that it may be fully. For in this way being would most assuredly be and not being would most assuredly not be, on the one hand, the being having a share of the being is when it is and, on the other, having a share of the not being that is when it is not – [162B] if it is to be fully. The not being having a share of not being that is not when it is, of being that is when it is not – if not being is in turn fully not to be.

Then since not being has a share of not being and not being has a share of being, the one also, since it is not, must have a share of being in order not to be. Evidently, then, being is in the one, if it is not.

And thus not being [is in the one], since it is not.

Is it possible for a condition to obtain and not to obtain without changing from that condition? Then everything of that sort – [162C] a condition obtaining and also not obtaining – signifies a change. But change is motion. Or what shall we say?

Aristoteles It is motion.
P And it was shown that the one both is and is not. And thus it is evident that a condition may obtain and not obtain for it. So evidently the one that is not is in motion, since it admits a change from being to not being.

But if it is nowhere among the beings, as it is (since it is not), it cannot shift about from here to there. Then it would not be in [162D] motion by changing place. Nor would it revolve in the same place. For nowhere does it touch the same. For what is the same is, and it is impossible for what is not to be in some one of the beings. Therefore the one that is not cannot revolve in that which is not.

And, whether it is or is not, the one cannot become other than itself. For, if it became other than itself, the account would no longer be about the one but about some other. But, if it does not become other, or revolve in the same, or change, [162E] can it still in any way be in motion? But what is not in motion must surely stay still, and what stays still is at rest.

So it appears that the one which is not is both at rest and in motion.

And then, since it is in motion, it must necessarily become other. [163A] For, in so far as anything is in motion, to that extent the same no longer obtains for it but rather something different. Since it is in motion, then, it becomes other.

But what is in no way in motion must in no way become other. Then in so far as the one that is not moves, it changes; in so far as it does not move, it does not change. Then the one that is not both changes and does not change.

Must not what becomes other comes to be different from what it was earlier and perish from its [163B] earlier condition? And must not that which does not become other neither come to be nor perish? And thus the one that is not, becoming other, comes to be and perishes, not becoming other, neither comes to be nor perishes. And in this way the one that is not comes to be and also perishes, and neither comes to be nor perishes.

The claim that the one that is not has in some way a share of being is followed immediately by an interesting anticipation of a high point in the *Sophist*. The anticipation concerns speaking or saying the *truth*. In quite literal translation, the anticipation reads, 'It must obtain just as we say. For, if it does not obtain in this manner, we would not be speaking the truth, saying the one is not (or speaking of the one which is not). And if (we speak the) truth, it is clear that we say the beings themselves (ὄντα αὐτὰ).' The *Sophist* passage (263B 4) states of a true sentence that it 'says the beings as they are.' True negative sentences are given the same treatment by the *Sophist*.

The claim in the present *Parmenides* text is that, given that the just previous statements are true, 'we must also be saying beings (ὄντα).' So the one, not being, is. 'For if, not being, it were not, but were somehow to let go not being, forthwith it would be.' If, that is, the one's not being were the ground for saying that it is not, and if it were to shed its not being, then, with the ground removed, it would be. Suppose that F is not-G. Were it to cease to *be* not-G, there would be no ground for the negative predication. Similarly, as the next statement indicates, the ground for saying that F is G is that it is not-not-G, that is, the ground for its being G is that it is not-not-G. Thus, as that statement says, F's being not-G requires that it *be* not-G. And F's being G requires that it *be* not-not-G. This is put as though *being* not-G were a fetter on F's being not-G. And *being* not-not-G would similarly be a fetter on F's being G.

Shades of the *Sophist*! But there is no indication in the *Parmenides* text of the problem of false belief, which is the ostensible occasion for the Sophist treatment of not-being. There, to justify claiming that, for example, Theaetetus is not flying, Plato takes one to be claiming that Theaetetus has a share of the different-from-flying. The logic involved is, however, the same in both dialogues. As we saw a bit earlier, Plato construes negation as negation of terms, rather than sentences. Thus 'F is not G' is construed as 'F is not-G,' with the 'is' playing the same role as the 'is' in 'F is G.'

The next move declares that it is impossible for a 'condition to obtain' in some manner and also not to obtain without a change from that 'condition.' (In fairly literal translation: 'It is impossible for there to be a having of some sort along with a not having of the same sort, with no change from the having.') Such a change Parmenides declares to be a motion and thus that the one that is not can be in motion.

Since the supposition requires the one to be negatively characterized, as so characterized it has no positive attribute and thus cannot be among those that *are*, that is, the 'beings.' Not being among them, it cannot change place. If it is simply not-F, not-G, etc., the indefinite character of each prevents any sort of localization. Nor, Parmenides goes on, can it revolve in the same place. For, as not-F (etc.), it cannot be among or touching those that *are* so as to be in the *same*. Indeed, if it were to become other or different, it would no longer be the one we are talking about. Hence, if it cannot be in motion or change, it must 'stay still' and be at rest. Parmenides concludes that the one that is not is 'both at rest and in motion.'

In all of this we are well into the liabilities and advantages of negative predication. The chief advantage, of course, is in the recognition, contra the historical Parmenides, that 'not-being is.' The chief disadvantage is in the indefinite character of negative predicates. To say what something is not rules out one affirmative predication; in the case of not-F, it rules out F, and so on for other cases. It does not rule 'in' any affirmative predication, for, as the *Sophist* makes clear, the 'parts of Different' are just that, namely, parts fitting into no general pattern.

Final Comment on This Supposition

It is hard to tell precisely when Plato discovered or worked out his solution to the problem of not-being. I assume, with most scholars, that the *Parmenides* is earlier than the *Sophist*, if only because of the clear reference of Socrates in the latter (217C) to being present at a conversation of Parmenides, a conversation employing the procedure of putting and answering questions. Given that assumption and given no earlier reference to his locating not-being in *difference*, it seems likely that its first such location is in the *Parmenides*.

I am inclined to think that the notion of *other* or *different* is crucial to the entire plan of the suppositions. Its employment even in the affirmative suppositions (working out the consequences *pros* or in relation to the 'others') simply destroys a major Parmenidean contention, namely, that not-being is not. When after the debacle of the first part of the dialogue Parmenides recommends to Socrates the suppositional procedure of Zeno, he insists that (a) Socrates must attend to the 'consequences' not only for whatever is supposed but also for those *other* than (that is, non-what-is-supposed) what is supposed and (b) Socrates must attend to the 'consequences' for the supposition that whatever is supposed *is not*. Plato thus lays the groundwork for the exhibition of his claim that not-being is.

Juxtaposing what I have called Parmenidean with Platonic versions of the one supposition serves a dual purpose for Plato. First, it enables Plato to do reasonable justice to Parmenides in the Parmenidean versions and to do it presumably in the manner of Zeno's treatise. The 'consequences' are in the main 'neither/nor' consequences and in this respect like the conclusions of Zeno from the 'many' supposition. And, if Zeno is entitled to conclude 'no many' from his argument(s), Plato is entitled to conclude 'no one' from the Parmenidean versions, though he does so with the consequence that the one cannot even *be*. Second, the Platonic versions follow Zeno's procedure and encourage the presumption that Socrates is receiving the sort of training or exercise that Parmenides has recommended. A major feature of that exercise is the treatment of *not-being*. It is clear enough in the *Sophist* that the standard resources of the earlier Platonic doctrine of forms and participation cannot respond to the *Sophist*'s attack on not-being. Without an adequate account of not-being, it is not possible to show how false opinion or false belief is possible.

Parmenidean Version: The Consequences for the One, If One Is Not (163B-64B)

Text:

Parmenides Once more let us go back to the beginning and see if the same or different consequences will be evident to us as those just now drawn. And so we ask, [163C] if one is not, what follows for it? When we say, 'is not,' is anything signified other that absence of being in that which we assert not to be?

Which is it then? When we assert something not to be, do we assert it somehow not to be or somehow to be? Or does saying 'is not' simply signify that what is not in no way is and in no way has a share of being? Then it must not be possible for not being to be or in any way [163D] to have a share of being.

Can coming to be and perishing be anything other than coming to have a share of being and perishing from being? And that which has no share of something cannot either seize it or lose hold of it. For the one then, since it in no way is, there cannot in any way be having, losing hold of, or coming to have a share of being. Then the one that is not neither perishes nor comes to be, since it in no way has a share of being.

And then [163E] it cannot in any way become other. For, in admitting this, it would be coming to be or perishing. If it does not become other, isn't it necessary that it not be in motion? And we cannot assert that what is nowhere is at rest. For to be at rest it is necessary for something constantly to be in the same.

And so once again we must say that what is not is neither at rest nor in motion.

And then none of the beings is in it. For, were it to [164A] have a share of a being, it would have a share of being. And so neither largeness nor smallness nor equality is in it. And neither likeness nor difference nor relative to itself nor relative to the others would be in it.

What of this? Can the others somehow be in it if nothing can be in it? Therefore the others are neither likes nor unlikes nor sames nor differents to, as, or from it.

What of this? Will there be of that, to that, a certain, this, of this, of an other, to an other, before, [164B] after, now, knowledge, opinion, sensation, account, name or any other being at all with regard to what is not?
Aristoteles There will not.
P Thus the one that is not has nothing obtaining in any way at all.

What we are seeing with this sixth supposition is the Parmenides whom we know from his poem and from accounts given by others, notably Plato in the *Sophist*. I have emphasized throughout that the Parmenidean versions of the several suppositions have as their key feature the denial of the possibility of any sort of predication, a denial that is obviously at work in the first supposition. Consistent with that denial but giving it a rather different twist, this supposition regards the attempt at predication as denying that there is any subject of predication at all.

Supposition one at least started with the subject of predication. But, in denying the possibility of predication, it ultimately denied that the one could in any sense 'be.' Supposition four took the others (non-ones) as to be in effect non-subjects. Here supposition six starts with a subject, the one, but construes the grammatical predicate ('is not') as indicating the complete 'absence of being' of that subject. So no subject. As we shall see, the eighth supposition, in common with the fourth, treats the 'others' as non-ones (and thus non-subjects). And it not only denies predication; it construes the grammatical predicate as indicating the complete absence of being of the others (non-ones). So the picture left by supposition eight is complete intellectual desolation.

Supposition six makes it clear that Parmenides did well to warn his followers (as the Eleatic Stranger of the *Sophist* says he did) against allowing that not-being in any way *is*. But, of course, the task of the Stranger in the *Sophist* is precisely showing that there is a good sense in which not-being *is*. And we have seen Plato taking on just that task in supposition five.

Platonic Version: The Consequences for the Others, *If One Is Not* (164B–65E)

Text:

Parmenides   Let us then go on to say what must hold for the others if one is not. I presume that others themselves must be. For if there were no others, one could not speak about the others. If there is speech about the others, the others are differents. Or would you use 'other' and 'different' [164C] to speak of the same?

And we say, I presume, that different is the different from a different and other is the other than an other? And thus for the others, if they are to be others, there is something of which they will be others. What, then, can it be? For they will not be others than the one, since it is not. Then they are others than one another. For this still remains for them except for them to be others of nothing at all.

Then they (ἕκαστα) are others than each other as multitudes, for they cannot be so individually, since one is not. But, [164D] it seems, each mass of them is unlimited in multitude; even if one were to take what seems the smallest, all of a sudden, like something in a dream, there would be many instead of what was thought to be one and, instead of smallest, immense relative to the chopped-up pieces of it. It is others made up of such masses that would be others of each other, if, though one is not, others are.

Thus there will be many masses, each appearing to be, but not being, one, if one should not be. And one will think, since they [164E] are many, that there is number of them, if each is thought to be one. And some will appear even, others odd, without really being so, if one should not be.

And, we assert, there will even be opined to be a smallest among them. But this is shown to be many and large relative to each [165A] of the many taken to be small. And each mass will be opined to be equal to the many and small portions. For it could not appear to pass from larger to smaller before reaching what is thought to be between. And this would be an appearance of equality.

Though having a limit relative to another mass, relative to itself it has neither beginning nor limit nor middle. Because, whenever anyone, in thought, grasps any of them as obtaining for one of them, there always appears another [165B] beginning before the beginning, a different end remaining after the end, and other and smaller middles that are nearer the middle due to the impossibility of grasping any of these as one inasmuch as one is not. So I think that whatever fragment there is that one would grasp in thought must be broken in pieces. For it would be grasped as a mass without one.

And so to anyone seeing anything of [165C] this sort from a distance and faintly it must appear one. But to one observing it intelligently near at hand and keenly each one will appear unlimited in multitude since it lacks the one which is not. Thus each of the others must appear to be unlimited and to have limit and to be one and many, if one is not while others than the one are.

And will they not be thought to be likes and unlikes? To one standing off a bit shadow paintings, all appearing to be one, appear to admit the same and to be like. [165D] But to one coming close they appear many and differents and, because of appearances of the different, differents in kind and unlikes of themselves. And thus the masses themselves must appear as likes and unlikes of themselves and of one another.

And also sames and differents, and touching one another and separated, and in every sort of motion and every sort of rest, and coming to be and perishing and neither, and all of those sorts, which it would be easy for us to mention even now, if [165E] with the one's not being, there are many.

Taking 'F is G' as our norm for affirmative predication, the sort of predication involved in supposition seven would have the form 'not-G is not-F,' with both grammatical subject and predicate being indefinite. (And, of course, it makes no difference which is in the subject and which is in the predicate place.) On the *Sophist* account both of these are parts of Different, that is, Different from G and Different from F. As we have noted, there can be no logical connection between these two. Parmenides remarks that, since there is no one (to be the object of a positive term), there is nothing for it but that they be differents from one another.

He proceeds to speak of the parts of Different with such terms as 'multitudes' and 'masses,' each 'unlimited in multitude.' This is, I believe, simply taking note of the indefinite character of the parts of Different. And, of course, each of these is made up of everything that is not F or not G in, for example, the Different from F.

One can, of course, produce grammatical sentences using various negative terms. 'Not-F is not-G' *looks* like a predication, and one may even try to work out the various permutations produced for the Platonic versions of the one supposition for these indefinite terms. It may look as though number is possible, so also large, small, equal, and the rest. But, given this remarkable dealing with indefinites, this would all be illusion.

Parmenides suggests that this is rather like seeing things that, from a distance, appear to be individuals of some sort but that, seen up close, are simply confused masses of indistinct particles. They may, even so, be taken as like and unlike. Parmenides counters this suggestion by suggesting that the situation is rather like that of 'shadow paintings' (scene paintings, *skiagraphia*, σκιαγραφία) which, from a distance, appear to contain figures that are the same and like one another. 'But to one coming close they appear many and differents and, because of appearances of the different, differents in kind and unlikes of themselves.'

It is tempting, given this characterization of scene paintings, to think that Plato has in mind something rather like an ancient version of impressionism. It is more likely, however, that he is describing the fairly elaborate use of shadows to produce at a distance the effect of depth and perspective, an effect that disappears when one gets up close. At any rate, this use of *appearance* to describe how grammatical possibility without logical or ontological support may be utterly misleading is quite remarkable. The upshot is, of course, that the 'both/and' possibilities built into proper recognition of sentences (rather than mere terms) have no support when both sentential terms are negative.

One may put the moral of this tale in a somewhat different way. Socrates is presumably to learn from this part of the exercise that sentences with both terms negative, though properly formed, cannot be given a truth value. Put in terms of the later *Sophist* arguments, though Different blends with the other 'greatest kinds,' it is impossible for any two parts of Different to blend with each other so as to give the ground for a sentence that is either true or false.

Parmenidean Version: The Consequences for the Others, If One Is Not (165E-66C)

Text of 165E–66B:

Parmenides   Once more, going back again to the beginning, let us say what must be the case for the others than the one, if one is not. Well then, the others will not be one. Nor will they be many. For then one would also be in many beings. For, if no one of them is one, all of them are no one, so that they could not be many. Since one is not in the others, the others are neither many nor one.

They do [166A] not even appear one or many. Because the others have no association ever or in any way with any of those that are not, nor is any of those that are not present to any of the others. For no part is in those that are not.

Thus there is no opinion of what is not present to the others, nor any appearance, nor is not being ever opined in any way about the others. Then if one is not, nothing of the others [166B] is opined to be one or many. For without one opining many would be impossible. If then one is not, the others neither are nor are opined to be one or many.

And so also neither like nor unlikes. Neither sames nor differents, neither touching nor separated, nor appearing as such others as we went through earlier. The others neither are nor appear to be any of these, if one is not.

Then, if we were to say in summation, if one is not, nothing is, would we not be speaking rightly?

In the first supposition (the Parmenidean Version of the consequences for the one 'if a one is') there was the saving grace at least of a term that presumably referred to something. With the other Parmenidean versions there was at least the *appearance* of referring to something. With this last Parmenidean version even the appearance has disappeared. No condition of intelligibility is satisfied.

In the last Platonic Version 'non-F' or 'Different from F' could be taken as having a reference to something, thus the *appearance* of making some sort of connection in predication. Here, however, with no reference to anything at all (not even an indefinite one), there is not so much as an appearance of any sort of connection. With the onset of predication in the second supposition and all of the permutations therefrom, the Parmenidean denial of predication is replete with 'neither/nors.' But the exploration of consequences on the present supposition does not even yield 'neither/nors.'

If Zeno's intention was to show how those who found Parmenides' conclusions absurd and laughable were guilty of even worse absurdity, this second part of the dialogue ends with the use of Zeno's own procedure to expose the aridity and fundamental absurdity of Parmenides' and Zeno's insistence on *one* and *no many* in the first part of the dialogue. Whether Plato's account of Parmenides' thought here and elsewhere does justice to the historical Parmenides is not easy to say. That Plato both here and in the *Sophist* pretty clearly gives the impression that he is doing so is beyond dispute.

166C

Text:

Parmenides Then let this be said and also that, as it seems, if one is or if one is not, it and also the others both relative to themselves and relative to one another both are and are not and appear and do not appear to be all in all ways.

This is, of course, not the sort of rousing finale one might properly expect after all that has preceded. The presumption must be that Plato at least thought that Socrates had been exposed to the exercise that Parmenides claimed to be needful. And it seems clear that, if I am right about the barrenness of the Parmenidean versions of the supposition, Plato did not require his Parmenides to state that. Not requiring its statement could be due to respect for the historical Parmenides and, perhaps, gratitude for the techniques exploited in the exercise. It was left for the Eleatic Stranger of the *Sophist* to commit 'parricide' and force the conclusion, in violation of Parmenidean dictum, that not-being *is*. Even so, it is clear from supposition five that, if one is not, not-being *is*.

There is a way of looking at the whole dialogue that expresses forcibly Plato's intention in writing it. It will be remembered that, when Zeno tells Socrates his motive in writing his book (128D), he remarks that people had found Parmenides' *supposition* (if one is) ludicrous. *His* (Zeno's) motive was to take what he took to be the detractors' supposition (if many are) seriously and to show that it was even more ludicrous. It is 'even more ludicrous' because the 'many' supposition is taken by Zeno to have contradictory consequences. It will be recalled that those contradictory consequences come from what Zeno takes to be the contradictory character of predication.

Looking at the dialogue in this light, we are required to take the Parmenidean versions of the supposition of the one as not allowing predication. What Plato does in the Platonic versions of the supposition of the one is to open a construction of that supposition that *does* allow for predication. This way, rather than directly responding to Zeno and falling victim to Parmenides' critical questioning, he can at once provide a response to Zeno, expose the aridity of Parmenidean monism, provide an appropriate stage for his account of the numbers, and be enabled to showcase his newly discovered account of non-being.

Without this last in mind, it would be difficult to find a motive for Plato's having Parmenides insist that the procedure must include the supposition that one (or whatever) *is not*. Indeed, given the imprecation against not-being in Parmenides' poem as well as the Eleatic Stranger's repetition of it in the *Sophist*, Parmenides himself would surely have refrained from any such insistence.

It is quite possible that Plato's motive in writing the *Parmenides* was to provide a plausible, perhaps an inspired, response to critics of the *Phaedo* doctrine of participation while exhibiting the basic forms (Being, Same, and Different) as the foundation of the intelligible structure of everything. We are about to look at other late dialogues in which those basic forms figure prominently and in just the places one might expect. In two of them (the *Theaetetus* and the *Sophist*) Socrates is made to express great respect for Parmenides, even though the *Sophist* is destructive of major features of Parmenides' thought.

From the above considerations I conclude that the reason for the great respect and, indeed, the reason Parmenides is portrayed as the skilful protagonist of the *Parmenides* is that reflection on Parmenides' poem and Zeno's treatise led him to abandon his middle period doctrine of the forms and participation. And it led him to what amounts to a creative revision of the Parmenidean supposition, a revision that finds in the duality of *one* and *being* an explanation of participation which is proof against the critique of the earlier doctrine put in the mouth of Parmenides in the dialogue. The respect accorded to Parmenides in the other late dialogues may well derive in part from that critique.

Again, if I am right, Plato hardly needed to do more than work through the exercise to provide an example for the members of the Academy. And it is quite possible indeed that Aristotle's comment in *Metaphysics* Gamma that exercise (*gymnastike*) as dialectical practice could be describing a procedure that became a regular feature of Academic training.

But the great exercise is surely more than that. Conceived as a response

The 'One' and the 'Others' on Both Versions of *If One Is Not* 141

to the problems raised in the first part of the dialogue and including, as it does, the generation of the numbers, the account of non-being, and the Coda with its account of change, the exercise signals a significant departure in Plato's mature thought. I shall try to make several details of that departure clear in the chapters to come. They will attempt to provide a coherent account that links the *Parmenides* with the other late dialogues.

In the next three chapters, it should be quite clear that Plato's late thought is suffused with the belief that there is nothing in the universe that fails to be within the intelligible order. With this in mind, one could easily think of Plato as endorsing Parmenides' claim that 'it is the same that can be thought that can be.'

9

The *Timaeus*

As I announced in the introductory chapter, this book has two aims: first, to provide a detailed interpretation of the *Parmenides*; second and related (with much already noted), to exhibit a remarkable set of intellectual interrelations between the *Parmenides* and several other dialogues commonly thought to be late. These are the *Timaeus*, the *Theaetetus*, the *Sophist*, and the *Philebus*. Attention also is paid to Books VI and VII of the *Republic* because of their obvious concerns with the nature of mathematics and their promise of dialectic's making ultimate principles known.

There has been little disagreement about the relative order of composition of the *Theaetetus*, the *Sophist*, and the *Philebus*; all are to be dated later than both the *Parmenides* and the *Timaeus*, and in the order just given. The relative dating of the *Timaeus* and the *Parmenides* remains a matter of controversy. Fortunately for my purposes, it makes no difference which was composed first; the special significance given in both to Being, Same, and Different and the place given to the mathematical construction of the world serve those purposes.

The Late Dialogues: A Preliminary Sketch

In the intellectual setting of the *Timaeus* Plato deliberately connects the *Republic* (with its remarkable analogies of the Line and Cave of Books VI and VII) and the mathematical cosmology of the *Timaeus*. And, as we have seen, at the beginning of supposition two of the *Parmenides* there is close and seminal (for the generation of the numbers) attention paid to Being, Same, and Different, the very forms invoked at the outset of the *Timaeus*. After the 'second start' (47E ff.) of the *Timaeus*, Plato gives us as mathematical a physical world as the *Parmenides* would lead us to expect. The

Theaetetus claims that it is the soul that perceives things, using the senses as external tools, and making use of the innate tools of the soul, namely, Being, Same, Different, and Number. And, of course, primary among the 'greatest kinds' of the *Sophist* in its remarkable dialectical heart are Being, Same, and Different. As well, the formal problem of the *Sophist*, the explanation of false belief, is solved by recognition of the 'parts of Different,' an explanation whose chief feature (as we have seen) plays a ubiquitous role in the *Parmenides*. The *Sophist* makes use of Collection and Division, and the *Philebus* explains the technique at some length. In so doing, the latter provides a rationale for taking Collection and Division as a procedure for arriving at definitions and explanations that give rational justification for the several 'crafts' (*technai*) broadly considered. As I have argued earlier in this book, it is a procedure that *presupposes* rather than investigates the major forms mentioned above. The fourfold division (Unlimited, Limit, Mixture, Cause of the Mixture) used in the *Philebus* is a plausible continuation of [a] development[s] attended to in this book's discussions of the *Parmenides*, the *Timaeus*, the *Theaetetus*, and the *Sophist*. Indeed, I shall claim in the *Philebus* chapter that mixture of Limit and Unlimited provides a Pythagorean simplification of the *Timaeus'* doctrine of the 'Receiver' and its mathematization.

The above is intended to set out very briefly the program for the remainder of the present work. I proceed to the discussion of the *Timaeus*.

The *Timaeus*

The formal setting of the *Timaeus* is that of a small gathering on the day following Socrates' presentation of the *Republic*. The discourse of Timaeus of Locris (probably not to be identified with any known historical figure) is preceded by Socrates' recapitulation of some features of the *Republic* and a brief presentation of Critias (with the promise of a longer presentation later). It is expected that Timaeus will discourse on the nature and origins of the universe, presumably supplying cosmic backing for some of the features of the *Republic*. Since the concern of this book is with the role of the *Timaeus* in the late philosophy of Plato, I do not attempt detailed commentary on the *Timaeus* but rather give selective attention to some important features of it. The selection is guided, of course, by what those features might tell us about the basics of Plato's late thought. I start, however, with reference to some portions of the *Republic* that, though not mentioned in the preamble to the *Timaeus*, are highly relevant to the latter.

The parts of the *Republic* that are of special relevance are those surrounding the famous images of the Line and the Cave in Books VI and VII. Both images are visual. Both divide *opinion* (*doxa*, δόξα) into an utterly naïve part and a less naïve part that corrects in some degree for perspective, lighting conditions, and other distortions. And both divide *knowledge* into a 'hypothetical' part that admits of illustration and a non-hypothetical part for which there is no illustration. The sun is said to be the cause of the *visibility* and the *becoming* of the objects of opinion. And the Form of the Good is said to be the cause of the *intelligibility* and the *being* of the objects of knowledge. I invite special attention to several matters concerning these portions.

First, in attending to the sun as cause of the visibility of objects, Plato appears to anticipate a feature of the *Timaeus* account of vision. Socrates says:

Neither vision (*opsis*) nor that in which it came to be, what we call the eye, is the same as the sun. But it is, I think, the most sunlike of the organs of sensing.

Did it not get the power that it has as something flowing from it [the sun]? Is it not therefore the case that the sun is not vision, but as being the cause of it, it is seen by vision itself?

In the *Timaeus* (45C–46C), Plato thinks of our ability to see as requiring an expanding cone of fire streams (*opsis*) issuing from the centre of the eye that, when they meet with the fire of the sun outside the eye, rigidify and become capable of transmitting impressions back to the surface of the eye. Without being rigidified by the sun's rays, the fire coming from the eye simply peters out. The sun is thus necessary for vision and, of course, can also be an object of vision.

Second, in discussing the lower part of the knowledge portion (that is, the major upper portion) Socrates observes that the *geometers* postulate or take for granted 'the odd and even and the various figures, etc.,' thus providing an example of the easy movement between arithmetic and geometry noted in the part of this book about the *Parmenides*.

Third and related, the very idea of the derivative nature of geometry calls to mind the generation of the numbers from the second supposition of the *Parmenides*. There, it will be remembered, the generation of the numbers was from the duality of the one that *is* and thus, of course, from Being, and, as we have seen, concomitantly from Same and Different. Aside from noting that geometers can and do produce and work with sensible illustrations (cf. Euclid's *Elements*, which contains a diagram for every proof) and that the dialecticians, dealing with what cannot be sensibly illustrated, presumably expose the frame of underivative knowledge, the *Republic* does not explain the derivation of geometric principles and does not expand on the highest form of knowledge. The exhibition of the primacy of Being, Same, and Different in supposition two of the *Parmenides*, the dialectical heart of the *Sophist*, and the exhibition of the basic principles of the *Philebus* do not require any sort of sensible illustration.

Fourth, it is worth noting that there does not seem to be any support in the late dialogues (that is, the *Timaeus*, the *Theaetetus*, the *Sophist*, the *Parmenides*, and the *Statesman*) for taking the Form of the Good in the *Republic* as indicative of a source of the foundations of intelligibility that lies somehow 'beyond' them. As we shall see, however, the *Timaeus'* 'construction' of the world soul from the foundational forms (Being, Same, and Different) and thus its identity with them removes the gap between the causal agent of the world and its pattern. More will be said about the human soul and its connection with the foundational forms in discussing the *Theaetetus*. And the *Philebus* will prove an appropriate place to end the discussion of the Neoplatonist account of the Idea of the Good.

Throughout his presentation Timaeus insists that his discourse is about a *copy* (*eikon*, εἴκων) and thus that the physical or visible universe is a copy. Given that the original or paradigm is the eternal order and that knowledge strictly speaking is *of* that order, Timaeus' exposition, in so far as it is of the copy as such, does not express knowledge. The standard translation understands it to be a 'likely story' or a 'probable story.' 'Probable' is misleading if it is taken in a modern sense, and 'likely' will do only if it is understood as 'of a likeness.' The exposition of Timaeus makes two somewhat different starts. The first, which largely concerns the nature and origin of the heavens, involves only the eternal order and the copy. The second, a 'fresh start' (48B), unpacks the notion of the copy by adding the complication of the Receiver (*hypodoche*, ὑποδοχή) and leads into the 'mathematization' of the physical world. (And we shall see the *Philebus* making use of Collection and Division, giving 'knowledge' of changing things a formal status, though a status rather below that of 'knowledge' of eternal things.)

The first start makes much of the distinction between what eternally *is* (*esti*) and what *comes to be* (*gignetai*), and Timaeus makes it clear that the former is somehow the cause of the latter. The latter is thus the locus of all change and is, of course, the copy. Timaeus speaks of the 'Maker and Father' of the copy who looks to the eternal for his model, and goes on to disavow the claim of knowledge for his account of the copy on the ground that there is only *opinion* (*doxa*) concerning it. This is a bit disingenuous, for much of the exposition concerns the requirements necessary for a copy to be a copy of the eternal order. I shall not, however, linger over the arguments that there can be but one copy or that the copy's order must be a temporal image of the eternal. My concern is rather with the notion that there can be no knowledge where the copy is concerned. Plato's point seems to be that, though we may have knowledge of the general features of the eternal order and thus a reasonably good idea of the general requirements for being a copy, there cannot be knowledge, strictly speaking, of the copy as such.

Timaeus presents us with an arresting image: that of the entire physical universe as an ensouled body or, if you please, an animal. That image joins the fundamental principles of intelligibility with the fundamental principle of motion: soul. It is an image that Plato evidently took to be correct and useful. And there is allusion to it both in the *Sophist* and the *Philebus*. The former is in the outcry of the Eleatic Stranger after the friends of the forms refuse to allow any sort of change in what is perfectly real.

But tell me, in heaven's name: are we really to be so easily convinced that change, life, soul, understanding have no place in that which is perfectly real – that it has neither life nor thought, but stands immutable in solemn aloofness, devoid of intelligence? (*Sophist* 248E–49A, Cornford translation.)

And what would satisfy the Stranger except the World Animal of the *Timaeus*? The latter is in that part of the *Philebus* in which the portions of earth, air, fire, water, and soul that we have are due to the immeasurably greater quantities of all of these in the universe (*Philebus* 29B3–30B8).

Timaeus' story about the soul of the World Animal uses the expository convenience of mixing ingredients together, the ingredients being in this case Being, Same, and Different, these being, as we saw in the *Parmenides*, the foundational principles of intelligibility itself (and, of course, those generative of the numbers). Starting at 35A1 there is a description of the composition of soul that has a striking resemblance to supposition two of the *Parmenides*.

And he made her (the soul) out of the following entities and on this wise. From the being which is indivisible and unchangeable and from that kind of being which is distributed among bodies, he compounded a third and intermediate kind of being. He did likewise with the same and the different, blending together the indivisible kind of each with that which is portioned out in bodies. Then, taking the three new elements, he mingled them all into one form, compressing by force the reluctant and unsociable nature of the different into the same. When he had mingled them with the intermediate kind of being and out of three made one, he again divided this whole into as many portions as was fitting, each portion being a compound of the same, the different, and being. And he proceeded to divide after this manner. First of all, he took away one part of the whole [1], and then he separated a second part which was double the first [2], and then he took away a third part which was half again as much as the second and three times as much as the first [3], and then he took a fourth part which was twice as much as the second [4], and a fifth part which was three times the third [5], and a sixth part which was eight times the first [6], and a seventh part which was twenty-seven times the first [7]. After this he filled up the double intervals [that is, between 1, 2, 4, and 8] and the triple [that is, between 1, 3, 9, and 27], cutting off yet other portions of the mixture and placing them in the intervals ... (*Timaeus* 35A1–36A2, Jowett translation).

It will be remembered from supposition two of the *Parmenides* that two number series were generated from the one that *is* by the use of Being, Same, and Different, two series generated by what I there called the 'two machine' and the 'three machine.' The 'parts' of the soul, with its make-up of Being, Same, and Different, here 'separated' correspond precisely (as far as they go) to the two different series of the *Parmenides*, and the *Timaeus* text goes on to talking about filling the intervals.

The *Timaeus* proceeds to describe the heavens as containing movements that accord with the features of the soul noted above, thus describing the movements as according with mathematical proportions and harmonies. Though the astronomy of this section is sophisticated and was highly influential in the ancient world, its detail as such is of little interest for my purposes. The astronomy of the *Timaeus* is virtually but not completely a priori. 'Not completely,' for it recognizes such features as the plane of the ecliptic and the need for retrograde motion of the planets. The whole visible universe is given a spherical shape, and this may be linked to the historical Parmenides' conception of Being (which we shall deal with in the discussion of the *Sophist*). The 'outer' sphere of the fixed stars is given the movement of the Same; the planets ('wanderers') are put in the plane of the ecliptic and given the movement of the Different. There is in this at least a verbal linkage with the principles in the construction of the soul. The movement of the sphere of the fixed stars is called 'same,' I believe, because it is totally inclusive, the counter movements of the planets are Different but occurring within the movement of the Same. What is of major importance for the present book is provision for the origin and derivation of mathematics within the soul of the universe together with the arresting idea of the whole universe as an ensouled body.

Still within Timaeus' first start we are told that the soul of the universe 'extends' everywhere within it, an 'extension' that is due simply to the extended character of the physical universe. This seems to be at least in part an explanation of the world soul's being in touch with everything and, somehow, being aware of everything. It is difficult not to think of this as the sort of awareness that a constantly productive agent might have and akin to thinking of the first principles' agent as bringing about and thus 'being aware' of derivative principles. And I shall argue, in discussing the *Theaetetus*, that human souls by virtue of their innate abilities or concepts are, on occasions of sensory input, aware of various things as being F, being the same as G, being different from H, and as being five or some other number. Given that those innate abilities include Being, Same, and Different, and given the superiority of the world soul, what more natural than to think of the world soul's being constantly aware in a *non-perceptual* way of the goings-on in the physical universe. Those goings-on are, of course, derivative from the productive agent and thus not 'discovered' by the world soul. Human conceptualization, making use of first principles, is thus like productive agency but lacking all or most of the detail for the physical universe while maintaining the ability to recognize its totally rational and non-arbitrary character.

Interestingly, Timaeus includes within the first start his account of human visual perception and of mirror reversal, though the former receives more extensive treatment in the second start. The visual account, as noted earlier in this chapter, involves fire rays diverging in a visual cone from the centre of the eye, which, when meeting with appropriate fire in the medium, rigidify and send back images to the surface of the eye. The mirror reversal account makes use of the visual account to explain left-right reversal in the image impinging on the eye. Both accounts are later given careful geometric treatment by Euclid in his *Optics* and *Catoptrics*. The *Timaeus* account of vision, historically called the 'extramission theory,' was, despite Aristotle's criticism of it, influential until at least the Middle Ages. It was not completely abandoned until Kepler took the eye to be a *camera obscura* and explained the clarity of vision, despite confusion of incoming rays, by the refocusing produced by the eye's lens.

Timaeus' second start adds a new element to the cosmic account, namely, the so-called *Receiver* (*hypodoche*, ὑποδοχή). The first start, Timaeus says, included but two 'forms' (*eide*, εἴδη): the eternal order and the changing copy. I have put 'forms' in quotation marks to indicate that here Plato is not using the term to mention the unchanging exemplars of the middle dialogues but rather the principles needed for the *Timaeus* account. And I have translated *hypodoche* as Receiver, thus preserving the idea of the 'receiving nurse' (to which Plato alludes) and avoiding the idea of a 'receptacle' as some sort of container. Timaeus is careful to speak of the Receiver as having no character of its own and being, as it were, completely plastic. A little into the exposition Timaeus uses the term *chora* ($\chi\omega\rho\alpha$) for the Receiver, and it is common to translate it as 'place.' This has, of course, given impetus to treating the Receiver as a receptacle. But the term *chora* is associated with a verb that has the sense of 'making room for,' and I think this is the proper clue for Timaeus' use of it.

If you will, the role of the Receiver, as having no character of its own, is to 'make room for' the numbers or, equivalently, the geometric solids. What I wish to claim is that, when the Receiver is somehow mixed with the intelligible numbers (or shapes), the product is a spatial array of figures. The contention is that Timaeus needs the Receiver in order to make the move from eternal mathematicals to spatially arrayed solid (that is, three-dimensional) figures. With the intelligible numbers (shapes) there are, as I pointed out in discussing the *Parmenides*, incredibly large and internally articulated sets of numbers that are capable, as it were, of joining with the Receiver in making completely filled in and determined spatial arrays together with articulating any number of such arrays through finite periods of time. And, as the earlier part of the *Timaeus* says, producing through the regularity of the heavenly movements what is there called a 'moving copy of the eternal.' I must note as well that Timaeus takes the finite periods of time to be replicated over and over again without end (the series of so-called Great Years).

I think that what we have here is Plato's mature conception of the physical and perceptible world (though we shall see reason for some emendation in the *Philebus*). Its constant production by and in the World Animal (that is, the ensouled universe) is the causal working-out of the principles of intelligibility itself within finite spatial and temporal parameters. It is finite or 'limited' (*peras*, $\pi\epsilon\rho\alpha\varsigma$) in order to avoid the threat to intelligible production posed by the 'unlimited' (*apeiron*, $\alpha\pi\epsilon\iota\rho\text{o}\nu$) as such, not the unlimited array of numbers.

Timaeus describes the physical world as consisting of an immense number of regular solids: tetrahedra (fire), cubes (water), octahedra (air), and icosahedra (water). Three of these have faces made up of triangles that allow for transformation from one kind to another. The triangles joining to make the faces of cubes do not allow this, though they do allow for transformation from smaller to larger cubes and vice versa. Timaeus further supposes that the whole universe rotates and, in so doing, crushes (presumably by centripetal force) the various solids so that there are no interstices and the kinds are scattered. But it is not my purpose to produce detail for this part of the *Timaeus*. It is, rather, to attend to two matters concerning it: first, the mechanical or quasi-mechanical picture it invites; second, its role in Timaeus' account of human perception.

It is indeed tempting to think of Timaeus' regular solids as moving about, striking one another, breaking up, and regrouping in various ways; and the descriptions given by Timaeus invite this picture. Even so, I think the picture is misleading. It is hard to believe that Plato was, at the time of the *Timaeus*, sufficiently naïve as to merit Aristotle's criticism of his allowing two-dimensional triangles to fly about and to treat real physical solids as made up of their faces. And the notion of merely mechanical interaction of the products of the mathematization of the Receiver is out of keeping with the notion of the derivation of the physical universe from the sources of intelligibility, even granting the so-called 'compromise with necessity.' The descriptions given by Timaeus are, I believe, part and parcel of the expository procedure of Timaeus. The fundamental Platonic scheme of the universe leaves no place for the incidental bumping of particles, even those in the shape of the regular solids. The so-called 'compromise with necessity' is rather to be construed as the recognition of a large number and a variety of rectilinear motions and the mathematical impossibility of more than one solid's delineating the same place at the same time in the 'space' produced by the mathematization of the Receiver. There are, moreover, two references in the *Timaeus* text to the 'shaking' (52E and 57C) of the Receiver. These are hard to explain on any interpretation I have seen and, if taken literally, would be damaging to my account. At least tentatively, I am inclined to take these as references to the sort of 'making room' that is suggested by the term *chora* (χώρα), which is used for the 'space' produced by the Receiver's *making room for* (χωρέω) the physical mathematicals.

The proper Platonic picture is, as we should expect both from the *Timaeus* warnings about the method of exposition and from the other late dialogues, that of a physical universe that maximizes intelligibility and justifies Plato's claims that the universe is as good as it can be. With this much said about ultimate principles, it is time to turn to the matter of the place of human beings in the world of the *Timaeus*. I begin with its doctrine of human perception.

Human Perception

The *Timaeus* distinguishes sharply between the physical processes in perception and the sensations produced by those processes. Before discussing the *Timaeus* account of this distinction, however, it will help that discussion and the discussion of other late dialogues to take time out to say something about perception and how Plato thought of it. In this it we shall need to anticipate some features of the *Theaetetus* and the *Sophist*.

In Greek as in English, 'perception' (*aisthesis*, αἴσθησις) is a general term covering seeing, hearing, tasting, touching, and smelling. And what we perceive are things, but always things as qualified in some appropriate sensible manner, that is, as coloured, as sounding, as hard, etc. This gives rise to a set of ambiguities or confusions that the history of philosophy has generously exploited, namely, that between the sensible qualification, the thing as perceived, and the thing as it is. There is nothing in Plato's works to suggest the much later development of the theories of 'ideas' or of 'sense-data' or 'sensa.' Attic Greek, however, does allow and Plato uses a distinction between *sensing* (*aisthesis*) and *sensed* (*aistheton*), which invites driving a wedge between a thing perceived and the sensible qualification, with the *sensed* taken as an *object* different from the thing perceived. But now let us keep a careful eye, as it were, on *sensing* (aisthesis), for relatively recent philosophy has commonly treated the term as used to refer to a 'mental act' that has a mere sensible as its object. As we shall shortly see, this is surely not Plato's doctrine.

If we suppose, as I do (and Plato does), that what are perceived are physical things (sensibly qualified), then, according to the *Timaeus*, they must be parts of the mathematized Receiver. And Plato regularly writes of the physical world as a sensible thing. In what manner could it be sensibly qualified? Only if it admits of qualification by items produced in beings that are capable of sense perception. We are, of course, such beings. If we take it that, as physical things affected in special ways by other physical things in our environment, our sense organs (physical parts of us) are so affected as to produce modifications in those organs, and if we think of those modifications as enabling our souls to represent things outside us, there is a way of taking the physical world to be sensibly qualified. Let a representation brought about by a modification of a sense organ be a 'sensing' or *aisthesis* as noted in the last paragraph. *Sensing* (*aisthesis*) and *sensed* (*aistheton*) are for Plato correlative terms and thus like *double* and *half* or *parent* and *child*. It is impossible for the one to be without the other. If, therefore, a sense organ is modified so as to bring about a sensing, there must be a *sensed* corresponding to that modification.

Timaeus speaks of the impact of the visual cone on the eye as going 'right up to the soul.' There is thus a *sensing* (that is, a representation produced by a modification of the sense organ) and a corresponding *sensed* (say, a shaped white thing). According to the *Theaetetus* account that is discussed in the next chapter, the *soul* perceives, using the sense organ and its product, the *sensed*, as a tool (*organon*). What the soul perceives is a white *thing*, perhaps a stick or stone, and this is, of course, a physical thing as sensibly characterized. And the *Timaeus* attempts fairly elaborate accounts of how it is that each of the sense organs can be appropriately modified and under what conditions, thus producing sensible characterizations in every sense modality. And it is clear from these accounts how it may be that different sensible characterizations of the same thing may obtain for the same person under different conditions and, of course, for persons with appropriately different sense organs. It is equally clear that no physical thing by or in itself is sensibly characterized. It can be so characterized only relative to a perceiver.

Throughout what I have called 'fairly elaborate accounts' there is a clear attempt to correlate sensible characterizations with appropriate physical changes, and it is reasonably clear what these correlates may be. In the case of touch, Timaeus correlates sensible characterizations as *hard* and *soft* with physically not yielding and yielding to the percipient's skin, *hot* to the tearing action of basic physical particles, and so on. (And shapes must be added to touch's list.) *Loud* and *soft* sensations are correlated to more and less forceful action of the air on the ear tissues. Except for vision the sensible correlates are correlates of physical actions on what are obvious physical sense organs. But vision poses a problem.

We see things at or from various distances, though there is no obvious impact on the eyes either of the tactual kind where our bodies are immediately impinged upon or of the kinds where a medium's changes impinge on our bodily organs. We have, however, already attended to the remarkable idea of the visual cone as made up of diverging fire rays coming from the centre of the eye and rigidifying when those rays meet with appropriate fire when emerging from the eye. Interestingly enough, Timaeus seems to think of the visual cone as an extension of a percipient's body and even expresses some concern that interference with the visual cone does not hurt or cause pain. As such an extension, the visual cone *is in effect a sense organ*, and Timaeus' doctrine is that vision is akin to touch. But the sensible correlates are colours and shapes. What produce the sensible colours are larger and smaller particles that either compact or split the rays in the visual cone. And the shape correlates are always coloured, of course, just as they are hard or soft for the tactual sense. If the ambient air (or water) is compatible and no obstruction to the visual cone, it is *invisible* or *transparent*. One must be careful here, however, for it is tempting to think of such invisibility or transparency commonsensically as something 'seen through' by the soul's use of the eye. For Plato it is rather the case that the commonsensical use of 'transparency' presupposes simply the absence of physical hindrance. And as well, if there is no appropriate fire in the medium, the rays coming from the eye simply peter out and do not rigidify, and there can be no seeing.

As I noted earlier, the idea of the diverging rays of the visual cone provides the basis for a geometric optics with interference of more or fewer rays producing sensible correlates of larger or smaller size. Concomitantly there is in this a theory of perspective as well as an explanation of the fuzziness of distant objects (intersection of fewer rays) as well as their disappearance from sight. All of this is picked up in Euclid's geometric *Optics*. Also as noted earlier, there is as well the possibility of an explanation of mirror reversals – picked up in Euclid's *Catoptrics*. Finally as noted earlier, there is the possibility that intrigued Plato as early as the *Protagoras* and as late as the *Philebus* that we can correct for size and distance perceptual judgments by using measuring sticks or their equivalent.

Let me emphasize one more time that what I have been calling *sensible correlates* are features of physical things only *in relation* to given perceptions. The doctrine of the *Timaeus* is that physical things in themselves have no such features. Thus all perceptual judgments assigning sensible correlates to physical things are false if we are speaking of physical things just by themselves – unless in making such assignments we are speaking of the *causes* of such sensible correlates. As regards this last, however, much remains to be said. And I turn to it.

As Plato acknowledges in the famous analogies of the Line and the Cave of the *Republic*, even at the level of opinion (*doxa*, δόξα), people learn. They progress from utterly naïve perceptual opinion (*eikasia*, εἰκασία) to a form of opinion (*pistis*, πίστις) that corrects for some features of point-of-viewishness and deception by lighting conditions and the like. Using the Cave analogy, people move from staring at shadows to 'looking at' the puppets that produce the shadows. I think the point being made is that individuals learn from experience to make a number of corrections to merely naïve perceptual episodes. Indeed, whole communities learn to do so, and, if they survive for long, enshrine a large number of corrections in the language they develop and speak. Without explicit worry (perhaps none at all) about the fundamental principles of intelligibility, successful craft routines and relevant speech for training and appraisal, modes of getting on in a community etc., develop over time. This, at any rate, appears to have been the experience of the Greeks. Thus without (or with only sporadic attention to) explicit concern for explanation of what would make craft procedures and successful speech possible, quite a remarkable culture came into being and flourished. One must grant, of course, that religious and cosmic speculation played a role in the Greek development of rational and philosophical inquiry. But for what I am about rehearsing the history of culture development is only tangentially relevant.

What I am concerned with is that the *Timaeus*' account of a mathematized physical world, its causal connections with what I have been calling 'sensible correlates' (despite failure of such correlates to correspond precisely with or to reveal states of the mathematized physical world as they are), and the development of language based heavily on the correlates serve as an appropriate introduction to the late Plato's development and use of the procedure of Collection and Division. I shall try to show in the next two chapters what I have claimed earlier, that is, that Plato does not use Collection and Division as a procedure for investigation of his timeless and changeless forms but rather as one that develops rational explanations and one that *presupposes* the intelligible world of principles but does not as such investigate intelligible numbers and the mathematized physical world we have been discussing in this chapter.

Two final notes on the *Timaeus*. First, I began the discussion of perception by claiming that what we perceive are physical things, commonly or normally physical things as qualified in particular ways. This is, of course, in accord with linguistic usage, whether that of Attic Greek or of twentieth-century English. People see, hear, touch, smell, and taste things: things that look or appear red, things that sound loud, things that feel hard or soft, things that smell pleasant or like roses, and things that taste sweet or sour. Even when asking such questions as 'Did you get a whiff of that?' 'Did you see the look of last night's sunset?' and the like, we presuppose that there is something that smells a certain way or that last night's sunset had a certain appearance. If I am right about the *Timaeus*, the things that we perceive, whatever names we give them, are, at bottom, sensible numbers. This sort of 'at bottom' issue is rather like the modern claim that 'at bottom' the several physical things around us, whatever names we give them, are whatever current microphysics says they are. Neither the modern claim nor Plato's treats the names the language gives to perceived physical things as positively mistaken. Rather those claims treat them as having fairly modest explanatory value. Modern science believes that its entities and the theory that deals with them have a great deal of genuine explanatory value. Plato can treat his mathematical physical things as in principle required for the intelligibility of the world, but he cannot claim that our best knowledge of mathematical principles gives us serious explanations of detailed changes in the physical world. The astronomy of the *Timaeus* and application of Plato's theory of the 'elements' quickly get us into trouble when treated as having detailed explanatory value. But we shall be at these matters again in the next chapters.

Second, I have been assuming throughout this chapter that Plato takes quite seriously the dictum that nothing comes from nothing; thus he believes in the eternity of the universe. The fiction of the demiurge as guiding and directing the coming to be of the World Animal and the detailed production of everything that is and comes to be is justifiable as an expository device. What guides Timaeus in his exposition is the requirement that the 'whole heaven' be and operate in accordance with basic principles of rationality. Within this requirement he needs the assurance that the *copy* can be in *principle* (though not in detail) explained as flowing from those principles. Included in all this, of course, is an 'in principle' explanation of humankind's place in nature.

10

The *Theaetetus* and the *Sophist*

The relevance of the *Theaetetus* for the present work is its place in the late philosophy of Plato and, of course, what it reveals of that late philosophy. Interestingly, of the four dialogues made up of the *Theaetetus* and the three explicitly contemplated early in the *Sophist* (*Sophist*, *Statesman*, and *Philosopher*) only the *Theaetetus* has (or was to have had) Socrates as protagonist. The setting of the *Sophist* is the day following that of the *Theaetetus*, and it has the same dramatis personae with the addition of an Eleatic Stranger (an about-to-be-reformed disciple of Parmenides) who carries the intellectual burden of both the *Sophist* and the *Statesman*. Though the *Philosopher* is announced in the *Sophist* and was to have had the Eleatic Stranger as protagonist, it was evidently never completed. I wish to attach some importance both to the shift of protagonists and to the remarkably different philosophical style that comes with the shift.

The *Theaetetus*

It has often been noted that the *Theaetetus* is a touching memorial to the brilliant and brave Theaetetus. It is very much worth noting as well that it is a memorial to the wise and good Socrates. It is the source of the depiction of Socrates as an intellectual midwife. It contains a long and heartfelt section on the purity of true philosophers and their disadvantage in law courts. And it ends with Socrates announcing that he must go to the porch of the King Archon to give a preliminary answer to the charge brought against him by Meletus, the charge that eventually led to his death. In the main, though not completely, the procedures followed and the doctrines of the *Theaetetus* signal no serious departure from those of the Socrates of the middle dialogues. They do, however, serve well to introduce those of the

Sophist. And with respect to its primary question, 'What is knowledge?' the dialogue is aporetic.

Early in the dialogue and on the way to making clear the complete relativity of Protagoras' 'man is the measure,' Socrates notes that we do not ordinarily believe it possible for something to be F and G, where these are incompatible, unless it has gone through a process of change; it cannot be both at the same time (and in the same respect). Protagoras, however, contends that one and the same wind can at the same time be correctly reported as both warm (to one person) and cold (to another) without undergoing a process of change. Before probing the *Theaetetus* further I should like to remind readers that the Coda of the *Parmenides* that was discussed earlier is quite clear about the impossibility of something's having incompatible features at the same time and respect. There, it will be remembered, change is taken to be catastrophic or, if you please, mediated by the 'instant' and is clearly taken to be a feature of our world. It is quite the clearest account of physical change in all of Plato. And it is echoed here on the threshold of the Protagorean/Heraclitean account of perception (the so-called 'secret doctrine').

The Protagorean/Heraclitean account is for Plato's purposes ingenious. It manages to be an initially plausible account of perception, and suggests how a process account of the nature of things might be given (whether or not it might be Heraclitus' own doctrine). Though the perception doctrine would be and is rejected by Plato, much of its relativism is compatible with his own account of the dependence of perception jointly on our sensitive faculties and the outside world (in the *Timaeus*). To the unwary Theaetetus the doctrine seems to make his definition of knowledge as perception plausible indeed.

Before moving on to Socrates' critique, it is worth noting that Plato is careful to say that, in the coming to be of the object of perception (156E), it comes to be 'not whiteness but a white thing' (for example, a stone). Without worrying the matter of what to say about *whiteness*, my concern is with the fact that, even in stating the Protagorean/Heraclitean doctrine, Plato treats perception (at least sight) as *of* physical things or of physical things as sensibly qualified. And there is a double issue here: first, how can any physical thing in itself be sensibly qualified? second, is the physical thing properly identified? Related is the idea that a perception is properly expressed in a perceptual judgment and is thus somehow of a complex or compound entity. (And this is not unrelated to the Platonic versions of the 'one' supposition in the *Parmenides* – all of them finding 'one beings' at the ontological core of things.) Interestingly, the linkage of *perceives* with *per-*

ceives that, *appears that*, and the like is exploited in the later discussion of Protagoras' doctrine.

Except for the *Parmenides* the concern of this book is not with detailed discussion of any later dialogue, and I shall therefore not attempt to follow all the moves of the *Theaetetus*, but keep my eye on what serves to introduce or comport with what I take to be the basic features of Plato's late thought. It should have been clear from Theaetetus' identification of *knowledge* and *perception* that the identification would not survive if perception were not expressible by the use of sentences rather than simple terms (quite aside from whatever else might be wrong with the identification). Thus the move of Plato's Protagoras to *seems that, appears that*, and the like was to be expected. The argument that the expert is much more likely than the non-expert to get a relevant future trend right and that it appears that way to most of us depends upon taking the expert's opinion as a judgment expressible in a sentence. Even Protagoras' claim that he is a better judge of which persons will judge themselves to have better experiences after Protagorean training is a judgment.

I must add that the *coup de grâce* given to the Protagorean/Heraclitean doctrine depends upon perception's being judgmental in character. This is the claim that it is impossible for absolutely everything to be changing in every way without ceasing. This is, of course, literally inconceivable and is akin to the remark attributed to Cratylus that you cannot step into the same river once (except, of course, that no term, in this case 'river,' could be used that suggested even the briefest stability). As we noted in the discussion of the *Parmenides*, the notions of motion as ever in a different and rest as ever in the same allow for something to be at the same time in motion and at rest. That is, say, a man who is running remains a man (thus in this way at rest) while continuously in motion. In order for something to be changing there has to be something that it *is* through the change. That it is changing in every way cannot be intelligible, for there is no *it* to talk about.

Probably the most important portion of the first part of the dialogue for my purposes contains Socrates' arguments and claims about the soul as perceiver, the unity of perceptual consciousness, and the role of the soul's abilities in perception. Presumably the Protagorean account of perception takes the several sense organs to be the perceivers, thus the eyes as seeing, the ears as hearing, and so on. Socrates elicits from Theaetetus (184B–86C) that it is, rather, the soul, *using* the eyes (ears, etc.) as instruments (*organa*), which sees, hears, etc. This admission, moreover, allows for the unity of perceptual consciousness in that it allows for the same person's being aware of the deliverances of the several senses.

For my purposes perhaps the most important admission of Theaetetus in this connection is the admission that not only does the soul *use* the deliverances of the senses but it also uses certain abilities of its own. Those abilities are, I believe, to be thought of as *conceptual* in that they play organizing roles in perceptual consciousness. They include Being, Same, and Different, and they are not unrelated to the forms Timaeus invokes in the construction of soul and not unrelated to the same items in supposition two of the *Parmenides*. The interest does not lie in the soul's ability somehow to be aware of the form Being, but rather to take it that something of which it is aware *is*, that is, is F (some feature or other). It does not lie in the soul's ability somehow to be aware of the form Same, but rather to take it that something of which it is aware is the *same* as itself or something numerically different. And it does not lie in the soul's ability to be aware of the form Different, but rather to take it that something of which it is aware is different from itself (in a different time or respect) or from some other.

What seems to be the crucial matter here is that the soul is not a passive recipient of the deliverances of sense; it is in this context rather a set of discriminating abilities that enable it to sort out the deliverances of sense. Without them our sensory connections with the outside world would simply be a phantasmagoria. Indeed, these discriminating abilities appear to be the source of nearly all of the everyday concepts we use in getting around in and understanding the world. I should also note again that Plato appears to take perception (that is, seeing, hearing, smelling, touching, tasting) to be *of physical things* or rather of such things as qualified in various ways. And there is no temptation to take Plato as holding that those things are congeries of colours, sounds, or whatever. Thus, though we might be more or less constantly revising our conceptions of various physical things, in making perceptual judgments we are making judgments about physical things as having some features or other.

In actual practice, given a long socio-linguistic history (which the Greeks also had), we tend to take for granted the concepts we acquired jointly through linguistic training and perceptual experience. And for most practical purposes there is no problem. With serious exposure to modern physical science, however, we find that the linguistic/conceptual apparatus we learned from childhood gives us little clue as to the 'real' nature of things. But even the most learned physical scientists among us find that they cannot for practical purposes and for many scientific purposes forsake the linguistic/conceptual apparatus they learned at their mothers' knees. No one in acquiring scientific sophistication acquires different sense organs and thus a different sense-life, though he or she may become more precise and cautious in the use of our language. The situation is similar in the thought of the late Plato. If I am right in my account of Plato's doctrine of physical things in the *Timaeus*, physical things are mathematized portions of the Receiver and thus perceptible only as causally affecting our sense organs. It is only after the acquisition of logical sophistication and much reflection that we begin to understand what sort of things that they must be. But Plato, like the modern physical scientist, does not, in acquiring sophistication, have some new and different perceptual appearances.

We shall shortly, in discussing the *Sophist*, be much into the celebrated procedures of Collection and Division. And, if I am right, we shall be dealing with a Plato whose use of these procedures depends upon finding the linguistic/conceptual apparatus we learned at our mothers' knees very largely trustworthy. My claim now, as earlier, is that Plato finds Collection and Division to be the admirable technique for coming up with responsible patterns of explanation that he says that it is in the *Philebus*. But, also as noted earlier, Plato finds that the rational use of Collection and Division depends upon or presupposes the intelligible ontological framework of Being, Same, Different, etc., with its production of the intelligible numbers and the physical world. Both the *Republic* VI and VII and the *Sophist* provide cogent reasons for our ability to explore and for the actual exploration of the general features of the intelligible world. Neither that exploration nor its results, however, take the place of, for example, the crafts of music, medicine, or ship-building.

Theaetetus' next move, namely, his identification of knowledge with true belief, introduces us for the first time to the problem of how false belief is possible. In effect, however, the problem was really introduced with the 'judgment' version of Protagoras' dictum of man's being the measure. Why does Plato do it again? I think that his chief reason for including both of the last sections of the *Theaetetus* is to prepare the way for what he does in the *Sophist* without involving Socrates in his later philosophical procedures. The worry about false belief is not banished even later in the *Theaetetus*. And the issue of how false belief is possible is a major one in the *Sophist*, a dialogue presumed to take place on the day following the *Theaetetus* discussion. The final section of the *Theaetetus* is an exploration of the thesis that knowledge might be true belief with an account (*logos*, λόγος). Detail of that exploration has been much discussed, and it is not strictly needed for what I am about. The dialogue ends on an apparently aporetic note, and Socrates leaves off to keep an appointment on the porch of the King Archon to meet the indictment brought by Meletus. The final sentence, however, informs Theodorus (Theaetetus' teacher) of Socrates' expectation of meeting with him on the next day.

The *Sophist*

The *Sophist* commences with that meeting, a meeting that includes the dramatis personae of the previous day with the addition of a Stranger from Elea. The Stranger's presence elicits from Socrates an expression of concern lest the Stranger be a Parmenidean disciple like Zeno, one whose business is refutation. We have, of course, met that Zeno in the *Parmenides*, and Plato, in the *Phaedrus*, refers to Zeno as 'the Eleatic Palamades,' further confirming Zeno's reputation. And, of course, Zeno is depicted in Aristotle's *Physics* as having produced the celebrated paradoxes, presumably in defence of Parmenides. Theodorus quickly assures Socrates that the Stranger is more reasonable and deserves to be called a philosopher. Immediately Socrates requests of the Stranger accounts of the Sophist, the Statesman, and the Philosopher. From the Stranger's asseveration that they are different there emerges a well-known pattern of expected dialogues. We are about to get the account of the Sophist from the Stranger, and Plato did write the *Statesman* (with the Stranger as protagonist). There is no evidence that the *Philosopher* was ever written.

After discovering that the Stranger prefers to proceed with an interlocutor, Theaetetus is chosen, and Socrates comments that he was once present when Parmenides himself used an interlocutor to carry out an 'elegant set of arguments' ($\lambda \acute{o} \gamma o \upsilon \varsigma \ \pi \alpha \gamma \kappa \acute{\alpha} \lambda o \upsilon \varsigma$). Since there was no such historical occasion, this comment obviously refers to the *Parmenides* and invites readers to keep that dialogue in mind as the *Sophist* proceeds.

The Stranger plunges into the procedure of Collection and Division immediately. Before we attend to what he actually does, a couple of comments are in order. First, it is not easy to see here, in the *Parmenides*, or in the *Statesman* just what need there is for the interlocutor. Except for a very few raised eyebrows and questions, the interlocutor in these dialogues has no role to play except to concur with the various moves in the discourse. There is the suggestion in the *Parmenides* that having someone respond lessens the strain on Parmenides. And the Eleatic Stranger allows that the exposition is 'easier' when the interlocutor is tractable, but he seems prepared to do the exposition alone. I fear that any attempt to explain Plato's use of protagonist and interlocutor in these dialogues would involve fairly profitless guesswork about Plato's motives.

Second, I have chosen to refer to the procedure used in the first part of the *Sophist* and all of the *Statesman*, and illustrated and described in the *Philebus* as Collection and Division (*synagoge* and *diairesis*, συναγωγή and διαίρεσις). The reason is that I think that both are involved in the proceedings of the *Sophist* and the *Statesman*. Deciding upon a kind under which one expects that what is being defined will fall (at whatever remove) is appropriately thought of as *collection*. Making proper divisions in and under that kind is, of course, appropriately thought of as *division*. I am aware that some commentators have reserved the term *collection* for the sort of activity attributed in the *Philebus* to Theuth, that is, for the initial recognition that various human sounds can be collected under appropriate kind-headings. The matter is not, of course, of great moment, provided that there is recognition that different but related processes are at work.

Among the matters that are of moment is the idea that division, properly done, provides one with genera/species hierarchies and, *pari passu*, with definitions. It may be appropriately noted that the Eleatic Stranger says that a major result of properly following his procedure is arriving at a *logos*. He does so immediately after modestly offering the *angler* as practitioner of a craft that may serve as a kind with which to begin. He then says, 'I hope that he provides us with a method and a *logos* for what we desire' (219A1–2). Mindful that the *Sophist* picks up from the previous day's *Theaetetus* conversation, which ended with unsatisfactory attempts at a characterization of *logos* in the formula 'Knowledge is true belief plus a *logos*,' it would not be surprising to find Plato starting with an attempt at a proper treatment of *logos*. What is more, the failures of knowledge as true belief and as true belief plus a *logos* in the *Theaetetus* are linked with the inability of either to explain how a person who has knowledge can offer a defence of his/her claim to know. The presumption of the *Sophist* account is that the result of a proper use of Collection and Division is the ability to make an appropriate defence.

The several uses of Collection and Division by the Stranger in attempting to define the Sophist make it difficult to take the claim that the ingredients in the several definitions are the eternal and unchanging Platonic forms. Even granting that the Stranger's move from *angling* to the more comprehensive *craft* (art, *techne*) and granting also that the divisions and subdivisions of the latter are well taken, the divisions of, for example, *acquisitive craft* seem remarkably tied to conventional Athenian institutions. There are some seven guises in which the Sophist appears in the divisions: merchant, retailer, salesman, hired hunter (of young men), intellectual separator of things (Socrates' craft), and maker of false images. The detail for arriving at these several characterizations or definitions is sufficiently tedious that Cornford[1] omits most of it from his translation and commentary. What I wish to emphasize are the points already made about the tie to conventional institutions and, as well, the rather loose texture that permits there to be seven different definitions.

In the Stranger's procedure of Division much, if not everything, depends upon conventional word usage. Let me hasten to note, as I have earlier, that I do not believe that the Stranger is talking about language or even about linguistic uses. He is *using* (unless clearly indicating otherwise) language to talk about various features of the 'world,' a world that is made available to us by means of our conceptual and linguistic abilities. Given our perceptual abilities used in conjunction with our basic conceptual abilities (noted in the *Theaetetus* discussion and hinted at earlier), civilized communities over time and with increased ability to cope have developed useful and tested languages. The Greeks, as countless scholars have observed, developed a excellent language. And the Stranger, in making his Collections and Divisions, draws heavily upon the distinctions that language makes possible. But there is no reason to suppose, nor does Plato give us reason to suppose, that the Stranger is talking about the forms as such (and certainly no reason to suppose that he is talking about language). Again, as I have claimed earlier, the procedure is calculated to arrive at useful definitions whose grounds in the language as used are indirectly connected with the mathematized physical world (and thus also indirectly connected with the intelligible world of forms and mathematicals). The connection is indirect because the human concepts embedded in the language are formed by the combined operations of simple perception and the innate concepts of the soul – another matter discussed earlier.

The procedure followed by the Stranger both here and in the *Statesman* draws heavily upon a large and varied set of distinctions, most of them either features of Greek common sense or features of a number of crafts (*arts, technai*). And I can find no place in which it is explicitly or even implicitly claimed that the objects mentioned or arrived at in the procedure are the eternal and changeless forms of the middle or late middle dialogues. Nor do I take this fact to imply that Plato has abandoned the forms. The eternal world of the forms and intelligible numbers is required for justification of the procedure. Plato, unlike a number of recent defenders of relativistic epistemologies, has the eternal order to lie behind and guide his procedure of arriving at explanatory definitions. The idea is akin to that of relatively recent attempts to justify the procedure(s) of induction by appeal to some a priori principle or other, except that Plato's is grounded in what amount to the fundamental principles of logic.

The Stranger's last definition of the Sophist, that is, as a maker of false images, raises a major and familiar problem from the *Theaetetus*: How is false belief possible? Most of the remainder of the dialogue is devoted to that problem and the issues it raises. Interpreting false belief or speaking as believing or saying *what is not*, the Stranger quickly gets to the admonition of Parmenides, viz., to refrain from saying or believing that not-being *is*. With that, it is made clear that the Stranger is about to commit intellectual 'parricide' on Father Parmenides.

We then come to passages that are distinctly reminiscent of supposition two of the *Parmenides*. They consist of a review of several of Plato's predecessors, who have laid it down that *the real* consists either of several things or one thing. The problem with all of them lies in the need for them to be able to say that whatever they have laid down *is*. In the attempt to do so, they will either simply repeat themselves or be forced to acknowledge, in addition to what they have laid down, whatever it is that *is* gets at. The reminiscence comes, of course, in the second supposition's taking the one supposition to be quite literally the supposition that the one *is* and thus working out the consequences for the *one-being* in full recognition of the duality of the one that *is*. It is in these passages that Parmenides is claimed to engage in self-refutation in saying that *one is*, for, in so doing, he is acknowledging more than one.

Interestingly, Aristotle runs through the possibilities for Plato's predecessors in the first book of the *Physics*. Without going into detail of what he does, the pattern of his analysis and argument is to take whatever is laid down as *real*, putting it in either the subject place or the predicate place and then letting the other place be occupied by standard commonsensical descriptive terms. Thus Thales might be taken, alternatively, as implying that water (or the wet) is green (is a horse, etc.) or that green things (or horses) are water (or the wet). Either procedure is taken to lead to paradoxes. Parmenides is given special treatment, largely, I believe, because not allowing the addition of predicates to the one invites no obvious paradoxes (thus justifying Zeno's comment about his defence of Parmenides). Even so, Parmenides is rejected for failure to recognize the need for any sort of predication. Aristotle is in *Physics* I working towards the recognition of the need for a subject of change which remains through the change and for a predicational pair of contraries to delineate the change. He takes this need as one that must be satisfied in order for there to be a science of *Physics*. I find it hard to believe that he did not have something akin to the *Sophist* passages under discussion in mind in writing *Physics* I. And I think it clear that the *Parmenides* treatment of supposition two lies in the background.

The Stranger turns from this critique of Parmenides and others to the so-called 'battle of gods and giants.' At the conclusion of this 'battle' the Stranger turns immediately to the need for recognizing Motion and Rest among the timeless forms. The interpretative issues here concern the transitions to and from the 'battle.'

I think that one must think of the giants as including those whose conception of what is *real* is a matter of presumably basic things that are taken as being or having perceptual features, notably from the pairs, hot/cold and moist/dry. Initially at least they are prepared to recognize as real only such perceptual features, taking them as somehow given. They are not, as the Stranger characterizes them, the standard materialists, that is, Leucippus and Democritus. And it is comparatively easy to get Theaetetus, who speaks for them, to concede that there are souls that are capable of wisdom and goodness. And he concedes (for them) further that these things are not as such sensible. The Stranger then elicits from the somewhat reformed giants agreement that a proper indication that something is *real* is that it is capable of *doing* or *undergoing* (if you please, affecting something or being affected by something). This constitutes a transition move in that those who take a thing or things having sensible features as *real* are now conceived as allowing soul and its features (which are imperceptible) as *real*. And they must, in so doing, allow that souls as changers and bodies as undergoers are both real.

The gods, the 'friends of the forms,' will not concede that doing and undergoing characterize what is real. Since they acknowledge only the eternal, unchanging forms, this is impossible for them. Indeed, they cannot even allow that there is knowledge of the forms, for this would allow them to be affected (that is, as *known*). At their reply, the Stranger bursts out (248E–49A) that theirs is a strange doctrine that cannot allow for change, life, soul, or knowledge in the universe, a universe that somehow exists, 'august and holy,' in its monolithic and unchanging splendour. What the Stranger wants, as he notes in allusion to a children's game, is *both*, that is, both the unchanging forms and also the entities necessary for change. And these are, in addition to the forms, soul and the physical world. To a reader who is familiar with the *Timaeus*, the World Animal comes to mind immediately. Here is recognition of the basic forms as the mind of the World Animal and, with the ensouled animal-world, the never-ending procession of the numbers and their informing of the Receiver (the *hypodoche*).

The Stranger's next move is again reminiscent of the *Parmenides*. He claims a need for forms of both Motion and Rest, where the *Parmenides'* formulae 'always in a different and always in the same' come to mind.

Thus, with soul and the physical world in place, it is entirely appropriate to call attention to the basic forms that provide the intelligible frame for the changes and restings from change that go on in the world. Though nothing is said in the *Sophist* context about changes occurring in a non-time (the 'all-of-a-sudden' of the Coda of the *Parmenides*), that sort of account is, I believe, assumed.

But the Stranger is on his way to the recognition that non-being *is*. To this end he needs to exhibit the interrelationships of what are here called the 'greatest forms,' namely, Being, Same, Different, Motion, and Rest. Here there is no talk of those forms 'having shares of' others, but rather of their 'blending' or their *koinonia* with one another. Thus, though they are *different* (that is, blend with Different) from one another, they all blend with Being and Same. In the course of exhibiting these interrelations, the Stranger speaks of what he is doing as *dialectic* and as *a* if not *the* proper task of the philosopher.

There is nothing in this set of arguments to suggest that what I take to be the three primary forms, namely, Being, Same, and Different, are to be construed as *genera*. As I have argued earlier (both in the discussion of the *Parmenides* and in that of the *Timaeus*), these are the ultimate forms that are responsible for the generation of the numbers and, as the basic ingredients of the mind of the World Animal, with the activity of its soul and the provision of the Receiver, the generators of the whole physical world. The recognition and articulation of the many genera/species trees comes with the systematic use of Collection and Division. And the presence of Being, Same, and Different in the human soul, together with perceptual experience, makes possible the articulate conceptual (and linguistic) life of human beings.

Different plays a special role and is, of course, the key to the problem of false belief. Although it does not play the role of a genus, it does have *parts*. Its parts, as we noticed in discussing the *Parmenides*, are each distinct from each and all of the other parts. And the parts are all of the form *different from X*, where X is replaceable by any term that may function as a subject or predicate. Thus, Different-from-Large, Different-from-Horse, and the like are parts of Different. The Stranger first attends to the special parts that belong with the greatest forms: thus Being is Different-from-Motion and Different-from-Same. Like other forms, various things may have shares of Different-from-X, whatever X may be. And, just as other of the greatest forms blend with Being, so also does Different and its parts. Thus Not-being (in the guise of Different) *is*.

The *Sophist* does not make the point, but I think it is worth noting that, in accordance with the Platonic construal of the supposition that 'one' *is*, one may legitimately say that Different *is* or even that Different has a share of Being. The use of the rather metaphorical *koinonia* or 'blending' can in principle be rescued from its metaphorical status. One suspects that, rather than get into the complications of the *Parmenides*, Plato in the *Sophist* was prepared to live with the metaphor. It might help, however, to have contentions of the *Parmenides* in mind while reading the Stranger's next comments, namely, those noting that, without the 'interweaving' (συμπλοκή) of the 'kinds' there would be no philosophical discourse and thus no philosophy. Indeed, the austere separation of things from one another would put us in a position like that of Parmenides without even the ability to say that something *is*.

The Stranger goes on to note (262A) that in discourse there are two kinds of terms: *names* (*onomata*, ὀνόματα) and *verbs* (*remata*, ῥήματα). These connect with one another, but more than one of each taken alone gives but a mere list. The point here is the same as that made by Aristotle in *On Interpretation* (also *Categories*), using the same metaphor of interweaving or intertwining. The Stranger follows up with offering a simple sentence consisting of a name and a verb, namely, 'Theaetetus sits,' and insisting that in order for this to be a proper sentence and thus true or false, the name must refer to something, in this case, Theaetetus. His test sentence for falsity is 'Theaetetus flies,' its falsity being assured by Theaetetus' having a share of Different from Flying. Indeed, it states something different from what obtains for Theaetetus, but what actually obtains, namely, Different from Flying, is not non-being, but rather a part of Different.

As I have noted several times in connection with the interpretation of the second part of the *Parmenides*, the treatment of the *others* was uniformly as non-*ones* or, more generally, as non-*X's*. I took this to be proper whether discussing the consequences for the one in relation to the others or discussing the consequences for the others. I also took a similar line in the interpretation of the supposition that *one is not*, thus construing the negative predicate as non-*F*, thus as a negative *term*. In all of this my guide was the *Sophist* treatment of Different. Given the interpretative success of this clue for understanding various parts of the *Parmenides*, I assume that Plato was in possession of this mode of handling the problem of non-being at the time of writing the *Parmenides*, though he may not have seriously considered its application to the problem of false belief at that time.

Given what I had to say about Plato's gratitude to Parmenides for the insistence of the need for the eternal forms and for the trenchant procedure of suppositions, it should be clear that Plato's generous comments about

168   The *Parmenides* and Plato's Late Philosophy

Parmenides in the early part of the *Sophist* can be taken seriously. Although the Eleatic Stranger, acting as Plato's spokesman, commits intellectual 'parricide,' the debt to Parmenides remains.

11

The *Philebus*

I have argued earlier that it is plausible to think that Plato's choice of protagonist for the *Parmenides*, the *Sophist*, and the *Statesman* signalizes a marked change in his thought, and that change has by now been appropriately explained. We come now, however, to what has been commonly taken to be an even later dialogue, and once again Socrates is the protagonist. Does this signalize a return to an earlier pattern of thought? I don't think so. I do think that the subject matter of the *Philebus*, namely, the choiceworthy life for a human being, is so appropriate for Plato's Socrates and is so much a sophisticated treatment of earlier Socratic themes that the choice of Socrates seems appropriate enough. It is even possible that the dialogue was intended to complement the Lecture on the Good, thus giving dialogic and lively form to a reportedly austere doctrine. Indeed, a major theme of the *Philebus* is that the life of pure intellect alone is an unsatisfactory one for a human being.

Nowhere in the earlier dialogues, even in Plato's masterful *Gorgias*, is there a serious effort to explain and justify the major features of the good (and thus choiceworthy) life of a human being. The earlier efforts were either justification of the vocation of Socrates, attacks on pleasure and pleasurable indulgence, or the special features of the life of the *Republic*'s guardians. The *Philebus* is the only dialogue in which Plato provides sufficient detail for a reader to understand how s/he might live and be satisfied with a life according to Platonist principles. Though the dialogue is replete with later Platonic metaphysics and is cast in the form of a contest with hedonism, its vision of a choiceworthy life for a human being is appropriate to the high moral purpose commonly attributed to the historical Socrates.

There is no historical context for the dramatis personae of the dialogue, though there is considerable context for the issue(s) under discussion. The ongoing question of the dialogue is: Is pleasure or mind (perhaps better, mind*ing*) the chief, if not the sole, good in a human life? At the commencement of the dialogue, Philebus, who is so totally committed to pleasure that he does not think the matter worth discussion, turns the argument over to Protarchus, a less unreasonable partisan of pleasure. Early on in the argument it is agreed that, should neither turn out to be the good for a human being, the matter of second and third place should be worked out.

In that connection, Socrates asks Protagoras if he would be willing to spend his life completely absorbed in pleasure and completely free from mind(ing), and Protarchus readily agrees. Socrates then astonishes him with noting that, without mind(ing), he would have no memory, anticipation, or even (present) awareness of the pleasure he (somehow) has. In addition to Protarchus' astonishment it is worth noting that there is a strong suggestion, if not the implication, that Plato takes mind in some form or other as the source of human consciousness, indeed, its very nature. Given a number of Platonic claims in this and other dialogues, it would seem that some sort of conceptualization or, if you please, proto-conceptualization is required for consciousness of anything. It is clear enough from the claim that Socrates makes as against Protarchus and Philebus that he is thinking of mind in very comprehensive terms indeed: he includes perception, thought, opinion, knowledge, memory, recollection, and probably more. And it is impossible not to keep in mind that in the *Theaetetus* we are told that it is the *soul* that perceives, using the sense organs and, as well, its own innate concepts, namely, Being, Same, Different, etc.

The dialogue moves to species of pleasure in order to get Protarchus to recognize that one species may be 'opposed to' another in the way that one colour may be 'opposed to' another, and it promises the same for mind(ing), though Socrates does not really concede the *opposition* of mindings to one another. In order to make it quite clear to Protarchus that pleasure may be many in some more important sense than that in which a man may be both one (as one man) and many (as having parts), Socrates turns to Plato's clearest statement of the procedure of Collection and Division. He describes it both as a 'road' that has often escaped him and also as the procedure responsible for significant discoveries or justifications in the *aretai* (crafts, but here used in the sense of the significant arts of civilization). It is actually a procedure for arriving at useful definitions.

The notion that there is a more important one/many problem than that of a man's being one out of many and many as containing parts is a clear allusion to Socrates' reply to Zeno in the *Parmenides*. It is obvious that we are getting into a matter concerning genera and species, but it is not clear what the status of genera and species may be. The temptation is to take them to be the immutable Platonic forms of the middle dialogues. This will not do, and I have given reasons for saying this in earlier chapters, in particular chapter 10. Nor will it do to say that they are *mere* hypostatizations of conventional linguistic usages, though I am prepared to claim that they are, in a way, entities by convention. My point is that the conventions that support them arise from human perception where perception is an activity of the soul using both the sense organs and also the soul's innate conceptual abilities. Given time and appropriate social organization, linguistic conventions have a reasonably strong claim to represent fairly well the mathematically informed physical world of nature.

Socrates begins by stating that, whatever it is you are seeking to define, you must first find a *one* that includes it. And he assures us that you can always find such a one, an assurance based (I believe) on the resources of the language. Having found it, you must determine what parts that one can divide into. Then you must select one of those parts and divide again, eventually coming down to what you were seeking to define. You must be sure that you have left no steps out and that you end by being able to say just 'how many' the one you started with is before you cease the process of Division, giving up in favour of the 'boundless' (*apeiron*) number of 'particulars.' This description is clearly a precursor of Aristotle's treatment of definition and its role in (what Aristotle takes as) *episteme* (knowledge, science) in *Posterior Analytics* II. Without getting into Aristotle's critique of it, I think it can be correctly noted that Plato's procedure serves a similar purpose. To develop a genera/species tree (alternatively, to find out 'how many' something is) is to provide oneself with a means of explanation. Such explanation is, of course, definitory and uses the apparatus of genus and differentiai (though Plato makes no formal mention of differentiai).

The detailed Division used in the Eleatic Stranger's definition of sophistry in the *Sophist* should provide an appropriate illustration of the procedure of Division. *Craft* or *Art* is the chosen *one* for the Division. *Craft* is divided into *Acquisitive* and *Productive*. *Productive Craft* is divided into *Divine* and *Human*. *Human Productive Craft* is divided into *Likeness-making* and *Semblance-making*. *Semblance-making Human Productive Craft* is divided into *Making with Tools* and *Making by Mimicry*. *Semblance-making by Mimicry Human Productive Craft* admits of Division into what is done with *Knowledge* and what is done in *Ignorance*. *Semblance-making in Ignorance and by Mimicry Human Productive Craft* divides into *Sincere* and *Insincere*. Finally, *Insincere Semblance-Making in Ignorance and by Mimicry Human Productive Craft* is practiced on the one hand by demagogic politicians and on the other by Sophists. The *Sophist* ends with the Stranger declaring, 'The art of contradiction-making, descended from an insincere kind of conceited mimicry, of the semblance-making breed, derived from image-making, distinguished as a portion, not divine but human, of production, that presents a shadow-play of words – such is the blood and lineage which can, with perfect truth, be assigned to the authentic Sophist' (268C–D, Cornford translation).

The presumption is that the Stranger's Division tells us just *how many* Sophistry is and thus provides an appropriate genera/species tree. The tree can 'explain' how it is that the Sophist is prone to speaking falsely: His craft is one producing in ignorance. The Sophist is also persuasive because he is skilled at semblance-making. And so on.

Since one may have a true belief that the Sophist is persuasive, s/he would have knowledge only if s/he had control of the genera/species tree or definition. Put in this manner, the account looks very much like the sort of account that Socrates and Theaetetus were seeking in the last part of the *Theaetetus*. And I think that Plato intended it to look this way when he wrote the *Sophist* as a sequel to the *Theaetetus*, though the *Sophist* does not explicitly say so. It is worthy of note as well that in introducing the Collection and Division passage in the *Philebus*, Socrates remarks that the procedure is a significant discovery and provides a path of enquiry that in the past has often eluded him. Certainly the criticism offered by *Parmenides* at the end of the first part of the Parmenides to the effect that Socrates has attempted definitions 'too soon' before having proper 'exercise' comes to mind. So also does the aporetic conclusion of the *Theaetetus*.

Even so, it may well be objected that the above-mentioned criticism of Parmenides refers to Socrates' attempts to define *forms* and goes on to express pleasure that Socrates would not allow the critique of Zeno 'to wander in and among the visibles but rather kept it to those which one grasps by argument and takes to be forms' (135D). It would therefore seem that allusion to this passage damages my claim that Collection and Division is not as such about Platonic forms. At least the start of a reply to this objection is to point out that the objects of enquiry by Collection and Division on my view are definitely not *visibles*. They are, rather, conceptual entities, perhaps best thought of as *surrogate forms*. They do indeed have a basis in the numbers that constitute the physical world and, of course, an ultimate basis in the fundamental forms. Those bases show rather clearly in the distinction that Socrates makes towards the end of the

Philebus, the distinction between the mathematics of various craftspersons and the mathematics of philosophers (56D3–57A4). Even Socrates' respected carpenters with all their measuring equipment produce at best imprecise likenesses of the mathematics of philosophers. A continuation of a reply might well point out that 'what one grasps by argument and takes to be forms' does not as such require that the surrogate forms of Collection and Division be the fundamental forms. Indeed, this is consistent with treating the surrogate forms as having a basis in the mathematical world and, ultimately, the basic forms. And, of course, it may well be that the Plato of the *Parmenides*, insightful as he is, had not yet taken Collection and Division as seriously as he did later on, when he came to the insights of the *Sophist* and the *Philebus*.

Once again I must say that the several claims of this book do not depend upon a small number of decisive texts (though some are rather decisive) but rather upon a doctrinal web drawn from texts woven from a number of late dialogues along with some texts of Aristotle. And those claims allege that the web explains the drift of Plato's thought and methodology at least from Books VI and VII of the *Republic* through the *Philebus*.

The assurance of there being a 'one' in each case is initially somewhat puzzling. We have, however, seen in the *Sophist* and the *Statesman* numerous examples of the Eleatic Stranger's finding 'ones' from which to make his divisions. In those dialogues many of the 'ones' as well as the divisions look almost frivolous and certainly metaphorical. As I have noted earlier, the possibility of finding 'ones' and making divisions appears to lie in the language and its related conceptual structure. Given an appropriately articulated language and a competent user, the 'ones' can be found and the divisions made. Does this make the procedure a 'merely linguistic' matter? Hardly, for the language has been formed over a long time, and it distils the widely variegated experience of many individuals. And, of course, it is being *used*, not mentioned. Finally, the language being used would seem to be a distillation of the variegated experience of individual souls making use of the innate ideas of the *Theaetetus* passage, and, of course, refining that usage.

Interestingly, the *Philebus* goes on to refer to some remarkable examples of Collection (*synagoge*). Socrates speaks of an Egyptian who first separated out from the boundless human sounds the several vowels and consonants. It is impossible to see how this could be done unless that Egyptian's soul had some general conceptual means of recognizing Sameness and Difference in a very large (indeed, in principle, unlimited) number of perceptions. It seems clear enough that Theaetetus' list of the innate conceptual abilities of the soul plays no small role in the late Platonic epistemological picture. Indeed, it must have been in Plato's mind ultimately responsible for all of the conceptual roles played by the descriptive terms of viable languages. These include not only the terms that have an obvious sense aetiology like those for colours, sounds, etc. but also sense-related arithmetic and geometric terms. But we need a little more exploration of the *Philebus* before we can do justice to these.

The *Philebus* is famous for a set of distinctions that have proved puzzling and difficult to relate to distinctions made in earlier Platonic dialogues. These are the distinctions between the Unlimited (*apeiron*), the Limit (*peras*), the Mixture (*miktos*) of the two, and the Cause (*aitia*) of the Mixture. Here the Unlimited is treated as whatever admits of more or less, in practice including all of the sensibles (as having in themselves no metric). The discussion of the Unlimited is reminiscent of the *Timaeus* treatment of the universe 'before' the demiurge has mathematized it. The limit is as such given no general characterization but the examples make it clear that what is involved is *number* in the broad sense that we have encountered before, notably, in the *Parmenides*. This, of course, includes ratio, proportion, and the like. It would seem, then, that the *Philebus* is making a similar point to one made in the *Timaeus*.

Mixture is, of course, the product of the joining of Limit and Unlimited with mind (or minding, *nous*) as the Cause of the Mixture. With all of this we are clearly in Pythagorean territory. And I think that we find Plato prepared to make a rather remarkable (and Pythagorean) simplification of the ontology of the *Timaeus*. The simplification consists in doing away with the Receiver. Negative evidence for this is the fact that there is no mention or even a hint of the Receiver in the *Philebus*, though there are several places in which mention of it would be relevant.

It will be remembered that the *Timaeus* needed the Receiver to 'make room for' the individualized numbers generated from the eternal numbers produced by the nature of the world soul – thus bringing about the world of space and time. It (the Receiver) was treated as featureless, having no nature of its own, and not derived from anything. In the *Timaeus* account, it is, as it were, a third 'form' (*eidos*) in addition to Being and Coming to Be. It will also be remembered that there seems to be no obvious place for sensibles in the *Timaeus* except as caused by the 'outside' world's impinging on the bodily senses. It is a bit strange that the *Philebus* gives the sensibles little attention even when invoking a doctrine of perception in the midst of to the discussion of 'true and false' pleasures (cf. 38C ff.).

Interestingly, the characterization of the Unlimited in the *Philebus* corresponds with Plato's earlier characterizations of sensibles, that is, as those admitting the more and less. What I want to suggest here is that the *Philebus* simplifies the *Timaeus* doctrine in taking the Mixture as doing the work of the Receiver *and* the more or less unexplained sensibles. Plato here takes the entire physical universe as made up of the Mixture. Obviously the mathematized Unlimited encountered in perception has impinged upon the percipient's body (also made up of the Mixture). The soul maintains the nature given it in the *Timaeus* (that is, Being, Same, and Different) and thus perceives or misperceives in a manner depending upon its situation. Finally, traces of an impingement remain for imagination and memory, as the *Philebus* account of perception requires and we shall duly note shortly.

All of this comports well with the Pythagorean tradition of a distinction between 'sensible numbers' and 'intelligible numbers.' And it comports well with the claim that the former 'imitate' (mimeomai, $\mu\iota\mu\acute{\epsilon}o\mu\alpha\iota$) the latter, that is, act in the latters' stead. It also fits with Aristotle's negative claim in the *Metaphysics* that Plato's doctrine of participation (*methexis*) is no improvement over the Pythagorean doctrine of imitation (*mimesis*).

On a cosmic scale, mind (*nous*) or the soul of the *Timaeus* World Animal produces the numbers and, in turn, the best imitation of the numbers in the combination with the Unlimited, thus accounting for the movement of the heavens and the other regularities of nature. And individual human souls, with a nature akin to the world soul, manage with greater or less ability to bring harmony and measure into their lives and tidiness into the various craft performances.

Plato probably intends for there to be a related ambiguity in the notion of the Cause of the Mixture. Clearly he takes Philebus' *pleasure* to belong to the Unlimited and his *mind(ing)* to be or belong to the Cause of the Mixture. Thus, in talking of the major ingredients in the well-lived human life, these are taken to be such ingredients. Equally there is taken to be an Unlimited and a Limit as well as a Cause on a cosmic scale, though, as noted above, it is difficult to find a place for the Unlimited except as that which, in its own nature, is always more or less and nothing definite. It could then be related to Plato's critique in the *Timaeus* of his predecessors, who took the basic features of the world to be sensibles, that is, the unlimited sensibles taken, as it were, on a wholesale scale (*Timaeus* 51B-D).

As I noted earlier, Kenneth Sayre's *Plato's Late Ontology* does a scholarly and imaginative job of explaining Plato's shift from the ontology of the middle dialogues to the Pythagorean ontology of the *Philebus*. After fairly extensive commentary on the *Parmenides* as a start towards explaining Plato's shift, Sayre continues with an extensive review of the literature concerning Plato's lost lecture on the Good, relying heavily on Aristotle's testimony for Plato's shift to Pythagoreanism in *Metaphysics* A. Sayre emphasizes in particular the testimony for Plato's distinction between the *one* and the *great-and-small* for the derivation of the forms, and he takes that derivation to obtain for Plato in the *Philebus* (though Plato himself makes no such claim) by way of the Limit/Unlimited distinction.

Sayre clearly disagrees with my assimilation of the 'Promethean discovery' to the Collection and Division of the *Sophist* and the *Statesman*, for he notes that the Philebus discovery makes serious use of the Unlimited (*apeiron*) whereas the earlier ones do not. This is surely correct, but I think that it mislocates the issue. First, there is good reason for Plato to have Socrates 'discovering' Collection and Division, for that procedure was clearly identified with the Eleatic Stranger after only a token appearance of Socrates (in the *Sophist*). Socrates reappears as the protagonist in the *Philebus* where the only build-up for that reappearance has been the promise of the *Parmenides* that Socrates will do better at defining only after serious 'exercise.' Second, the *Philebus* clearly distinguishes two sorts of *knowledge*, one of which is *of* eternal things and the other *of* physical things. Examples of the latter include medicine, music, and practical arithmetic, the first two of which are given as examples of the 'Promethean' procedure. Third, Sayre follows Gosling in revising the Oxford text at 16D2 from 'for you will find it is there' to 'if one is there you will find it' (121). The reading is strained. What motivates it is the understandable belief that staying with the Oxford text is tantamount to legislating to nature. As we have seen, it is my belief that the terms of a rich language that has proved its 'objectivity' (as it were) embody a genus/species structure. We are, however, speaking of a language in use and thus of the semantic reference of the relevant terms – what I have called 'surrogate forms.' Fourth, throughout his book, Sayre treats soul as conscious of various things (forms, sensibles) without any sort of conceptual or representational vehicle. This makes it difficult, if not impossible, to account for learning – indeed, to account for Plato's consistent use of relational ('*pros*') terms for perception and knowledge.

Interestingly, after putting pleasure in the Unlimited, Plato points out that pleasure arises in human beings only as a result of the Mixture. Since, in earlier accounts of perception (for example, in the *Theaetetus*), Plato puts pleasure among the sensibles, he is very likely taking it to be on a par with (sensed) colours, sounds, etc. (These would have to be so-called 'physical' pleasures and not those of the soul alone. But of these latter more shortly.) I presume that it is said to arise from the Mixture because of its connection with the body, and this would parallel the connection of sensed colour with external objects of sight. Indeed, it is in this context that Socrates links physical pain with imbalance or disharmony in the body and physical pleasure with appropriate return to balance or harmony. Bodily pleasure and pain are as sensibles used as means of the soul's awareness of bodily changes. Later he notes that a great many such changes occur that do not reach the soul and thus are not felt as either pleasures or pains.

We are now ready for some of the most worked-over pages in all of Plato's works, namely, those dealing with so-called 'false' pleasures. We are introduced to them by Protarchus' noting that pleasures (and pains) of anticipation are those of the soul only, for they may occur when no relevant body change is going on, indeed, when the body condition is producing an 'opposite.' Such pleasures, it is quickly pointed out, seem to require that there is no such thing as bodily desire, for desire is for a bodily condition different from if not opposite to a relevantly present bodily condition. (A parallel comment, *mutatis mutandis*, concerning aversion seems appropriate as well.) Desire is thus treated as an anticipatory pleasure. Before getting seriously into false pleasures, however, Socrates turns to some animadversions on perception, memory, and recall (recollection).

What he says is that, when one perceives something, there comes to be a bodily trace that remains after the perception. When one *remembers*, that bodily trace is somehow activated, whether called up by some association or by the perception of the same or a similar thing. When one *recalls* (or recollects), the soul deliberately calls up the memory trace and may combine memory traces in a variety of ways. Plato seems to use the term in such a way that recall or recollection does much of the job of what we should think of as imagination, so that one may recall (recollect) things that never happened and imagine things that will not occur or are unlikely to occur in the future.

He goes on to cite an example of mistaken perception, that is, taking an object seen at a distance for some other thing than what it actually is. Presumably, in this sort of case the mistake lingers in memory and may (or will?) even be verbalized (whether internally or said out loud). And Plato suggests that it is as though there were a scribe in the soul writing down the words and, as well, a painter who gives graphic illustration to the words. So a false perception may linger in memory *and* imagination. At least part of what Plato wishes to show in all of this is that a blurred sense presentation may lead to incorrect conception, thus a false perception and false belief. But this is embedded in a section of the dialogue that is attempting to show that there can be false pleasures. How is this possible?

Plato seems in the passage to be claiming that, even as seeing something at a distance may be or lead to a false perception, so the pleasure of imagining something may, through an analogy to spatial distance, be a false pleasure. Remembering that desire is the pleasant anticipation of something, we may think that Plato has it in mind that we may rather easily be misled by the proximity of what is anticipated and/or by its being a manifest pleasure boon. Even as one may have a false fear due to the proximity of what is anticipated and/or by its manifest fearfulness. What seems to induce false pleasures or false fears is the undue influence of desires and aversions in favour of their satisfaction. Their victim is a victim of an overweening desire or aversion that prevents rational deliberation and choice. In the fear case, there is no bear, burglar, or whatever. In the pleasure case, there will be no lottery win, or whatever. In both cases the person involved allows his/her passions to subvert rational abilities and has done so, as it were, intentionally. In Kantian terms (though without Kant's context) s/he has a bad will or, at least, an irrational one. And this is probably why Plato (in this context) treats him/her as not beloved by the gods. In the simple case of misperception produced by distance there is simple mistake, not the expression of an undisciplined will.

So much for false pleasures of anticipation. After arguing that pleasure cannot be reduced to absence of pain, Plato goes on to consider the possibility of true pleasures. Oddly he does not explicitly consider the possibility of true pleasures of anticipation, though he does not rule out the possibility that those beloved by the gods do actually have such true pleasures. Indeed, it is difficult to see how in the manifold choices of everyday matters, a good person could in Plato's view fail to have the motivation of measured and restrained anticipatory pleasures. But, as we shall shortly see, this may need some qualification in the light of pleasure's not being, as a 'becoming,' unqualifiedly choiceworthy.

Socrates takes it for granted that the peculiar pleasure of knowing (both coming to know and exercising the ability) is a 'pure' and thus true pleasure. Moving to the pure pleasures of perception, he says a number of things that are strange sounding to modern ears at least. Here the pleasure involved is linked with *beauty*. And the beauty he has in mind is that of items that are not beautiful relative to anything else. He starts with things having simple geometric shapes, the presumption being that these are not relative to (*pros ti*) any other shapes. Ensembles of shapes, however, would seem to have their beauty only relative to other such ensembles. At any rate, they would admit of comparison with other ensembles.

When he moves to colours, sounds, etc., he is at pains to make it clear that he is not talking about the intensity but rather of the purity of the beauty and thus the pleasure. The example that he dwells on most is that of pure white colour. To understand what Socrates has in mind I think that we must have in mind his concept of colour (cf. *Timaeus* 67E ff.), which appears to take white (bright?) as the one colour that is not an admixture of any sort. And I think we are not dealing with the physical causes of colour sensation but with the sensation itself. And, of course, we are not dealing with a modern conception of the colour spectrum or with photon transmission of the physical colours. We are, I believe, dealing with a conception that has white (or white/bright) at one end and a variety of admixtures going down to black (or black/dark) at the other end. This would make the colours other than pure white *relatives* (to one another) and thus failing in purity. My comments here are somewhat speculative, and I cannot make a relevantly related case for 'pure' tones or odours.[1] Plato makes no case for tones' dependence upon the variants of pitch, timbre, and overtones, nor does he make a relevant case for odours. These are simply treated as sensations the lack of which is not at all painful. He does, however, come back a second time to the colour case as though it were a better paradigm than the others for the sensation sort of 'true' pleasures.

The discussion of mixed emotions evokes the attack on tragedy in Book X of the *Republic*, but it is not limited to the theatre and audience response. Assuming that Plato takes the emotions as springs to action along with appropriate feelings, it is tempting to think of the emotions as varieties of desire (pleasurable anticipations) and aversion (painful anticipations). Just how Plato justifies taking some of them to be pains and others to be pleasures is left fairly unclear, but it is clear that Plato finds the mixed emotions to be unsatisfactory components of a well-lived life and based in large part on lack of self-knowledge.

Rather artificially placed in the treatment of pure and impure pleasures is what appears to be a bad argument, though Plato says that he got it from someone else. It is rather simple. It is noted that pleasure of whatever sort is a *becoming* (a *genesis*, a coming-to-be). As such it must always or ultimately be for the sake of something else, to wit, something that *is*. So it cannot be the good (for a human being), for that good, as such, is sufficient and complete. But it was agreed much earlier in the dialogue that neither pleasure nor mind(ing) is the good for a human being, and it has not been claimed or shown that at least some pleasures fail to be goods (though not *the* good). Nor has it been shown that some pleasures may not come to be for the sake of yet other pleasures. There is, further, no guarantee that whatever a pleasure may be for the sake of in a human life it will have the sort of permanence that Plato usually associates with *being*, for the concern is with a human life. Even so, there is nothing to prevent an impermanent condition of the soul from being something for the sake of which something else occurs or is done and that provides a full stop.

The argument proceeds by moving to the mind(ing)s to test *them* for purity even as the pleasures have been tested. Socrates first notes that, if arithmetic, measurement, and weighing were taken from the several crafts (arts, *aretai*), nothing would be left except 'empirical' association, routine practice, and guesswork. And he cites music, medicine, agriculture, and the arts of the ship pilot and general as having relatively small shares in the use of mathematics. But then he turns to building, his model craft for the use of mensuration. Here the use of various instruments for measurement gives building the greatest accuracy among the practical crafts. Even so, Socrates is immediately moved to distinguish between arithmetic and geometry used in building and kindred practical crafts and the arithmetic and geometry of the philosopher. As he puts it, the former work with 'unequal units,' the latter strictly with units that differ in no way or degree from one another. Unfortunately, Socrates talks of unequal units in terms of armies and oxen and is not specific about the building craft in which there is some inexactness due to observation and imperfection of instruments. Even so, the distinction Socrates is making should be clear from our earlier discussion of the foundations of arithmetic and geometry in the *Parmenides*.

'Pure' arithmetic and geometry in the *Parmenides* flow from the duality of the 'one-being' with the addition of Same and Different. What is adumbrated there is a fairly elaborate combinatorics with purely theoretical 'units.' There is in it no hint of their use in any sort of practical affairs, though in later parts of the second supposition as well as other suppositions that sort of use is clearly indicated. As the *Theaetetus* passage concerning the soul's seeing using the eyes *and* the innate concepts of the soul itself indicates, *number* (as among those innate concepts) makes at least elementary numbering a natural feature of our perceptual judgments. Such judgments as such do not, of course, give their makers any insight into the intellectual foundations of arithmetic, though they may be and commonly are the beginnings of the arithmetic (and geometry) of the practical arts.

Socrates is then moved to include 'the power of dialectic' among the pure and exact forms of mind(ing). Given its concern with *being*, the *'real'* (the 'truth'), and what is eternal and unmixed by nature, it is described as 'the truest knowledge.' Beyond this sort of description of dialectic's objects no further comment is made about it. I am inclined to think that the characterization of dialectic that was noted in the *Sophist* chapter obtains here. It is the working out of the interrelations of the 'greatest kinds' that is demonstrated in the *Sophist*. Given the scheme that anchors intelligibility in the greatest kinds, proceeds to the intelligible mathematicals, then, in combination with the Unlimited produces the physical world, and finally allows for sense apprehension on the part of finite ensouled bodies, it matters little whether we speak of 'lesser kinds' or of intelligible mathematicals. It matters only if we are worried about what sort of derivation the lesser kinds have from the greatest forms. Here the use of the intelligible mathematicals and *their* derivatives, the physical mathematicals, gives us a clear route. And we can clearly note the ways in which the post-*Parmenides* Plato is and is not like the early and middle Plato.

Before we turn to the conclusion of the *Philebus*, it may be worth alluding to two matters that came up earlier in the dialogue. First, Socrates gets Protarchus explicitly to acknowledge that the earth, air, fire, and water of our bodies have their source in the vast quantities of each that are in the universe and to acknowledge that our souls also derive from a plentiful source in the universe. No account is given of how these transactions or transfers have occurred. Though it is strange to give individual souls treatment paralleling the acquisition of bodily stuffs, it seems clear enough that Socrates is thinking of individual souls as like or kin to the world soul. And one is reminded of the *Timaeus* story of the ingredients (Being, Same, and Different) of the world soul and the same but inferior ingredients of individual human souls. Second, Protarchus in an earlier section readily acknowledges – indeed, insists – that the universe is not only well governed, it is governed as well as it could be. And this comports with statements made elsewhere by Plato as well as with the *Timaeus* image of the World Animal and the *Sophist* claim that intelligence (nous) is the active heart of things.

The first stage of the dialogue's finale personifies the mind(ings) and the pleasures, asking each to determine which of the others it prefers to be joined with. And, of course, the pleasures want all of the mind(ings) – at least partially for the reason given early in the dialogue, namely, that pleasure without consciousness is quite unsatisfactory. The mind(ings), however, will accept only the pure or true pleasures, finding the others simply to be nuisances and hindrances. With this result we are, says Socrates, on the road to the good for a human being. It therefore remains to follow the road.

The first move is to provide a certification for the mixture of mind(ings) and pleasures gotten through the consent of the personifications of each.

To this end Socrates speaks of truth (*aletheia*), proportion (*summetria*), and the fine (*kalon*) as necessary features of any such mixture that is to be both genuine and enduring. Truth seems to require that there can actually be such a psychological mixture, though Protarchus' remarks about the deceptions of pleasure suggest that integrity is required for the endurance of any such mixture. Then it is claimed that proportion is requisite for any mixture to endure. Without it some part may destroy the mixture by dominating it. The 'fine' is a little tricky. *Kalon* is a term that, depending upon context, may be translated as 'noble,' 'honourable,' 'beautiful,' or 'fine.' Its standard opposite, however, gives the chief clue to its inclusion. That opposite is *aischron* – the 'dishonourable,' 'shameful,' or 'disreputable.' Since allowing the opposite of the fine in any mixture that purports to be the good for a human being would be quite unacceptable, the reason for the inclusion of the *kalon* seems clear enough. Socrates in context asks for the inclusion of all three as though they were one, and obviously regards the three as necessary and sufficient conditions for any enduring mixture of psychological components that purports to be the good for a human being.

This much done, Socrates proceeds to list the factors in the good life in order of their importance. He puts measure (*metron*), moderation (*metrion*), and the opportune time (*kairos*) as first. Whoever uses them must possess the ability to calculate factors in a situation, to avoid extreme or precipitate action or undue emotion, and to seize or wait for the appropriate time to act. These would indeed seem to be the most important general abilities one must possess in order to live well and thus produce the human good.

Second he puts proportion (*summetron*), the fine (*kalon*), the completed (*teleon*), and the sufficient (*hikanon*) 'and all others of that kind.' Earlier in the dialogue Socrates and Protarchus have agreed that, whatever the good for man should be, it must be *complete* and *sufficient*. It cannot be lacking in anything (or, at any rate, anything important). Just what proportion consists in is a bit unclear. My guess is that Plato is thinking that the good for a human being must include a suitably proportioned set of concerns and activities. It must balance civic, family, and other responsibilities appropriately. The second appearance of *kalon* has, I believe, the same rationale as the first. There must be nothing dishonourable or shameful in the good life for a human being. There is as well the overtone of Beauty. The life of a good person can appropriately be thought of as beautiful. Finally, it would seem that the *completeness* and *sufficiency* requirements must be such that, even if a life should be cut off prematurely, it could be thought of as meeting them.

In the third place Plato puts mind (*nous*) and (practical) wisdom (*phronesis*). The list is a bit curious in that the first two list ingredients or features of the well-lived life, and this third (and, as we shall shortly note, the fourth) refers to the abilities needed to bring about the first two. Earlier, it will be recalled, mind in the fourfold classification was listed as the Cause of the Mixture of Limit and Unlimited. Plato does not at the present point refer to the fourfold classification, but it seems clear enough that the first two ingredients either are or require a good mixture of Limit and Unlimited. So mind and (practical) wisdom are still being thought of as cause of the well-lived life. I have put parentheses around 'practical' in connection with *phronesis*. The reason is that the fourth place is given to the whole set of what we should regard as practical abilities. Putting *nous* and *phronesis* in the third place strongly suggests an honorific role for each. Here reside the abilities to do philosophical arithmetic and geometry and to practice dialectic. The person who possesses only the abilities listed in the fourth place and lacks these in the third, though s/he may live reasonably well, would seem to be living an incomplete and insufficient version of the good life for a human being.

Listed fourth are the sciences (*epistemai*), crafts (*technai*), right opinions (*doxai orthai*). These would seem to be those making use of Collection and Division, the crafts learned through apprenticeships (including the useful mathematics of the builders), and the exercise of common sense. As noted earlier, what is envisioned in the dialogue is the good life for human beings who must cope with the necessities of providing for life in the sublunary physical world. Once more there is in the dialogue the suggestion that Collection and Division presuppose rather than get at the order of the eternal rational entities.

As expected, the painless and pure pleasures come in fifth. And there is no place at all made for false and mixed pleasures. Though there is mention of the pleasure of intellectual activity, it is a bit strange that Plato in the dialogue makes no mention of *eudaimonia*, the special sense of satisfaction that Plato gives to his guardians in the *Republic* and that Aristotle treats as the accompaniment of virtuous activity.

Given the initial format of the *Philebus*, that of a contest between pleasure and mind(ing), it is easy to reach the end of the dialogue and miss its serious significance. There simply is no other dialogue in which the good life for a human being is described and explained. And this description was written after and against the backdrop of the great period of Plato's mature epistemology and metaphysics. The choiceworthy life obviously includes the ability to use the results of Collection and Division, calculative abilities,

184   The *Parmenides* and Plato's Late Philosophy

preference for order and tidiness, avoidance of disruptive pleasures, and what is most important, recognition that such abilities and choices are grounded in the great order of things. What is at stake here is not simply morality or enlightened self-interest. It is, rather, the recognition and acceptance of one's place in the great scheme of rationality and its complement, beauty or nobility.

Afterword

The eleven interpretative chapters of this book are at once an effort to explain the text of the *Parmenides* and an effort to provide plausible linkage of that explanation with the texts of other important late dialogues. It is difficult not to believe that Plato himself intended the linkage. First, the start of the *Parmenides* is clearly linked with the *Republic* in that Glaucon and Adeimantus are given the role of greeters of the party from Clazomenae. And, of course, the setting of the *Timaeus* just as clearly links that dialogue with the *Republic*. Second, the favourable references to Parmenides obviously link the *Theaetetus* and the *Sophist* to the *Parmenides*. That the meeting of Socrates and Parmenides is the invention of Plato makes the references all the more significant. In all likelihood Plato intended the readers of the *Theaetetus* and the *Sophist* to have the *Parmenides* in mind while attending to the claims and arguments of both dialogues. Third, though the linkage with the *Philebus* is less obvious, the 'fit' of the two dialogues is remarkable.

If any image dominates the mature philosophy of Plato, it is the *Timaeus*' image of the World Animal. In order fully to understand that Plato really does think of the entire world as a living, ensouled, rational, and everlasting body, one must shed preconceptions of mechanism and/or deism. And one must recognize that Plato takes quite seriously the dictum that nothing comes from nothing. One must understand as well that the fundamental forms (Being, Same, Different), thought of as the mind of the ensouled World Animal, are capable (in the manner exfoliated by the generation of the numbers section of the second supposition of the *Parmenides*) of constantly generating the eternal numbers. Think of the eternal numbers as mixed with the Unlimited and thus generating the world of space and time. Add the requirement of limitation in space and time and the assumption of the best (that is, the most intelligible), and one has, in brief, the universe of the mature Plato.

When, after the so-called gods of the *Sophist* refuse to accept the Eleatic Stranger's mark of the 'real,' and the Stranger impatiently demands that life and soul be importantly in the 'all,' what can Plato have in mind if not the World Animal of the *Timaeus*? When Socrates in the *Philebus* gets Protarchus to agree that the earth, air, fire, water, and soul in human beings are all tiny in compariston with those of the whole and that they are all derived from the whole, what does he have in mind if not the World Animal of the *Timaeus*?

For epistemologically minded moderns there may well be the complaint that 'sensibles' (however construed) have not been given their proper place in my account of the mature Plato. To this I must reply as I did in the commentaries, namely, by noting the role Plato gives them in perception with the provision that they be used by the soul only in conjunction with the soul's innate concepts. And by noting that, in the absence of the soul's explicit consciousness of the forms, they play a critical part in the activity of Collection and Division. To this I must add a possible clarification that I did not make in the commentary. Plato's epistemological ontology in this connection is in effect the same as that of Wilfrid Sellars in making the distinction between the 'manifest image' and the 'scientific image.' We cannot, of course, get out of the manifest image (that is, sensations), but it would be a mistake to take the deliverances of sense as more that *indicative* of the real order of the world.

I must also note that the picture I have drawn of the mature Plato, with its very heavy emphasis on the mathematical ground and character of the whole universe, justifies Aristotle's (in *Metaphysics* A) calling Plato a Pythagorean and makes it plausible that Plato's successor in the Academy, Speusippus, is being faithful to the mature Plato in making mathematics the key to philosophical understanding. That the issue of mathematics in the Academy after Plato's death was a major controversy is quite clear from Aristotle's *Metaphysics* M and N (and elsewhere).

Though he does display eclectic tendencies, the great astronomer/geographer, Ptolemy, in his best-known work does make use of major features of the mathematical Platonism that I have been describing. The *Almagest* assumes that the 'fixed stars' travel together in their circumscribing sphere, that the earth is at the centre, that the several planets travel in circles, each with uniform velocity, and that the observed orbits of the planets can, given the exercise of ingenuity on Euclidean geometry, conform to the circularity and uniform velocity requirements. Despite a number of problems with the system, Ptolemaic astronomy stood up well for hundreds of years, providing for intelligible navigational guidance and calendar-making and giving human beings a sense of their place in the universe. Appropriately enough, its replacement went hand in hand with the development of the classical mechanics – another system that took mathematics as the key to understanding the universe.

Let me end this book, however, on quite a different note and one that takes us back to Plato's respect for and debt to the historical Parmenides. I have tried in this book to highlight the remarkable image of the great world system as totally rational and to note that the ultimate sources of intelligibility produce always for the best, though the conditions of space and time require occasional conflict. Even so, from the fundamental forms, through the generation of the intelligible numbers, thence to their being mixed with the Unlimited (*apeiron*), there is and can be nothing that *is* that fails to be a source of intelligibility or the intelligible product of such sources. Thus whatever *is* must be consistently thinkable all things considered, and whatever is consistently thinkable must *be*.

When we look at the *Parmenides* and Plato's expressions of respect for Parmenides in the *Theaetetus* and the *Sophist* in the light of the above, some important interpretative matters come into focus. A major motive of Plato in writing the *Parmenides* was to show how, despite his rejection of Parmenidean monism and despite the Eleatic Stranger's 'parricide,' Plato intends to honour and defend Parmenides' fundamental insight as expressed in the latter's *The Way of Truth*. That insight could stand as a motto for Plato's mature philosophy: *It is the same that can be thought that can be.*

APPENDIX
Other Approaches to the *Parmenides*

The Neoplatonist Interpretation

What was to become the standard interpretation of the *Parmenides* and other late Platonic dialogues was elaborately stated in the *Enneads* of Plotinus[1] in the third century, CE. Indeed, it became common to have the Neoplatonism of Plotinus, and some others, in mind when making reference to Platonism as such. Augustine, for example, popularized that usage. And Neoplatonism continued to be the dominant form given to Platonism at least until the nineteenth century. In the late Hellenistic and early medieval periods the reasons for this dominance are on the whole to be found in Neoplatonism's adaptability to religious apologetics. In the Christian West, the dominance of Augustine's apologetics and inspirational writing was almost complete. In the early and burgeoning Muslim world the peculiar mix of Aristotelianism and the Neoplatonist *Theology of Aristotle* and the *Book of Causes* contributed to the continuation of the Neoplatonist understanding of Platonism. When Ficino made his Renaissance translation of and commentaries on Plato's works into Latin, the Neoplatonist reading of Plato was given the stamp of virtual orthodoxy.

Aside from the intrusion of Gnostic and various syncretistic doctrines into such works as Proclus' commentary[2] on the *Parmenides*, the chief objection of twentieth-century commentators on the dialogue is to Neoplatonism's finding the source of intelligibility in the world in the 'superessential One,' a non-intelligible taken to be 'beyond Being.' Rich as that tradition has been with its invitation to mysticism and negative theology, it has seemed to recent commentators – including the author of this book – to have no justification in the works of Plato. Nor has the Hegelian adaptation[3] of the Neoplatonism thesis found any recent support.

The major textual support for the Neoplatonist interpretation of the *Parmenides* is to be found in what I have been calling the Parmenidean Version of the suppositions that one is or is not – notably the first supposition. Since at no point in the last part of the dialogue is there any straightforward impugning of any of the consequence sets, there is a presumption that Plato intends the 'neither/nors' to be taken seriously. On the Neoplatonist reading of the dialogue, the reason for there being no predication for the one of the Parmenidean versions is that the one is taken to be 'beyond' the possibility of predication and thus 'beyond Being.' And in the standard versions of the Neoplatonist reading, the *one* that is 'beyond Being' is identified with the form of the Good in the *Republic*, where Plato appears to take the form of the Good to be the source of both the intelligibility and the very being of the forms, thus inviting its later identification with a transcendent God of faith. Given the manifest difficulty of the *Parmenides*, it is all too easy to think that the text, especially with its obvious connection with the *Republic*, should be given a Neoplatonist reading. It is thus not at all surprising that the Neoplatonist reading was the standard one for so many centuries.

The whole thrust of the interpretation of the *Parmenides* given in the preceding chapters is that detailed explanation of the dialogue's text requires a very different reading from that of the Neoplatonists. And that very different reading fits very well with the texts of the *Theaetetus*, the *Sophist*, the *Timaeus*, and the *Philebus*. As F.M. Cornford wrote in the preface to his 1939 commentary[4] (of which more shortly): 'I sympathize with the Neoplatonising school in so far as they are convinced that the dialogue has a serious purpose. But I also agree with Professor Taylor's demonstration that Plotinus' scheme finds no support in the *Epistles*, and is inconsistent with Plato's theology as known to us from the *Timaeus* and the *Laws*. Further, only some of these writers have shown how the whole series of arguments can be given a valid meaning. Some have been content to pick out a sentence here and there which can, without its context, be used to support their thesis ... The impression left is that anyone who sets out with the Neoplatonic preconception is bound to read into many of the arguments a meaning, sometimes startling in itself, which is not suggested by anything in the text, and to abandon others as pointless sophisms' (ix). In spite of Cornford's comment it is worth noting that the general scheme of Plotinus can be read as endorsement of Plato's late mathematical vision of the whole universe, including the idea that the whose is an ensouled body.

F.M. Cornford's Interpretation

Cornford's 1939 translation of and commentary on the *Parmenides* was for many years the standard work in English and remains a volume that repays serious study. He takes the first part of the dialogue as serious criticism of the earlier Platonic doctrine of forms and participation, and he works through the second part in detail and with imagination.

In spite of giving lengthy treatment of the work of the historical Parmenides (including translation and interpretation of the fragments of the poem) and the Pythagoreans, Cornford's commentary fails to recognize the nature of Plato's debt to the Pythagoreans, and he does not offer a convincing account of the several suppositions. He takes Plato's effort at the generation of numbers very nearly at face value, but he does not appear to appreciate its true character or its relation to the *Timaeus* and the *Philebus*.

He gets into quite a bit of improvisation, much of it devoted to distinguishing various senses of terms so as to make the 'arguments' valid. As this last sentence suggests, Cornford takes the claims of what I call the Platonic Version to be *arguments* in the strict sense of requiring true conclusions from true premises. Often, however, he is forced to recognize that what is at stake are what I have called 'compatibilities' (that is, logical possibilities) rather than strict arguments. Not seeming to recognize that the several compatibility sets are based on taking, first, the *one* and, second, the *others* as logical subjects, he is forced to improvisation on different senses of 'others' in order to make the arguments or compatibilities plausible. Throughout the treatment of the second part of the dialogue, he treats the variations on *one* and *others* as *forms*. From the point of view developed in the present book, this leads to considerable artificiality, an artificiality that is needless if one recognizes that Collection and Division is not as such a procedure for arriving at definitions of *forms* (though it surely is a procedure for arriving at definitions).

He takes the *one* of the first supposition (a Parmenidean Version) to be different from the *one* of the second (a Platonic Version), not recognizing that what is at stake is the difference between a term and a proper predication. He does note, however, the barrenness of the Parmenidean Version. I think that at least part of Cornford's reason for taking the *one* of the first to be different from that of the second is his taking Plato to be exploiting several senses of 'is,' including 'exists' among them. It will be remembered that in this book there has been no reason to think that Plato recognized any such sense of 'is,' though he was quite aware of failure of reference and came up with the ingenious treatment of 'is not F' as 'is different from F.' The difficulty with *exists* for a contemporary is, of course, *existence's* treatment as an operator in modern logic and the puzzles engendered by attempting to treat it as a proper predicate or property. I think that what Cornford wanted to do was to treat the *one* of the Parmenidean Version as non-existent and that he was led thereby to fail to recognize it simply as a *term*. The problem with the Parmenidean Version is, in a word, not an 'existence' problem; it is the denial of predication.

Cornford ends by claiming that the abruptness of the *Parmenides'* ending recognizes the impossibility of continuing and discussing 'the relevancy of this ocean of arguments' to the questions raised at the beginning. The student must think out these matters for himself. If he does, he will discover much that throws light on the later dialogues: the *Theaetetus*, the *Sophist* and *Statesman*, and the *Philebus*' (245). Unfortunately, Cornford does not offer much help in determining the direction of such thinking.

Reginald Allen's Interpretation

Between the appearance of Cornford's 1939 book and the publication of Reginald Allen's *Plato's 'Parmenides': Translation and Analysis*[5] in 1983 there is no significant literature on our dialogue unless one counts the stir over Gregory Vlastos' 1954 paper on the so-called Third Man. I have noted earlier that, despite the importance of the Vlastos-inspired literature, there is little in it that helps in understanding the *Parmenides*.[6]

Taking 'aporetic' as indicative of a carefully articulated and circumscribed invitation to sophisticated readers to think through problems, Allen takes the *Parmenides* to be aporetic. 'The *Parmenides* is aporetic; it presents metaphysical perplexities, not positive doctrine. To undertake to solve the problems it raises without close attention to Plato's later dialogues in their relation to it would be like trying to reconstruct Aristotle's metaphysical view from Book B alone' (289). Allen has a point, but it is pejorative to claim that the *Parmenides* only raises problems and equally pejorative to imply that the interpretation of the later dialogues is not materially aided by attention to the text of the *Parmenides*.

Interestingly, he takes there to be *nine* suppositions, since he takes the one following supposition two as a distinctly different one. Rather than take it as a comparatively simple Platonic account of change, Allen holds that what I have called the Coda is a reconciliation of suppositions one and two, since it requires that 'Unity must sometimes have a share of Being, since it is, and sometimes not have a share of Being, since it is *just* one'

(261). Unity can come to be one only from having been many and vice versa, and this is taken to obtain for the other pairs of opposites. Taking this seriously, Allen thinks (264-5), leads to the world of Cratylus, who claimed that one could not step into the same river once. Incidentally, regular translation of *to hen* (τὸ ἕν) by 'Unity' is in itself an interpretation, virtually requiring that the *Parmenides*' One be thought of as a form.

As one might expect, Allen takes suppositions three and four to be related (though concerned with the 'others') as suppositions one and two are related. In the discussion of supposition three, Allen links Aristotle's references to a Platonic *dyad* or *great and small* to the *Parmenides*, finding it in the infinite divisibility of Unity (that is, the One) and the infinite generation of numbers from Unity in supposition two and associating it with the idea of a 'participant' (in the forms) in the *Parmenides*. And he thinks that the 'debacle' of the dyad/participant in the *Parmenides* invites the solution of the *Timaeus*, namely, taking the 'participant' to be 'the eternal Receptacle that mirrors forth the eternal Ideas' (272). The problem here, despite the insight of the linkage of the *Parmenides* with the *Timaeus*, lies, I believe, in Allen's not recognizing the general pattern of the suppositions, in the case of suppositions three and four, recognition of the 'others' as non-*F*'s or, if you please, negative subjects. It also lies in his not recognizing the numbers (*ta mathematika*) as between the forms and the sensibles, thus making possible the proper informing of the Receiver (receptacle).

He reads the summation of the affirmative suppositions as a presage of the conclusion of the entire dialogue. The consequences of those suppositions are mutually contradictory and, thus, as Allen reads them, absurd. After going through the negative suppositions, he claims that 'whether the hypothesis that Unity is is affirmed or denied, the result is absurdity' (275). The dialogue is thus at most to be taken as aporetic. But he does think that there is a moral to the *Parmenides*' tale. On his interpretation, 'Plato anticipated Aristotle in recognizing that being is not a genus, and more generally, that unity and difference are not genera either. On this hypothesis, Plato saw that it is nonsense to speak of what it is to be being, or what it is to be different, or what it is to be one, apart from determinate essences, which are and are one and are different from each other. Being, unity, difference are not definable essences, not genera, but unrestricted in scope, the transcendentals and syncategorematic terms of later metaphysics' (290).

Needless to say, since I have consistently argued that Being, Same, and Different are the grounding principles of Plato's world, I must agree that they are not 'definable essences,' but I can hardly agree that they are 'the transcendentals and syncategorematic terms of later metaphysics.' The talk of 'transcendentals' is derived from Aristotelian metaphysics and presupposes the denial of categorial (Aristotelian) status to Being, Same, and Different. The claim that they belong among the 'syncategorematics' of later metaphysics is more complicated, but, once again, the medieval concern with them belongs within an Aristotelian frame. It is, to say the least, difficult to see how Plato's *Parmenides* can be made to fit into this alleged historical development. Allen's reading of the *Parmenides* is thus remarkably Aristotelian.

Kenneth Sayre's Interpretation

Kenneth Sayre's *Plato's Late Ontology*, published in 1983, though directed to the illumination of the *Philebus*, contains a plausible and well-defended interpretion of the *Parmenides*. Sayre takes the first part of the dialogue as containing a set of inconclusive (indeed, 'eristic') arguments against the reply of Socrates to Zeno. They are inconclusive in that they are rather more dialectical articulations of a Plato who is dissatisfied with the middle period doctrine of the forms and participation rather than destructive of that doctrine. As Sayre sees it, a more mature Socrates would have found ready responses to Parmenides' destructive critique. An attentive reader of this volume will recognize that I am not really out of sympathey with this line of claim. I think, however, that the critique of Parmenides is simply a deliberate attempt to state anumber of more or less standard and well taken objections (probably discussed in the Academy) to the middle period doctrine of separated forms, centred on the literal meaning of 'have a share of' and the radical separation of forms and things 'having shares.' Plato displays no interest in defending the doctrine, and the historical Socrates (especially a very young Socrates) could hardly have held it. But Plato is obviously interested in taking forms as in some manner fixed objects of thought.

Sayre's treatment of the longer second part of the dialogue is largely anticipatory of his interpretation of the *Philebus*. That interpretation (discussed in the *Philebus* chapter of this book) correctly, I believe, takes the Philebus to be a clear declaration of Plato's Pythagoreanism. Using Aristotle's *Metaphysics* A's evidence of Pythagoreanism, including the well-known claim that Plato 'generates' the forms and also sensibles from the One and the Great and Small, Sayre takes the generation of the numbers in supposition two of the *Parmenides* as confirmation of Aristotle's claim. In the course of his exposition Sayre invokes proposition 15 of Book V of Euclid's *Elements* as evidence of Eudoxus' anticipation of the 'Dedekind

Cut' and thus of the theory as a means of handling proportions applicable both to commensurable and incommensurable magnitudes. Though there is no doubt of the importance of the theory as a means of handling problems of irrationals and its likely relevance to issues of greater, smaller, and equal, it is not clear to me that it is useful in understanding the second supposition.

Throughout his exposition, Sayre translates *hen* as 'Unity' rather than as 'One.' As an attentive reader of the present volume will readily understand, this translation hampers both the generation of numbers of supposition two and the general pattern of the suppositions. If, as in Euclid, the numbers are understood to be *multitudes* and their parts to be *factors*, the generation of numbers goes in self-replicating twos and threes (presumed to join in producing the primes, despite Aristotle's claim of no primes). And the enormous variety of parts, parts within parts, etc. makes possible the mathematical pattern of virtually anything together with its changes.

Mitchell Miller's Interpretation

Mitchell Miller's *Plato's 'Parmenides,'* published in 1986,[7] is a dense and complex book that combines literary analysis with close textual analysis. He is sufficiently taken with the figures of Cephalus (arriving from the birthplace of Anaxagoras), Glaucon, and Adeimantus to make a great deal of the connection(s) with the *Republic*. This is enough, when buttressed with some textual analysis, for him to find Parmenides' prediction of the mature Socrates (who will not despise hair, mud, and dirt) virtually satisfied in the Socrates of the *Republic*.

He thinks that the reason the immature Socrates of the *Parmenides* is unable to respond satisfactorily to the argument of Parmenides in the first part of the dialogue is that he (Socrates) has not yet sufficiently freed himself from material or commonsense images of the forms and participation. Though the mature Socrates of the *Republic* continues to use such images, Miller thinks he does so only because of the need for them in explanations made to the philosophically immature Glaucon and Adeimantus. As Miller sees it, a major point of the great exercise of the second part is to provoke in Socrates a proper understanding of the complete immateriality of the forms.

Like most interpreters (including the author of this book) Miller thinks that the target audience for the *Parmenides* was the membership of the Academy. Indeed, it is hard to imagine what other audience would be either sufficiently qualified or interested to follow the complicated set of arguments and distinctions. (And one might add Aristotle's characterization of *gymnastike* in *Metaphysics* Gamma as evidence that something like the great *Parmenides* exercise was a standard feature of Academic training.) Like Reginald Allen, Miller takes the exercise of the *Parmenides* as *aporetic* and thus designed to provoke thought and attempts at problem solving in the members of the Academy. Whether or not this aporetic claim is supported by Plato's alleged aversion to written philosophy (in the *Phaedrus*), there seems little, if any, *textual* evidence for it in the *Parmenides*. As we have seen in the detailed interpretation offered in the present book, Plato is quite obviously at pains to leave relatively few loose ends either in argument or in exposition. And he is equally obviously using Zeno's procedure to make a number of points, not the least of which are the account of numbers and the treatment of negation.

Miller distinguishes the 'consequences' of the eight suppositions as 'neither/nor' and 'both/and,' but he does not find the 'neither/nor' consequences barren. He finds them to be indicative of the totally non-material conception of the forms in that they do not admit of any division or multiplicity. The 'both/and' consequences, especially those of the second supposition, he takes to be indicative of things having shares of forms, thus divisible, in motion, etc. Those sections which take the one or a form to be divisible (and which the 'immature' Aristoteles unwittingly accepts) are to be treated as attempts to provoke deeper thought in the Academic reader, that is, thought that goes under the 'surface grammar' of the text. Here, as elsewhere, for example, in discussing the procedure of Collection and Division in the *Sophist* and *Statesman* as appropriate investigation of the forms, when the general lines of the interpretation seem threatened, Miller is prone to invoke the sort of special insight that he takes as needed to grasp, for example, the transcendent Form of the Good in the *Republic*.

No brief summary can do justice to Miller's dense but imaginative effort to provide detail for the great exercise. I must note, however, that it is an interpretative desideratum to work with the simplest interpretation that explains the text and is faithful to it. Miller's explanatory baggage requires too much *ad hoc* treatment of the text, usually in the guise of penetrating the 'surface grammar' of the text. I think, as well, that Miller's effort to find the Socrates who has benefited from Parmenides' tutelage in the Socrates of the *Republic* reads too much into the introductory part of the text. It is enough to recognize that evocation of the *Republic* in the introduction is to remind the reader of the comprehensive picture of *Republic* VI and VII. It may indeed be the case that a major function of the *Parmenides* is to provide the means for giving detail to that comprehensive picture. Curiously,

Miller has nothing to say about the *Philebus*, where, if anywhere, one finds a Socrates who is made to confess previous failure at finding satisfactory definitions and who introduces the method of a veritable intellectual 'Prometheus.'

Constance Meinwald's Interpretation

Constance Meinwald, in an articulate and carefully argued book published in 1991,[8] offers a novel and ingenious approach to the explanation of the *Parmenides*. What makes it novel is her drawing of and application of a distinction between what she takes to be two kinds of predication, one of which she applies to what I call the 'Parmenidean versions' (the neither/nor ones), the other to the 'Platonic versions' (the both/and ones) of the one supposition. So doing, she gets the required eight suppositions (which she calls 'sections'), and she holds that the application of the two kinds of predication enables her to be entirely faithful to Parmenides' instructions for the proper exercise of Socrates.

She calls *pros heauto* (πρὸς ἑαυτό) a predication that holds just in case what is predicated is the same as the subject term or is part of the definition of the subject term. The former is, of course, a mere identity and thus uninteresting. The latter is interesting because it will hold only if the predicate is a part of the definition of the subject term and thus always true. Meinwald's contention is that the negative predications in the Parmenidean Version will be false unless they are construed as *pros heauto*. And she takes this to explain how it is that the negative results of the Parmenidean Version of the one supposition can be true, since she takes them all to be *pros heauto* predications.

She calls *pros ta alla* (πρὸς τὰ ἄλλα) predication such predication as is not *pros heauto* and that may or may not hold for a given subject whether at a given time or at different times. And she maintains that the predications of the Platonic Version are *pros ta alla*. Furthermore, she introduces what is in effect a doubling version of *pros ta alla* predication that she labels 'displays.' With it she construes 'Socrates is bald' and 'Socrates displays baldness' as equivalent.

The work that 'displays' does for Meinwald is found in what I have called its 'doubling' use. As such it is key to her solution of what many consider the major issue of the dialogue, namely, that of giving a defensible account of *participation* or *having a share*. It is taken as allowing both for form predication and individual predication. As such it allows Meinwald to deny that 'participation' has a single sense but go on to account for the two different senses by means of place occupation in a *displays* relation. Thus, for example, 'Displays (Socrates, Motion)' and 'Displays (Motion, Unity),' using the same logical device, presumably account for individual and form predications by shifting the place occupied by 'Motion.'

This is a tidy package, and, though I think I have stated it fairly, I have not done justice to the considerable detail that she offers in its development and defence. Even attending to that detail, however, it is difficult not to think of it as having a rather contrived tidiness. First, while there is little doubt that the Plato of the *Philebus* (with its account of Collection and Division) would have agreed that there is the sort of predication that Meinwald calls *pros heauto*, its application to the 'neither/nor' suppositions of the *Parmenides* is dubious indeed. Second, and related, the weight that Meinwald gives to *pros* is egregious. The term does not appear at all in the text of supposition one. When it does appear in supposition two, it patently has to do with pairs of contraries (or contradictories) that are taken to have joint application to the one as related to (*pros*) itself or as related to (*pros*) the others. The occurrences of *pros* in connection with an abstract term are rare and explicable in context, though Meinwald seizes them as justification for her two basic modes of predication. Third, the invention of *displays*, though ingenious and supported by some 'intuitive' equivalences (for example, that between 'Motion is one' and 'Displays (Motion, Unity)') appears to be *ad hoc*.

Since from the point of view of the present work, genera/species trees obtained through Collection and Division do not articulate different levels of forms, their relevance to the several suppositions of the *Parmenides* is, at best, tangential. From the same point of view there can be what Meinwald calls *pros heauto* predication, for Collection and Division will produced the required trees. And, of course, there can be what she calls *pros ta alla* predication. The distinction, however, will be idling for getting the required eight suppositions, for it presupposes and does not explain the intellectual structure that makes Collection and Division a defensible procedure, the very structure that the exercise is designed to explain.

Lest some of the above be thought of as special pleading, let me note that Meinwald does not attend to the relevance of the *Sophist* claim that, if Parmenides were to claim that One *is*, he would be admitting two entities and thus engaging in self-refutation. And, of course, the context of the *Sophist* gives no support to taking 'One is' as *pros heauto* predication. Doing so, by the way, would have saved the Eleatic Stranger from committing intellectual parricide. Later in the *Sophist*, when the Stranger is explaining the *koinonia* or 'blending' of the 'greatest forms,' he could hardly think of their interrelationships as requiring or even allowing *pros heauto* predication. Indeed, he is at pains to require that none enters into the definition of any of the others. And it would be egregious to claim that those interrelationships could be expressed by means of *pros ta alla* predication.

There is little evidence in her book that Meinwald has given serious attention to the possibility that Plato, at the outset of supposition two, means just what he says when, in distinguishing the second from the first supposition, he notes the difference between 'if one one' and 'if one *is*' and declares the second to require that the one 'has a share' of being. What the text requires is that *being* is neither the same as nor a part of the definition of *one*. Nor does Meinwald give more than a passing nod to the generation of the numbers in the second supposition, despite its natural introduction to *in itself* and *in another* and despite Euclid's use of the number classification and Aristotle's recognition of it in *Metaphysics* A.

Concluding Remarks

Quite aside from my critical comments concerning the several interpretations of the *Parmenides* dealt with briefly in the above, I think it worth notice that none of their authors except some of the Neoplatonists has made a serious attempt to fit that dialogue into the pattern of Plato's later thought. It should be noted, however, that Cornford wrote pathbreaking translations/commentaries on the *Timaeus*, the *Theaetetus*, and the *Sophist*. Even so, those were completed earlier than his work on the *Parmenides*, and none can be construed as making anything like detailed linkage with the *Parmenides*. I must also note that, attractive as Hellenistic Neoplatonism was and despite its inclusiveness, it can hardly be regarded as a dispassionate effort (or set of efforts) to link the text of the *Parmenides* with the texts of other late Platonic dialogues. And the modern Hegelian-inspired Neoplatonic efforts are as much concerned to defend Hegel as to explain the texts of late Platonic dialogues.

Notes

Preface

1 Princeton NJ: Princeton University Press, 1983.
2 The appendix takes note of, in particular, the work of Neoplatonists F.M. Cornford, Reginald Allen, Kenneth Sayre, Mitchell Miller, and Constance Meinwald. The effort is not to offer detailed summaries but rather to comment on the use of rather different interpretative clues. The list is not exhaustive of proposed interpretations, but I believe it includes the most plausible lines of interpretation.
3 *Theaetetus*, 154B–C. The point (among others) is that nothing can be F and G (where these are contraries or contradictories) at the same time and in the same respect. To become G from being F, it must change.

Introduction

1 John Burnet, *Platonis Opera*, vol. 2 (Oxford: Clarendon Press, 1901). Text is from the reprinting of 1957.

2: Zeno's Stricture, Predication, and 'Having Shares' (126A–35C)

1 'Zeno's Stricture and Predication in Plato, Aristotle, and Plotinus,' in *How Things Are*, ed. James Bogen and James E. McGuire (Dordrecht: Reidel, 1984), 21–54.
2 See Peter Strawson, *Individuals* (London: Methuen, 1969).
3 Gregory Vlastos, 'The Third Man Argument in the *Parmenides*,' *Philosophical Review* 63 (1954), 319–49.
4 See especially chapter 9.

5 See my 'Becoming and Intelligibility,' *Oxford Studies in Greek Philosophy,* Summer, 1988, 1–35.
6 See bibliography listing, along with reference for Vlastos' 'Third Man' article.
7 Commentary on Aristotle's *Metaphysics,* 62, 29–33.
8 'Knowledge and the Forms in the Later Platonic Dialogues,' *Proceedings and Addresses of the American Philosophical Association* 52 (1978), 735–58.
9 Alexander Nehamas, 'Self-Predication and Plato's Theory of Forms,' *American Philosophical Quarterly* 16 (1979), 93–103.

3: The Needed Exercise and Supposition One

1 The Neoplatonist interpretation of the dialogue depends heavily on denying any sort of predication for the 'one.' That interpretation takes predication as assimilating a term to a 'higher' level. Since the Neoplatonist 'one' is taken to be the highest level and generative of everything that is in any way, it cannot be a subject of predication. The denial of predication that I am taking to be uniform in the 'Parmenidean' Version of the one supposition is, to the contrary, a denial based on the impossibility of predication when there is but a single term. It thus provides no support for Neoplatonist mysticism or, in the religious appropriation of Neoplatonism, the *via negativa.*

As is noted in the appendix, others have attended to the apparent denial of predication in the 'Parmenidean' Version. Constance Meinwald (in *Plato's 'Parmenides,'* New York and Oxford, 1991) treats the apparent denial as the always false attempt to apply *'pros ta alla'* predication where only *'pros heauto'* predication is appropriate. These terms are explained in the appendix. What is of interest at the moment is simply noticing that others have seen the need for distinguishing what I call Parmenidean from Platonic versions of the one supposition.

2 It may be useful to point out that not only does Meinwald attempt to give a sense to the negatives of supposition one but Cornford does also. He does it by distinguishing what he takes to be different meanings or senses of 'is.' Again, appropriate detail is to be found in the appendix to this volume.

4: Supposition Two as the Clue to the *Parmenides*

1 *Physics* 186A 30–2. See also '*Physics* I: Sense Universals, Principles, Multiplicity, and Motion,' in *Motion and Time, Space and Matter,* ed. Peter K. Machamer and Robert G. Turnbull (Columbus: Ohio State University Press, 1976).
2 H.H. Price, *Perception,* rev. ed. (London: Methuen, 1950), chapter 6.

5: Supposition Two, Part One (142B–48D)

1 See in this connection Jeffrey B. Gold, 'The Ambiguity of "Name" in Plato's *Cratylus*,' *Philosophical Studies* 34 (1978), 223–51.

10: The *Theaetetus* and the *Sophist*

1 F.M. Cornford, *Plato's Theory of Knowledge* (London: Routledge & Kegan Paul, 1935).

11: The *Philebus*

1 See Eleanor Irwin, *Colour Terms in Greek Poetry* (Toronto: A.M. Hakkert Press, 1974). Though her interest is rather more the meanings of Greek colour terms as used by Greek poets, the discussion of the theoretical literature in her first chapter is very useful indeed. So also is her very complete (for 1974) bibliography.

Afterword

1 Wilfrid S. Sellars, 'Philosophy and the Scientific Image of Man,' in *Frontiers of Science and Philosophy*, ed. Robert Colodny (Pittsburgh: University of Pittsburgh Press, 1962).

Appendix: Other Approaches to the *Parmenides*

1 Plotinus, *Enneads*, trans. A.H. Armstrong, 6 vols. (Cambridge MA: Harvard University Press, 1966).
2 *Proclus' Commentary on Plato's 'Parmenides,'* trans. Glenn R. Morrow and John M. Dillon (Princeton: Princeton University Press, 1987).
3 F.M. Cornford, *Plato and Parmenides: Parmenides' 'Way of Truth' and Plato's 'Parmenides'* (London: Routledge & Kegan Paul, 1939). Rpt. Library of Liberal Arts (Bobbs-Merrill), viii–ix.
4 Ibid, ix.
5 Minneapolis: University of Minnesota Press, 1983.
6 Gregory Vlastos, 'The Third Man Argument in the *Parmenides*,' *Philosophical Review* 63 (1954): 319–49. Relevant literature: Wilfrid S. Sellars, 'Vlastos and "The Third Man,"' *Philosophical Review* 64 (1955): 405–37; also Sellars, 'Vlastos and "The Third Man": A Rejoinder,' *Philosophical Perspectives* (Springfield IL: 1967): 55–72. See also Colin Strang, 'Plato and the Third Man,'

Proceedings of the Aristotelian Society, Supp. 37 (1963), 147–64, and P.T. Geach, 'Third Man Again,' *Philosophical Review* 65 (1956), 72–8.
7 Mitchell H. Miller, Jr, *Plato's 'Parmenides'* (Princeton: Princeton University Press, 1986).
8 Constance Meinwald, *Plato's 'Parmenides,'* (New York and Oxford: Oxford University Press, 1991).

Bibliography

Allen, R.E. 'The Interpretation of Plato's *Parmenides.*' *Philosophical Review* 69 (1964). Rpt. in *Studies in Plato's Metaphysics*, ed. R.E. Allen. London: Routledge & Kegan Paul, 1965, 373–92.
– 'Unity and Infinite: *Parmenides* 142b–145a.' *Review of Metaphysics* 27 (1974): 697–724.
– *Plato's 'Parmenides': Translation and Analysis*. Minneapolis: University of Minnesota Press, 1983.
Annas, Julia. 'On the Intermediates.' *Archiv für Geschichte der Philosophie* 57 (1975): 146–66.
– *Aristotle's 'Metaphysics': Books M and N*. Oxford: Clarendon Press, 1976.
– 'Aristotle on Substance, Accident and Plato's Forms.' *Phronesis* 22 (1977): 146–60.
– 'Knowledge and Language: The *Theaetetus* and the *Cratylus*,' in *Language and Logos: Studies in Ancient Greek Philosophy Presented to G.E.L. Owen*, ed. Malcolm Schofield and Martha C. Nussbaum. Cambridge: Cambridge University Press, 1982, 95–114.
– 'Die Gegenstände der Mathematik bei Aristotles,' in *Mathematics and Metaphysics in Aristotle*, ed. Andreas Graeser. Bern: Haupt, 1987, 131–47.
Augustine. *Contra Academicos*, trans. and intro. Mary P. Garvey. Milwaukee: Marquette University Press, 1957.
Burnet, John. *Platonis Opera*, vol. 2. Oxford: Clarendon Press, 1901.
Burnyeat, Myles F. 'Plato on the Grammar of Perceiving.' *Classical Quarterly* N.S. 26 (1976): 35–54.
– *The 'Theaetetus' of Plato*, trans. M.J. Levett, intro. and commentary Myles F. Burnyeat. Indianapolis: Hackett, 1990.
Cherniss, Harold. *Aristotle's Criticism of Plato and the Academy*. Baltimore: Johns Hopkins Press, 1944.

- 'The Relation of the *Timaeus* to Plato's Later Dialogues,' lecture at Harvard University, 1956, printed as delivered in R.E. Allen, *Studies in Plato's Metaphysics.* London: Routledge & Kegan Paul, 1965, 339–78.
Clagett, Marshall. *Greek Science in Antiquity,* Abelard-Schumann, 1955. Rpt. Toronto: Collier-Macmillan, 1963.
Cooper, John. 'Plato on Sense-Perception and Knowledge (*Theaetetus* 184–186).' *Phronesis* 15 (1970): 123–46.
Cornford, Francis M. *Plato's Theory of Knowledge: The 'Theaetetus' and the 'Sophist.'* London: Routledge & Kegan Paul, 1935.
- *Plato's Cosmology.* London: Routledge & Kegan Paul, 1937.
- *Plato and Parmenides: Parmenides' 'Way of Truth' and Plato's 'Parmenides.'* London: Routledge & Kegan Paul, 1939.
Curd, Patricia K. 'Some Problems of Unity in the First Hypothesis of the *Parmenides.*' *Southern Journal of Philosophy* 27 (1989): 347–59.
- '*Parmenides* 131C-132B: Unity and Participation.' *History of Philosophy Quarterly* 3, 125–36.
Forrester, James. 'Plato's *Parmenides*: The Structure of the First Hypothesis.' *Journal of the History of Philosophy* 10 (1972): 1–14.
Fowler, D.H. *The Mathematics of Plato's Academy.* Oxford: Oxford University Press, 1987.
Freeman, Kathleen. *Ancilla to the Pre-Socratic Philosophers.* Cambridge MA: Harvard University Press, 1948.
Gaiser, Konrad. 'Plato's Enigmatic Lecture on the Good.' *Phronesis* 25 (1980): 5–37.
Gill, Mary Louise. 'Matter and Flux in Plato's *Timaeus.*' *Phronesis* 32 (1987), 34–53.
- *Aristotle on Substance.* Princeton: Princeton University Press, 1989.
Gosling, J.C.B. *Plato: 'Philebus.'* Oxford: Clarendon Press, 1975.
Hackforth, R. *Plato's Examination of Pleasure.* Cambridge: Cambridge University Press, 1957.
Hampton, Cynthia. *Pleasure, Knowledge and Being.* Albany: SUNY Press, 1990.
Heath, Thomas L., trans., intro., and commentary. *The Thirteen Books of Euclid's 'Elements.'* 3 vols., 2nd ed. Cambridge: Cambridge University Press, 1926. Rpt. New York: Dover, 1956.
- *A History of Greek Mathematics,* 2 vols. Oxford: Clarendon Press: 1921. Rpt. New York: Dover, 1981.
Irwin, Eleanor. *Colour Terms in Greek Poetry.* Toronto: A.M. Hakkert Press, 1974.
Kahn, Charles. 'The Greek Verb "To Be" and the Concept of Being.' *Foundations of Language* 2 (1966): 245–65.
- *The Verb 'Be' in Ancient Greek.* Boston: Reidel, 1973.
- 'Some Philosophical Uses of "To Be" in Plato.' *Phronesis* 26 (1981): 105–34.

Kirk, G.S., and J.E. Raven. *The Presocratic Philosophers*. Cambridge: Cambridge University Press, 1964.
Klibansky, Raymond. *Plato's 'Parmenides' in the Middle Ages and Renaissance. Medieval and Renaissance Studies* I, part 2: 1943.
Knorr, W.R. *The Evolution of the Euclidean Elements*. Dordrecht: Reidel, 1975.
– 'Problems in the Interpretation of Greek Number Theory: Euclid and the "Fundamental Theorem of Arithmetic."' *Studies in the History and Philosophy of Science* 7 (1976): 353–68.
Letwin, Oliver. 'Interpreting the *Philebus*.' *Phronesis* 26 (1981): 187–206.
Lewis, Frank. 'Parmenides on Separation and the Knowability of the Forms: Plato's *Parmenides* 133A ff.' *Philosophical Studies* 35 (1979): 105–27.
Lindberg, David C., ed. and trans. *John Pecham and the Science of Optics*. Madison: University of Wisconsin Press, 1970.
Matthen, Mohan. 'Greek Ontology and the "Is" of Truth.' *Phronesis* 28 (1983): 113–35.
Meinwald, Constance. *Plato's 'Parmenides.'* New York and Oxford: Oxford University Press, 1991.
Miller, Mitchell H., Jr. *Plato's 'Parmenides.'* Princeton: Princeton University Press, 1986.
Mills, K.W. 'Plato and the Instant.' *Proceedings of the Aristotelian Society* 48 (1974): 81–96.
Moravcsik, Julius. 'Forms, Natures, and the Good in *Philebus*.' *Phronesis* 26 (1979): 81–104.
– 'Forms and Dialectic in the Second Half of the *Parmenides*,' in *Language and Logos: Studies in Ancient Greek Philosophy Presented to G.E.L. Owen*, ed. Malcolm Schofield and Martha C. Nussbaum. Cambridge: Cambridge University Press, 1982, 135–53.
Mourelatos, A.P.D. *The Route of Parmenides*. New Haven: Yale University Press, 1970.
Mueller, Ian. *Philosophy of Mathematics and Deductive Structure in Euclid's 'Elements.'* Cambridge MA: MIT Press, 1981.
– '*Parmenides* 133A–134E: Some Suggestions.' *Ancient Philosophy* 3 (1984): 3–7.
Mueller, Ian, ed. *Peri Ton Mathematon*. Edmonton: Academic Printing and Publishing, 1992.
Nehamas, Alexander. 'Self-Predication and Plato's Theory of Forms.' *American Philosophical Quarterly* 16 (1979): 93–103.
– 'Episteme and Logos in Plato's Later Thought.' *Archiv für Geschichte der Philosophie* 66 (1984): 11–36.
Neugebauer, O. *A History of Ancient Mathematical Astronomy*, 3 vols. Berlin, Heidelberg, New York: Springer, 1975.

Owen, G.E.L. 'The Place of the *Timaeus* in Plato's Dialogues.' *Classical Quarterly* 3 (1953): 313–38.
- 'Plato and Parmenides on the Timeless Present.' *The Monist* 50 (1966). Rpt. in *The Pre-Socratics*, ed. A.P.D. Mourelatos. Garden City, 1974, 271–92.
Plotinus, *Enneads*, trans. A.H. Armstrong, 6 vols., Loeb Classical Library. Cambridge MA: Harvard University Press, 1966.
Proclus. *A Commentary on the First Book of Euclid's 'Elements,'* trans. and intro. Glenn R. Morrow. Princeton: Princeton University Press, 1970.
- *Platonis Parmenidem Commentarium*, ed. V. Cousin. Paris, 1984.
- *Proclus' Commentary on Plato's 'Parmenides,'* trans. Glenn R. Morrow and John M. Dillon. Princeton: Princeton University Press, 1987.
Ross, W.D. *Plato's Theory of Ideas*. Oxford: Oxford University Press, 1951.
Rossvaer, Viggo. *The Laborious Game: A Study of Plato's 'Parmenides.'* Vorlaget: Oslo University, 1983.
Runciman, W.G. 'Plato's *Parmenides*.' *Harvard Studies in Classical Philology* 64 (1959). Rpt. in *Studies in Plato's Metaphysics*, ed. R.E. Allen. London: Routledge & Kegan Paul, 1965, 149–84.
Ryle, Gilbert. 'Plato's "Parmenides."' *Mind* 48 (1939). Rpt. in *Studies in Plato's Metaphysics*, ed. R.E. Allen. London: Routledge & Kegan Paul, 1965, 97–147.
Santas, Gerasimos. 'The Form of the Good in Plato's *Republic*,' in *Essays in Greek Philosophy*, vol. 2, ed. J. Anton and A. Preus. Albany: SUNY Press, 1983, 232–64.
Sayre, Kenneth. 'Why the Eight Hypotheses in the '*Parmenides*' Are Not Contradictory.' *Phronesis* 23 (1978): 133–50.
- *Plato's Late Ontology: A Riddle Resolved*. Princeton: Princeton University Press, 1983.
Sellars, Wilfrid S. 'Philosophy and the Scientific Image of Man,' in *Frontiers of Science and Philosophy*, ed. Robert Colodny. Pittsburgh: University of Pittsburgh Press, 1962, 35–78.
- 'The Soul as Craftsman,' in Wilfrid S. Sellars, *Philosophical Perspectives*. Springfield IL: Charles C. Thomas, 1967.
- 'Reason and the Art of Living in Plato,' in *Essays in Honor of Marvin Farber*. Buffalo: University of Buffalo Press, 1973.
Striker, Gisela. *Peras und Apeiron: Das Problem der Formen in Platons Philebos*. Göttingen: 1963.
Taylor, A.E. *The 'Parmenides' of Plato*. Oxford: Oxford University Press, 1940.
Teloh, Henry. 'Parmenides and Plato's *Parmenides* 131A–132C.' *Journal of the History of Philosophy* 14 (1976): 125–30.
Toomer, G.J. *Ptolemy's Almagest*, trans. Toomer. London: Duckworth, 1984.
Turnbull, Robert G. 'The Argument of the *Sophist*.' *Philosophical Quarterly* 14 (1954): 2–14.

- '*Physics* I: Sense Universals, Principles, Multiplicity, and Motion,' in *Motion and Time, Space and Matter*, ed. R.G. Turnbull and P.K. Machamer. Columbus: Ohio State University Press, 1976: 28–56.
- 'Knowledge and the Forms in the Later Platonic Dialogues.' *Proceedings and Addresses of the American Philosophical Association* 52 (1978a): 735–58.
- Review of Gregory Vlastos, *Plato's Universe*. *Journal of the History of Philosophy* 16 (1978b): 99–103.
- 'The Role of the "Special Sensibles" in the Perception Theories of Plato and Aristotle,' in *Studies in Perception*, ed. R.G. Turnbull and P.K. Machamer. Columbus: Ohio State University Press (1978c), 3–26.
- 'The Later Platonic Concept of Scientific Explanation,' in *Plato and the Sciences*, ed. John Anton. Albany: Eidos Press, 1980, 75–101.
- '*Episteme* and *Doxa*: Some Reflections on Eleatic and Heraclitean Themes in Plato,' in *Essays in Ancient Greek Philosophy*, vol. 2, ed. J. Anton and A. Preus. Albany: SUNY Press, 1983, 279–303.
- Review of R.E. Allen, *Plato's 'Parmenides.'* *Ancient Philosophy* 4 (1984a): 206–17.
- 'Zeno's Stricture and Predication in Plato, Aristotle, and Plotinus,' in *How Things Are*, ed. James Bogen and J.E. McGuire. Dordrecht: Reidel (1984b), 21–54.
- 'Becoming and Intelligibility.' *Oxford Studies in Greek Philosophy* (1988): 1–35.
- 'The "Third Man" Argument and the Text of *Parmenides*,' in *Essays in Ancient Greek Philosophy*, vol. 3, ed. J. Anton and A. Preus. Albany: SUNY Press, 1989: 203–26.
- 'Platonic and Aristotelian Science,' in *The Science of Ancient Greece*, ed. Alan C. Bowen. New York and London: Garland, 1991, 43–59.

Vlastos, Gregory. 'The Third Man Argument in the *Parmenides*.' *Philosophical Review* 63 (1954): 319–49.
- 'Plato's "Third Man" Argument (*Parm*. 132A1–B2): Text and Logic.' *Philosophical Quarterly* 19 (1969): 289–301.
- *Plato's Universe*. Seattle: University of Washington Press, 1975.

Wedberg, Anders. *Plato's Philosophy of Mathematics*. Stockholm: Almqvist and Wiksell, 1955.

Wundt, M. *Platons 'Parmenides.'* Stuttgart and Berlin: Verlag W. Kohlhammer, 1935.

HIEBERT LIBRARY

3 6877 00160 9485

B
378
.T78
1998